Education

Quality basic education:
the development of competence

Joan Freeman

Prepared for the
International Bureau
of Education

In the series 'Educational sciences':

Landsheere, G. De. *Empirical research in education.* 1982. 113 p.

Zverev, I.D. *Teaching methods in the Soviet school.* 1983. 116 p.

Kraevskij, V.V.; Lerner, I.Y. *The theory of curriculum content in the USSR.* 1984. 113 p.

Léon, Antoine. *The history of education today.* 1985. 117 p.

Bronckart, Jean-Paul. *The language sciences: an educational challenge?* 1985. 105 p.

Mialaret, G., et al. *Introduction to the educational sciences.* 1985. 106 p.

Camilleri, C. *Cultural anthropology and education.* 1986. 171 p.

Siguán, M.; Mackey, W.F. *Education and bilingualism.* 1987. 147 p.

Bhola, H.S. *World trends and issues in adult education.* 1989. 177 p.

Duric, Ladislav. *Essentials of educational psychology.* 1989. 163 p.

First published in 1992 by the
United Nations Educational,
Scientific and Cultural Organization,
7, Place de Fontenoy,
75700 Paris, France.

ISBN: 92-3-102788-3

Printed in Switzerland by Presses Centrales SA, Lausanne.

Preface

This book is a major publication of the IBE on basic education following the World Conference on Education for All (WCEFA, Jomtien, Thailand, 1990). The author, Dr. Joan Freeman, president of the European Council for High Ability, has already written many books and scientific papers on the development of children's abilities and talents. This book is designed to remind the reader about the importance of the qualitative dimensions of learning in basic education; the central issue in quality is the development of competence in the individual learner. As clearly recommended by the WCEFA, the focus of basic education in this book is on the learner. An active and participatory learning process and acknowledgement of achievement are essential elements in building up the learner's competence.

The content of Dr. Freeman's book, however, goes beyond the basic premises and objectives of the World Conference on Education for All. What really makes this publication unique is the fact that the characteristics of basic learning and those of high ability (usually associated with gifted children) are placed in a continuum. Talents and giftedness are viewed from the perspective of individual differences in the upbringing of all children, not a minority of children nor a group of elitist learners. The author argues that talents and gifts cannot arise spontaneously. She believes that all children have the right to develop their full potential, and whether this goal is achieved or not depends on educational, psychological, social and physical means and support provided to the learning child. Encouragement and stimulation provoked by mothers and teachers for his/her learning, flexible and adaptable curricula, various aspects of school organization, learning experiences – all these factors affect the task of competency-building in the learner.

In this book Dr. Freeman, a talented scholar, has examined the findings of recent scientific research on the development of children's abilities and skilfully transformed them into practical and clear ideas, suggestions and information for use by parents, educational practitioners, planners and decision-makers. The readers of the book will find this book stimulating, insightful and useful in conducting their daily educational activities.

The International Bureau of Education is very grateful to Dr. Freeman for her contribution to a clearer and more profound understanding of the nature of how children's abilities and competency develop. Our special thanks should also be extended to Dr. Pieter Span of the University of Utrecht for his comments on Dr. Freeman's manuscript.

Readers are reminded that the ideas and opinions expressed in this work are those of the author and do not necessarily represent the views of UNESCO. Moreover, the designations employed and the presentation of the material throughout the publication do not imply the expression of any opinion whatsoever on the part of UNESCO concerning the legal status of any country, territory, city or area, or of its authorities, or concerning the delimitations of its frontiers or boundaries.

Contents

Introduction

In writing this book, it has been my intention to provide an overview of how the psychology of child development can improve today's education, and especially to show how this can be of practical use for the promotion of children's competence. Whatever abilities children are born with, if they can be helped to use them in the most effective way, both their level of performance in life and their personal happiness are likely to be greatly improved.

The best education is not only about imparting knowledge but also about opening children's minds. Through the influence of developmental psychology, there is now considerable stress in education on extending its objectives well beyond the mere acquisition of information. Concern for each child encourages the growth of a competent person who is curious and is able to learn, so that education does not end with school or college, but continues throughout life. Motivating pupils to learn is the first priority of formal education; the single most important measure of its success is how far individuals are encouraged to continue learning, and to take responsibility for it themselves as adults.

The real value of psychology in education is through providing a scientific basis for making decisions which will guide children's' progress – such as when to intervene and when to step aside. This comes from understanding the developmental processes through which most children pass, as well as the best conditions for them to thrive. Although no power on earth can endow every new-born baby with stable life conditions and wide educational opportunities, educators are becoming much better equipped to help children help themselves to what is available. The application of psychological knowledge to education can help teachers to develop effective general strategies for their work: they can also become better able to make use of specific techniques to increase both their own and their pupils' competence.

There is enough evidence now to show how we should seek to promote both general competence and outstanding talent in children. Although in most of the world such provision is not readily available, it is always possible to help children take greater charge of their own lives, using whatever facilities already exist both in school and at home. The key to this is in teaching methods – particularly the use of flexible approaches to the different needs of all pupils. The fewer avoidable frustrations children have to face in their learning, and the more appropriate that process is for them, the happier they will be to learn and keep on learning.

The major priority in education should be to help both teachers and children understand and improve the way they use their minds. To do this, teaching procedures should be designed to promote curiosity and problem-solving attitudes. From the very first lessons, knowledge can be taught so that it can be used in an adaptable way, to include realistic problems which are meaningful to the pupils. This is not only beneficial to all children's thinking, but is particularly suitable for those living in harsh conditions. Such children may not only have little access to schooling, but what they do receive has often been largely a matter of memorising and reproducing information which seems distant from their everyday lives. Such teaching methods will have to change if all children are to be enabled to reach beyond a minimal level of competence – adequate for survival in limited circumstances but unable to be transferred and used in others.

Research data from psychology, the social sciences, neurobiology and medicine suggests that the quality of an individual's early life has a considerable influence on the development of that person's brain and mind. Those early conditions, which include the level of sensory stimulation, appear to be closely related to coping skills and health in adult life. Beyond the basic needs of food are: the degree of support that children get from the people who are most significant to them – usually their families; the teaching and educational material they have to learn with; and the increasing degree of control they are able to take, as they grow up, over their own working and living environments.

For achievement, such matters as self-confidence and satisfactory personal relationships can be as important as the mastery of actual skills and knowledge, however well these are taught. Children who feel good about themselves and feel confident about aiming high are psychologically well placed for development, especially compared with those who are inhibited by poor concepts about themselves and their place in the world.

Emotional influences have a vital effect on children's intellectual development as well as on that of their other abilities. Feelings of being worthwhile affect ideas of self-efficacy, and are the basis of behaving in a competent way. On the other hand, emotional problems may result from feelings of rejection, and from the pressures of parents, teachers, peers or circumstances, so that children may then develop psychological defences against expected hurt, and these can then handicap them throughout life. Curiosity and problem-solving attitudes in learning do not occur naturally in all children; for most, these need to be encouraged by specifically directed teaching. There are many reasons, such as lack of self-confidence, poor living conditions, poor teaching or cultural dictates, that can inhibit children from being curious and asking the necessary questions.

Throughout this text, special consideration is given to the education of highly able children, especially those who may not be recognized as such because of their circumstances. This focus is intended to stimulate in both parents and teachers a general awareness of the special potential of these children and of what is needed for its development; it can help to encourage the eventual emergence of a higher proportion of more lively-minded and creative adults. The importance of this aspect of education has become clear to me during my long involvement and research with such children, watching them grow up in a variety of different circumstances. There is also expanding international interest in the special needs of the highly able, not just during the school years, but over the human life-span.

Study of the highly able is beneficial to all individuals, because it highlights their special ways of functioning, which can be learned by other children. For example, valuable learning strategies which the highly able find out for themselves, such as the way they often seek out principles first and add the details later, can help in teaching more average pupils. The special educational needs of the highly able, such as enrichment of the basic curriculum, and the provision of adequate learning materials for high-level performance, also overlap with those of other children in the classroom. The talented do have a rather special quality – something the world needs – and they also have as much right to fulfil their all-round potential as anyone else.

It was because there did not seem to be adequate recognition and provision for such individuals that the European Council for High Ability (ECHA) was founded – to speak for them, and to change attitudes and provision for them across Europe as well as in other continents. ECHA is a dynamic communications network which co-ordinates scientific work in the area of high ability, working through national correspondents, special interest groups, co-ordinated by the ECHA Centre at Bildung und Begabung, 45, Ahrstrasse, Bonn, Germany. It holds biannual international conferences, as well as more frequent smaller seminars and presentations at other scientific meetings around Europe, and publishes the academic *European journal for high ability* twice yearly, as well as state of the art information and the quarterly *ECHA news.*

In my role as first President of ECHA, I have been privileged to see children of all abilities growing up and being educated in widely varying world circumstances, some of which offer them severely limited possibilities of education and resources for developing competence. In the ex-communist countries of Europe, for example, not only do teachers face severe shortages of physical resources, but have had to overcome the training which, for more than a generation, obliged them to think and teach in specifically structured ways. In the *favella* slums of Brazil, teachers are forced to use their ingenuity, such as offering food to entice children into the school who would otherwise have to earn money to survive. In South Africa, children in the shanty towns are struggling with the break-up of the system of education based on *apartheid*.

We have in the past seriously underestimated the human potential for learning. The decoding and learning of language, for example, is a brilliant feat that is accomplished by everyone, including slow learners. Those who are now seen as highly able are to some extent the ones who have had the best opportunities to learn and develop. The learning and coping skills of individuals determine how well they can take part in activities that are important not only for their own lives, but also for the prosperity and welfare of their community. Poor-quality education is debilitating; high-quality education enhances everyone's life. And learning does pay; an educated population can advance economically. However, improving education to improve the competence of the world's children is not only a question of money, but of changing attitudes; I hope this book will go some way towards doing that.

For the purpose of this book, and wherever appropriate, personal pronouns have been simplified in the text: babies, infants and schoolchildren are usually referred to as 'he'; primary schoolteachers are usually referred to as 'she'; others are neutral where possible, but otherwise, either 'he' or 'she' are used in random order, as in life. This practice has been adopted to avoid resort to ungainly sentence structures involving he/she, him/her, his/her and his/hers. This is designed to make reading easier, and no prejudice is intended towards moves within the United Nations system to adopt non-sexist language in its publications.

ACKNOWLEDGEMENTS

My special thanks for his contributions to the book's production go to Professor Pieter Span, who helped me sort out what was to go in it as well as reading the manuscript; he spotted the missing bits, made sure it was up to date, and added greatly to its style and value. It was Toshio Ohsako who first approached me to write it for UNESCO's International Bureau of Education, and I thank him for his initiative and constant support; John Fox's careful editing is much appreciated. And I am, as always, glad of the encouragement and generous editorial help of my husband, Hugh.

PART ONE:
INDIVIDUAL DIFFERENCES

CHAPTER I

The roots of
children's competence

ENVIRONMENT AND HEREDITY

All children have abilities and the capacity to learn: even the most severely mentally handicapped in institutions learn to respond to the rattle of the food trolley. Whatever they start out with, the overwhelming conclusion of research findings is that it is never too soon to start helping children develop their abilities. But competent performance at any level is defined by both heredity and environment, those two major boundaries of potential and educational opportunities, and it is their interaction, their proportional effects, that are of particular concern in education.

Each child's situation is different in both genetic potential and in the way each one reacts to different experiences, such as to the people who look after them. None can be made to perform better than genetic inheritance will allow, and under-achievement is always possible, but outstanding individuals can appear unexpectedly in families of low cultural level. In biological terms, such genetic changes would be expected from time to time, because mental abilities (in so far as they are innate) are likely to be transmitted in the same way as physical characteristics. It will probably never be possible to predict such spontaneous changes, because the deciding conditions are extremely complex, for example, one out of every five children carries a new gene mutation inherited from one of the parents.

Discovering exactly how different kinds of influences are received by different kinds of children is also extremely difficult. Parental divorce, for example, might either cause a temporary halt to a child's development or have lifelong effects. A great deal of information which has accumulated from many cultures provides a useful guide to what level of performance can be expected at any age. In the practice of education, it is essential to know the normal pattern of children's development, as a comparison for any individual's development, while understanding that what is 'normal' is only an average, rather than an absolute measure.

Comparing a child on a developmental scale of the average covering thousands of children indicates the *rate* of development, not any individual *patterns*.

Some psychologists (Eysenck, 1971; Jensen, 1972) have concluded that, on average across large populations, heredity is responsible for about 80 per cent of our potential – leaving about 20 per cent to work with. Others claim that environmental effects account for far more, if not all human performance (Howe, 1990; Ceci, 1990). Of course, if we could measure accurately just what a child needs, we could give each one an educational programme designed to be of the greatest personal benefit. For instance, if it was known that a child needed specific genes for musical ability to play an instrument, then those who do not have them would not need to waste time on music lessons. If, as seems more likely, musical appreciation and performing ability are to some extent the products of environment, then there should be a more generous spread of musical opportunity amongst all children.

Since such questions remain unanswered, it would be unjust to deny any educational opportunity to any child. Both Eysenck and Jensen are now particularly well known for their association of race with ability, focusing on intelligence, but their research results are questionable and open to other interpretations, leading to entirely different conclusions. In addition, because of the strong feelings associated with such arguments, clear thought on what education to give children of different races is sometimes lost, and certainly the effects of culture cannot be discounted either in assessment of ability or in any resulting statistical analyses. Besides, it may well be that the recognized ratio of inherited to acquired ability is not fixed and absolute, but that it varies between different children, so that any fixed educational programme would be inappropriate and detrimental to some.

Although the potential for talent may be present at birth, for most children it will not 'automatically' emerge over the course of time, unless the right conditions are present. Such influences as under-expectation, sex-role stereotyping and social attitudes are all possible limitations on development. For example, a high rate of unemployment in a depressed economy may mean that poor bright children, who are the most likely to get whatever jobs are immediately available in the area, may see little point in staying on at school, so that they neglect their studies and leave as soon as they can. Unless the children of high potential also have an eagerness to learn, they will not put in the thousands of hours of work that are needed to develop their talent to a level of recognizable achievement.

THE MATURATION OF HEREDITY

Three different processes need to be distinguished here: 'maturation' implies an inherent, preordained 'unfolding' of potential which is already there, while 'growth' involves gain of some sort and is a part of maturation. Both are part of 'development', which can be defined as the changes which occur as the result of the maturing child's interaction with his environment.

Before birth, the quality of nourishment, the mother's age and her emotional stress can affect the development of the foetus; prematurely born babies are less likely to develop well in many ways, such as intelligence and height. By the time of birth, a baby is capable of a complicated range of well-practised movements, and exhibits its own individual ways of carrying out life processes, such as breathing, feeding, reacting to bright lights, and including personal tastes. All this has to be organized in the processes of growth for ease of action, and the context in which this takes place is important. Physiological research shows that intellectual growth cannot take place until the appropriate physical growth is there. It is clear, for example, that voluntary behaviour which takes place via the central nervous system (including the brain) only develops new functions when the nervous structures are sufficiently mature.

All mental abilities, such as thinking, although they are dependent on maturation of the nervous system, need teaching, unlike others, such as standing up or sphincter control, which simply 'unfold'. The greatest interference with normal maturation is probably caused by starvation which, whilst preventing bodily growth, also obstructs intellectual development. Both the duration of starvation and the child's stage of development while this is taking place affect the eventual outcome. Interferences in nervous maturation may also be caused by genetic disorders, poisons, diseases, or physical injury. Because both mental and physical growth are affected, it is vitally important to remedy the effects of poverty as early as possible in a child's life.

As well as the great differences between children of the same age, and between the developmental rates of different abilities in one child, every child has an individual tempo and style in growth, which is as personal as their face. Human development is not smooth; it happens in fits and starts, with pauses in between. Even national averages can change within a few years as children mature earlier, and this itself varies between cultures. For example, in the Western World over the last twenty years, the age of onset of menstruation in girls (menarche) has advanced by around six months. To get the best response from teaching, it would need an educator to know where each child is in terms of the development of any particular ability – an impossible ideal.

Emotional implications of maturation. Until puberty, obvious changes of bodily size in boys and girls are much the same: new shoes for bigger feet are part of the pleasure of normal growing up. But after puberty, changes towards an adult shape and the accompanying surge of hormones become obvious and not always welcome, such as when the sudden increase in strength and size causes clumsiness and embarrassment. Generally, all the pubertal and adolescent changes take place together, so that if a boy is a late maturer, he is late in all respects, and that will probably be his life-pattern. Looking at, say, 12-year-old girls or 14-year-old boys, it is easy to see their variation in maturity, even though their chronological ages may be the same. Emotional maturity tends to follow suit.

Growth of height and strength is particularly important to boys in most societies. Early-maturing boys are able to become dominant, and usually remain so, but on the other hand, a boy's self-concept can be affected badly if his maturation is slow, and he remains smaller and weaker than his peers. Later-maturing boys and girls are likely to stay at school longer, and the boys tend to become more sensitive men (Tanner, 1978). Slow maturation also seems to be more common in boys who are obliged to be dependent on their parents for longer, as part of the long preparation for an educated adulthood.

Adolescent girls are generally further along the road of emotional development than boys of the same age. On the whole they appear to be less psychologically disturbed by the changes of adolescence – perhaps because they are actually physiologically 'older' already. However, their school marks often begin to suffer at about the age of 14 or 15, particularly in societies which exert social pressures for them to assume the traditional female role, encouraging them to feel that their school work is not important for their futures. Before that age, given the same opportunities and encouragement, girls will pass exams better, including those for selection to a higher level of education, which is why, when there are equal places for girls and boys, the scales have to be tipped in favour of the boys. Thus, girls with marks higher than some of the boys may be excluded from such schools, as happened in the United Kingdom at a time when children were selected for an academic education at the age of 11.

Extreme rates of maturation, whether unusually fast or slow, are always difficult for a child, but the effects are considerably cushioned by the support of a loving and secure family relationship. The underdeveloped boy who finds total acceptance at home may avoid repercussions from the rejections of his class-mates which such adolescents can experience.

Educational implications of maturation. A child's maturation puts an upper limit on his educational achievement: if the task requires mental operations of which he is not yet capable, he will fail. He may, never the less, sometimes get the right answer by other means, such as by memorising a method in arithmetic without understanding. Another cause of failure may be that the child has simply never had adequate learning experience on which to build new learning.

Bigger children are likely to be more able than smaller children of the same age, and slower maturing children are at a disadvantage in a competitive school situation, regardless of their potential. Yet even when allowance is made in examinations or intelligence tests for exact chronological age, no account is taken of developmental age. By the completion of growth, the late maturer will probably have caught up, but this will be too late as far as the school is concerned, so that any future opportunities may also be affected. In spite of this information, ability tests, including intelligence tests, compare one child's score with those of many children of the same chronological age, and an individual child's personal style and progress over time are often disregarded. Medical reports could be a valuable asset in education.

THE EARLIEST LEARNING ENVIRONMENT

Although there are many environmental influences on a baby before it is born, including drugs such as nicotine and alcohol, or severe shortages of food, the earliest education is based on human communication of all kinds. The right experiences during the first two years, especially speaking and listening, are crucial to the development of high-level abilities. There is no lack of evidence that the style which parents use in caring for their babies has a strong effect on their eventual intellectual development and outlook.

The way in which birth itself is conducted might be influential on the development of babies' abilities, but the evidence is confusing. For example, the actions of medical drugs on a newborn's responses are uncertain, because each one has a different effect at various stages of the birth, and on mothers and babies respectively. Strong pain-killers can interfere with the initial responses of both mother and baby, with possible poor consequences for their emotional bonding in the longer-term; yet tranquillizers, by reducing anxiety, have been found to have a beneficial effect on mother/baby bonding (Rosenblith & Sims-Knight, 1989).

It is possible that different kinds of 'social' birthing experiences make a difference, but, as yet, there is no evidence that being born by candlelight is more beneficial than in the glare of electricity, or that being either cuddled or slapped at birth has any short- or long-term effect – in spite of people's strong feelings on such matters.

Family attitudes

Each family is unique – a small group which mediates the wider forces of society – so providing a mini-culture of its own in which the child develops. The composition of families varies from isolated one-parent units in big cities, to large families which are well integrated within a local community, African families where there is more than one 'mother', polygamous families, etc.

The term 'socio-economic status' (SES) incorporates an extensive network of attitudes. It indicates a group of influences which provide a picture of a life-style – the context and opportunities in which a child can develop. It affects many areas of life, such as how people spend their time, how much they feel in control of their lives, what kind of reinforcement children are given for their behaviour, and how children might choose to cope in situations of uncertainty.

All long-term studies have shown the cumulative effects of family attitudes (e.g. Douglas, 1968; Bloom, 1985; Freeman, 1991a). These have provided evidence that a child's capacity to do well at school is heavily dependent on encouragement from parents, the type of home and neighbourhood, and on the academic record of the school. The inhibiting effects of low SES on intellectual growth are cumulative and clear. As the children get older, there is a widening gap in average intelligence scores between children of lower and higher SES levels respectively, including children of potentially high achievement.

Parents who have themselves been brought up in impoverished circumstances may lack familiarity with easy verbal communication, which affects their children's intellectual growth. Cultural disadvantage usually brings three main psychological handicaps – in the areas of perception and attention, verbal and intellectual abilities, and motivation. Parents may, for example, give orders more frequently than explanations, and are less likely to discuss daily events with their children. Where the children's questions are ignored or rejected, and play-material is scarce, their development will be accordingly narrowed, and bright children may have to develop complex strategies to get verbal interaction from their parents. It is not so much money as attitude which counts; strictly economic differences between families have little effect on children's achievement when attitudes are similar, except in extreme cases.

The intellectual poverty of children from unstimulating homes is already noticeable by the age of five years. Perceptual deficiency in children who are not talked to by their parents is shown by the fact that they recognize fewer objects and situations; not only are their interests limited, but they are less able to describe them. Piaget (1932) pointed out three important stages in early development, which are still acknowledged today.

THE STAGES OF DEVELOPMENT

Stage 1. An infant is essentially responsive, motivated by needs. The orienting response (seeing where you are) is present at birth, so that any changes in perceptual input will attract the infant, who will react in turn.

Stage 2. An infant shows interest and tries to maintain any pleasant input, such as being jogged on an adult's knee.

Stage 3. An infant seeks novelty by a trial-and-error process, such as dropping things from its high-chair, and making new sounds. From the beginning, 'the more a child has seen and heard, the more he wants to see and hear' (Piaget 1953). This is the start of deep (intrinsic) motivation which, given the right encouragement, should develop continuously.

Relatively isolated babies who live in old-style orphanages or spend long periods in large hospital wards will suffer intellectually. They are the victims of a silent process of neglect and deprivation of human contact and stimulation – and their cultural deficits become their cognitive deficits. No matter how carefully the institutions are run, we know that it is extremely rare for a child to emerge from them functioning at a high level of competence and ability. Although those who live in poor overcrowded conditions often have other children around to see to their early needs for stimulation, when they begin to move and need opportunities for exploration, their perceptual development can be set back, just as later on, when a child begins to speak, it can be difficult to find opportunities to talk with adults. Yet, in contrast, we also know that specifically designed care can have great positive effects on children who had previously been deprived of the most essential human experiences (Clarke & Clarke, 1976).

An adaptation from the study of animals (e.g. by Conrad Lorenz, 1965) implies that there are certain specific times in development when a child is sensitive to certain influences. Danger points in physical development were revealed at the time of the thalidomide tragedy – if the mother took the drug at a specific time in the development of the foetus, the baby was born with deficiencies related to that time. Maria Montessori designed a system of early childhood education using the idea of critical periods or prime developmental times (Montessori, 1964), while Tinbergen showed that an infant duck's attachment to its mother had to be made at a critical time. The same was also shown by experimental work with baby monkeys and different kinds of substitute mothers (Harlow & Harlow, 1966). Intellectual progress is 'at risk' from between seven to thirty-six months, because that is a period which is particularly sensitive to lack of good stimuli.

Even in the United States, probably not more than 1 in 10 children get sufficient educational input at that time for the fulfilment of their potential (White, 1985). Since research can only be done with deprived babies, such as those in old-style orphanages, however, it is difficult to separate the effects of long-term deprivation from those of adverse experiences at precise times. Obviously, one cannot ask parents to deprive their children of possible learning experiences, so that outside the laboratory it is necessary to use large population studies to find out how environment affects children.

Maria Montessori wrote that if those special times are used well then good learning will occur, but if not, the moment could pass and the child may not have the chance again. It could be that some stages of development may be critical, whereas others are merely sensitive and are times when a child is more open to learning. Precise information on the effects of differing amounts of deprivation on these times is lacking. Montessori found that children were more receptive to colour, shape, sound and texture between 2 to 6 years than at other times. She said that if a child is taught something too early, this may result in a dislike for it; too late, and the child may have already have lost interest.

STIMULATION TO ENCOURAGE EARLY LEARNING
* Noise, if it is not meaningful to the baby, can have different effects. Loud and clashing noises produce confusion; background music can be soothing.
* A variety of activities and experiences is important, particularly through parents who are responsive to their child in play and conversation. Children's verbal abilities are clearly related to family verbal interaction.
* Learning materials should be generously provided.
* The example which parents set is more effective than any expectations they might have for their children.

Imitation. The ability to imitate is extremely important in learning. So fundamental and universal is this human ability that its absence in newborns is a sign of retardation. It is the way children learn in a non-literate society, success being followed by the rewards of praise and further responsibility.

Imitation is not only a means of learning; it is also an emotional bonding process which begins from the first day of life, when the two-way imitative 'conversations', which mothers and babies enjoy. Mothers introduce their babies into their culture, such as one would do for a helpless foreigner. In her attempts to bring the baby into the cultural picture, she establishes a 'dialogue' with him. To do this, she is sensitive to what her baby initiates, as well as suggesting and demanding certain behaviours from him. She encourages the activities of which she approves, discourages those she considers inappropriate, trying to extend the baby's grasp of what is appropriate by being sensitive to signs, which she can reinforce, that he is understanding what is wanted of him. It is not just physical behaviour that she is moulding, but a conceptual learning system. The mother/baby dialogue is most certainly a two-way process, its success depending on the sensitivity and tolerance of both parties – neither can remain unaffected. The normal child becomes a novice version of the adults in his family, while the mother, by putting into action her *assumption* that the child is creatively intelligent, acts as a skilled applied psychologist.

These social interactions continue throughout infancy, well before babies begin to produce words, usually at the age of about a year, and they can be started by either of the pair, or with others members of the family. For example, mother looks at baby and baby catches her eye; then she leans forward and says 'Who's a lovely baby then?'. Baby purses his lips and coos. She copies. He does it again. And so on, until interest fades. The style of the mother/baby relationship can be set within a week or so, and is very much influenced by this earliest social life.

Babies initiate as well as imitate, making their own mark on their world. For example, demanding babies receive special family attention and resources, and if these are of an appropriate nature, these can stimulate the infant's intellectual development. But this option is not open to all babies – interaction is the key. It is only in families where the parents are good communicators that the baby's demands are likely to be beneficially effective. This implies a decidedly active role for the baby, but one which positively involves the parents too. It is open to question, though, whether demanding babies are those with the potential for high ability, and whether parents should stimulate passive babies into demanding more, on the grounds that this will encourage intellectual development.

By seven to nine months old, all the basic emotions can be detected in a baby, each contributing to the way in which intellectual behaviour is built up. Emotional deprivation, which may occur at any level of society, can severely damage both personal and intellectual development. It takes considerable energy for a child to remain emotionally balanced in an unstable psychological situation, and it is correspondingly harder to focus on a specific endeavour, to concentrate, and to be competent. This diversion of energy can be observed, even in physical maturation, when an infant is slow to stand and to walk, because of the psychological demands involved. Language development can also suffer, the child falling back into an earlier style of communication until the acute stage is over.

Whatever a child's ability, when this emotional instability happens early in life it can put a brake on learning how to learn, affecting general learning and how it is used. The results may be seen in school, where even children of high potential who are suffering emotionally do not reach the high levels of attainment that might have been expected of them.

In many, if not most, societies, mothers provide a baby's introduction to the prevailing culture by mediating its experiences of the outside world. It is this mediating facility which Feuerstein has recognized and applied with success, not only to children with learning problems, but to children of very high ability (Feuerstein, 1990, and see Chapter 2). Babies are highly sensitive to the kind of care they receive; by two weeks old, they will respond to the mother's characteristics, such as voice and smell, and by six weeks, will become distressed if the social contacts between them are even slightly disturbed. Between three and six months, a baby starts to discriminate between the expressions on people's faces, and from three to nine months, will search for clues from other faces.

The mother's emotions play a role in this mediation, which can significantly affect the intellectual growth of the baby. Even infants of ten weeks can recognize the difference between happiness, sadness or anger in the mother. Her happiness encourages them to explore, joy in one producing joy in the other, whereas her distress causes them to withdraw, sadness producing sadness or anger. The implications are profound: if an infant is unresponsive, it may be a sign of autism, often mistaken for deafness, or real deafness, or it could be due to neglect or abuse. A negative emotional atmosphere inhibits good learning, but positive emotions have an encouraging effect, not least in concern for others, such as helping, sharing, empathizing, and showing physical affection for the benefit of others (Abroms, 1985).

Any condition that causes stress to infants increases their need for their mothers, and decreases their urge to explore. What is more, when toddlers experience a series of anxiety-arousing experiences, the effect is cumulative. Sensitive parents are aware of when the baby's attention begins to diminish, and change their behaviour to keep its interest, such

---

COMPETENCE AT HOME COMES FROM:
- Security and love;
- Praise for genuine effort;
- Tolerance of individual weakness, and patience for mistakes;
- Encouragement;
- Some discipline to provide structure;
- Teaching and listening;
- Encouragement to play;
- Facilities to try things out.

as a change of voice or holding the toy in a different light. Infants cared for in this way are more likely to persist with their own explorations later on, especially as the tasks become more complex.

Roles

Learning life's complex roles is part of the socialization which all children undergo in all cultures. Social roles are similar to dramatic parts, and although the player may not realize it, keeping up a role is generally a two-way process, even in childhood. It involves teaching by adults, as exemplified by the admonition to a small boy not to cry because that is what girls do, which affects the development of how he sees himself in the eyes of others.

People are socially distinct in the way they use language and thought, for example, speaking the same language with a different accent. Children learn their wider social roles, however ambiguous they may be, through their parent's life-styles: the son of a factory-worker is more likely than the professor's son to find his eventual livelihood on the factory floor. But a child must still keep to the role of a child, however wise beyond his years he may be. Should he step out of that role and make independent decisions of which his parents disapprove, this will be termed 'bad behaviour' and corrected, because only in the adult role is one expected to make such decisions. Consequently, reaching maturity involves shaking off a number of outgrown roles, usually during adolescence, which is one of the reasons why problems occur at this time.

A child's position in the family, be it first, second, or fifth, can have a considerable effect on role-expectations. First-born and only children strive harder to please their parents because they identify more strongly with them, and in general they achieve more than their siblings throughout life, including having higher IQ scores. Even their leisure time pursuits often have an educational aspect. There are also recognized personality characteristics for each child's position in the family. First-born and only children are more likely to be more concerned with the effect they have on adults, more responsible and score more highly on intelligence tests; the second-born is easier going and has more friends; the third-born is often more difficult to live with; and the fourth-born is often 'babied' and so learns to be more dependent.

Gender roles. No-one would deny that there are differences between the sexes but, even within the last fifteen years, much that had been taken for granted about the respective behaviour of human males and females has been questioned and changed. In most parts of the world girls are taught to be restricted in their physical behaviour; in Western dress, this means that a girl's skirt not only gets in the way of climbing trees, but obliges girls to stay upright so as not to show their underwear, whereas boys in trousers are free to adopt any position. Girls are often expected to be weak, both psychologically and physically, and boys are expected to be strong in both. Girls' questions in a mixed-sex classroom are often ignored by both male and female teachers in deference to boys' questions, especially in mathematics and science (Kelly, 1988).

Up to the age of 2, American boys and girls scream and cry equally, but by the age of 4, boys hit and shout more (Erikson, 1963). In play, boys are often more concerned with height and downfall movement (such as cars and rockets) and its swift halting (such as by policemen). Girls are concerned with static interiors which could be simply enclosed, and which are peaceful. In their early years, while being cared for by women, boys identify with them; later, because they have to alter this to identify with men, the change can cause them lifelong problems. At their first school, so many teachers are women that the identification problem continues; it should therefore be beneficial to both boys and girls to have more equal numbers of men and women teachers in primary schools.

Even in Norway, a country that has a reputation for advanced gender equality, an experiment with 7-year-olds found considerable stereotyping (Ve, 1991). The researcher attempted to change primary schoolchildren's attitudes by getting them to carry out the other gender's activities for a year – with only moderate success. The little boys even drew the curtains in their classroom so that others passing by would not see them doing the washing-up, although the girls took to working with tools very well. The real breakthrough only came when all the children made their own dolls, which the boys took home and cared for without a trace of shame. It was concluded that it was the involvement in and meaningfulness of their own creations which made all the difference. The parents were delighted with the changes, but it is to be hoped that the effects are generalizable and will last.

It is possible that gender stereotypes are based on very small differences in developmental predispositions between the sexes which are greatly exaggerated in the stereotyping for the benefit of one sex or the other (Hinde, 1991). Vocational choice is the end-product of this role division. All around the world, girls tend to become low-paid, low-status workers, with the expectation of home-making and motherhood as the basis of their self-fulfilment. Boys are more likely to take further training to qualify them for their higher-status jobs and expectations of working outside the home until retirement. Western, long-term, follow-up studies have found that while parents often encourage sons to take jobs for which they were not suited in various ways, daughters are still pressured to take jobs which are generally below their ability.

Personality development

Personality is concerned with individual reactions to the world, involving abilities, emotions, perceptions and physique, and can be measured through behaviour, including responses to a test situation. For easier study, psychologists have arranged aspects of personality into traits such as dominance, sociability, aggression, etc. Some of these traits may be genetically inherited and so unalterable, while others are shaped by experiences. For example, both dominance and submission in children are closely related to the effects of early discipline, although some counselling help can be offered to either the aggressive or the very shy child.

Children who have personality traits such as fear and anxiety, which make it difficult for them to mix with others, have often had unfortunate life experiences that need to be understood to help them. Adjustment is a continual and relative process – there is no such thing as perfection, nor would it be desirable that children adjust more than is essential to living in what may be an unhealthy environment.

There seems to be a connection between personality and school achievement, although intelligence and motivation are, of course, involved. Extraversion is good for school success up to about 11 years-old, stable extraverts being the most likely entrants to selective schools. At about 13, extravert girls achieve better than other girls, but around that age it is the introverted boys who take the lead from extravert boys. University entrants are likely to be high-ability introverts who also have good studying habits and perseverance.

MOTIVATION TO LEARN

Motivation is not a vague general feeling; it implies the seeking of a goal, and the willingness to put in the energy required to reach it. That drive towards a goal, even in quite small children, comes from a complex mixture of self-concept, expectation, social pressure, curiosity, etc., and varies with feelings of success and failure. Human beings have very few instincts to drive their motivation, other then the biological ones for food, etc., so that most motivation 'drivers' are learned and psychological. With adulthood, those psychological needs become more refined so that symbols, such as high status, can become the goal.

Motivation to learn is directly affected by social influences, primarily the family, as it moulds the child's earliest outlook. Probably the major emotional influence on motivation to become competent is self-esteem. This starts in infancy, when good feelings about themselves enable babies to take some control over their behaviour and expectations, and to associate learning with pleasure. There is evidence that 4-year-olds who have high self-concepts are not only more intelligent and socially responsible, but better able to plan ahead, which is a vital part of competence (Mischel, Shoda & Rodriguez, 1989). But there are difficulties in measurement here, for example in accounting for the effects of influences such as gender, classroom setting, and socio-economic status.

Motivational factors are as important to human accomplishment as intellectual ones. The existing body of research on deep meaningful motivation, as distinct from superficially trying to please, seems to be particularly relevant for high levels of competence. Ryan, Connell & Deci (1985), for example, analysed over 200 studies on motivation, from which they formulated a theory of human motivation, which included personality factors. They found that when children feel competent, it motivates them to exercise and elaborate their abilities.

Empowering children by giving them a feeling of competence and a goal to aim for (even examinations) generally increases both their motivation to study and the accompanying increase in level of work. Too much adult control can undermine this by constant dependence on someone else's decisions, because it removes their 'locus of control', the place from which power comes (Rotter, 1966). Over the years, experimental research in schools has shown many times that motivation and achievement levels go up when children are encouraged to take more control over their own learning in the classroom. If they see control of their learning as outside themselves, with the teacher or some other authority figure, they will be less involved and motivated to work. The urge to learn is also improved when poorly motivated youngsters are empowered to help others, as when unsuccessful adolescents take on the role of tutors to younger children.

Every pupil should have achievements to be proud of which are in addition to the basic school curriculum, and not necessarily those things of which the parent or teacher is proud. Ideally, it should be part of the school's provision to encourage pupils to venture out to new areas of learning, or parents and the children themselves will have to find the way. Adequate motivation for learning is normally present in children, but if it is not, the cause often lies in life outside school, for example in family circumstances or peer relationships.

Children who believe that intelligence can be developed are more likely to take risks, and are better motivated to learn than those who believe intelligence is unchangeable. To enhance children's sense of competence, they should be discouraged from attributing their difficulties to basic stupidities, but encouraged to believe that learning, in terms of skills and strategies, can indeed be learned. As children see that they are developing greater competence in learning, they will be more likely to invest energy and reap enjoyment from it.

The goals towards which children are motivated affect their learning. Entwistle (1987) thinks in terms of three main approaches to studying – 'deep', 'surface', and 'strategic' – and believes that these are related to distinct forms of motivation. A deep approach is closely related to intrinsic motivation, where interest or relevance is clear to the learner. A surface approach is mainly concerned with fear of failure or 'test anxiety', while a strategic approach involves both achievement motivation and vocational motives. It has been shown many times that there is a close relationship between the approach adopted and examination results; motivational factors often seem to be more important than the technical aspects of instruction. Pupils who are deeply, intrinsically motivated become more interested and better organized; they spend more time studying, structure their notes carefully prior to revision – and get the best results.

Self-efficacy and motivation. Bandura's self-efficacy theory is concerned with explaining aspects of children's achievement motivation and their social behaviour in school (Bandura, 1977). Self-efficacy is seen as a psychological mediator, which intervenes between cognitive processes and action, while an efficacy expectation is the conviction that one's behaviour will produce a desired outcome. Such expectations would influence people's choice of activities, how much effort they will expend, and how long they will persist at it.

Competence is not a fixed property that one does or does not have in one's behavioral repertoire. Rather, it involves a generative capability in which cognitive, social, and behavioral skills must be organized and effectively orchestrated to serve innumerable purposes (Sternberg & Kolligian, 1990).

Although both the self-concept and self-efficacy are formed through experience, there are probably more differences than similarities between the two. Self-concept is a relatively imprecise emotional construct, whereas self-efficacy is a cognitive construct, based on narrower and more consistent definitions. These are situational rather than general, and so might lead to more precise, valid and useful findings on the psycho-social development of the child. Self-efficacy is mainly derived from how well one performs a challenging task, in which success has been found to produce the highest, strongest, fastest, longest-lasting and most generalized increases in self-efficacy. The evidence of the accomplishment provides potent feedback about abilities. Learning by imitation, although a weaker source of self-efficacy, has been shown to promote it, as can verbal persuasion and emotional arousal, which can convince people that they will succeed at a task.

Individuals who perceive themselves as highly efficacious are expected to act, think, and feel differently from those low in self-efficacy, though the levels will vary over time and across tasks. They are more likely to set themselves challenges, persist longer at difficult tasks, expend more effort, and have fewer stress reactions when tackling difficult or threatening tasks.

School-related self-efficacy has been measured in children as young as 4 years old with specifically constructed tests, assessing both academic and social self-efficacy in children. This is also true for sports. Teachers too are more likely to use methods about which they feel efficacious than those which have been identified by others for them to use. This being the case, trainers of teachers could spend their time more valuably raising teachers' own self-efficacy in specific teaching strategies. This could be, for example, through teaching try-outs, such as micro-teaching, which provide opportunities for doing well, rather than merely trying to convince other student-teachers.

Improving motivation through feedback. Knowing how well one is doing allows sights to be set at an appropriate level, avoiding both certain failure and too-easy success. Both success and failure tend to perpetuate themselves. A teacher can modify feedback to give a child the feeling of success, and so alter her outlook on learning.

The best kind of motivation is intrinsic – that which is generated by interest or relevance in learning, and which is fired by children's belief in their own effectiveness. Such energizing assurance in one's ability to tackle a task comes best from positive personal experiences, especially from feedback that children have received on how well they did. Some of it they can see for themselves, but if other people's responses are to be effective, they must always be genuine, whether good or bad. Sincerity is the key; false praise, such as telling children they have done well when they know they have not, will not enhance their intrinsic motivation. A particularly undermining kind of feedback is telling a child that the right answer was just lucky – unlikely to enhance anyone's feelings of personal competence. Children who believe they can work hard and get better results are more likely to put that belief into action than children who depend on fate.

Despite the importance of feedback, the situation is not entirely controllable by adults. Children can interpret feedback in different ways, depending on the psychological context and the child's personality. Telling one child he is doing badly may be interpreted as an excuse to stop work because it does not seem worth the effort, while for another, the response may be an increase in motivation to prove 'them' wrong. Paradoxically, too much praise, particularly in a system of close supervision, may tell a child simply that he is doing as the teacher bids, rather than personally exploring the area of study and so developing his own competence. This can undermine intrinsic motivation, because it then becomes psychologically impossible for the child to feel in control of his own progress in learning.

All children, whatever their ability, want to feel effective and engaged by challenge, which must include a risk of failure. The highly able need challenge at least as much as any others. Experimental work has shown that if children are given a superficial reward, such as money or sweets, they are far more likely to choose the easiest ways of succeeding, whereas if they are enjoying the activity for itself, they choose harder tasks, usually just above the level of previous success. No child can reasonably be expected to work hard in all areas of the curriculum, since individual interests are influenced by many things. But when children are interested in what they are doing, they have a natural tendency to take on challenges that exercise and expand the limits of their competence.

Positive feedback can be very effective, particularly a positive attitude on the part of the educator, who can praise something, identify some success and offer a reward such as a treat. Negative feedback, such as sarcasm, punishment, detention and the like, is much less effective: the child may have been seeking extra attention, and such punishment may simply fulfil what was wanted.

Group pressure. All groups or institutions, whether family, school or ability group, exert a certain pressure on their members. For example, if the overriding peer-group feeling is one of rebellion, it would take a strong member to respect established authority. Group competition can have a marked effect on group performance but, if carried to extremes, can be psychologically damaging. Teachers are normally supported by society in their efforts to motivate the classroom group towards learning, but at the same time may face peer-group pressure which runs counter to those efforts.

Social influences on achievement

The social environment affects a child's educational development continuously, particularly with regard to aspirations. This is not only affected by the immediate family, but by broader cultural variations which filter through, such as the intensity and style of religious influence, a high regard for criminality, or the move to individuality of the 1960s. Yet, the parents' hopes and expectations for their children, even if they are not made explicit, can have a remarkably self-fulfilling effect, and the examples of parent's behaviour even more so. The son who is expected to fulfil his parents' ambitions often does his best, and the girl marked for marriage and home-making tends to do just that.

Research begun in America by McClelland et al., (1953) on the 'Need for Achievement' (NAch), pointed out some detailed features of upbringing which promote a child's urge to achieve. He suggested that parents should help children judge and relate what they are aiming for within their developing frames of reference. A simple example would be if a small boy is building a tower by piling up bricks. If his parents expect him to add more than he is able to balance, then the tower will collapse, but if they suggest a number which is too easy for him he will neither get satisfaction from the success nor any praise for it, and so may lose interest. If their expectation is set just above what he believed he could do, and he achieves it, then he feels the glow of success and wants to aim even higher.

The boy is thus developing expectations – a frame of reference – about what he can accomplish. A touch of uncertainty helps, although parental encouragement must be reasonably realistic. If he does better than expected he will advance – positive reinforcement from proven ability – if worse, he will lower his aim. The crucial aspect in improving his achievement is for him to know how effective he has been in relation to his own self-evaluation so that he can alter his aim accordingly. An emotional example would be when a child is put in a situation of relative maturity before he is ready, such as children who are placed in a class a couple of years in advance at school, which may result in poor development of reference points; the child becomes overdependent on the approval of parents, teachers or friends. A child's self-confidence, emotional reaction, and frame of reference, are also affected by causes over which parents can have no control, including personality factors and the wider cultural influence.

Achievement in school. A child's wish to achieve in school, in terms of motivation, persistence and the value placed on education, is not only personal, but is associated with the traditions and attitudes of the school itself, such as the effectiveness of the teaching methods, and respect for pupils. A pupil's motivation to achieve is driven by goals, notably the perceived relevance and value of school lessons, so that underachievement due to poor persistence in the face of difficulties may result from loss of interest. A little anxiety (not too much) sometimes improves effort and results, but only in specific circumstances, such as exams. But the temptation is always there to do other things than study.

Personality characteristics of the successful school pupil present a picture of an individual who is law-abiding, diligent and conscientious. Such a pupil is well socialized, with high levels of self-control, accepts the goals and authority of the institution, and enjoys intellectual pursuits. The pupil will be relatively responsible and dependable, with control of gratification, more introverted than most, with boys tending to display qualities which are sometimes thought of as feminine, such as consideration for others. Though not all successful children who are successful at school go on to do as well at higher education, most of them do.

CHAPTER II

Intelligence

THE BRAIN

Both the physical make-up of the brain and the way it operates affect a person's intelligence. For our present purposes, the brain can be thought of as a highly complicated switchboard in a telephone system, with the major difference that thought messages are transmitted almost instantaneously. It operates by using special, densely packed, nerve cells or neurones with long fibres (of up to three metres) called axons which reach out to other axons. Each one takes in and sends on messages to other neurones by an electric current that jumps across the gap (synapse) between them; storage seems to take place through changes in the protein structure.

Thinking is the result of around ten billion neurones constantly exchanging information and, in theory, there is no limit to the amount of material the brain can cope with. One neurone can probably connect with as many as a thousand others at the same time, and the more information-passing fibres any one neurone has, the greater its ability to transmit information. On that basis, if we could increase the branching of the information-giving fibres, we could improve intelligence. Indeed, it is possible that very intelligent people have more of these branching fibres than the less intelligent, which would explain how they can process information so much more efficiently. It seems that the more a learner uses a particular nerve route – whether for mental arithmetic or gymnastics – the quicker the jump across the synapse gap between axons becomes, and the more refined the skills.

When learned behaviour becomes entrenched by this increasing smoothness of action, it becomes unthinking and automatic, as happens in much of our daily behaviour, and is called a habit. Habits are constantly reinforced, both because they are the 'easiest' form of behaviour, and because of the complexity of causes which bring them about. This makes the breaking of a habit difficult, and strong motivation is needed to change one.

Psychological research on rats has shown that the thicker the fatty coating around each axon, the quicker they conduct information and the more intelligently the rats behave. This thickness is found to increase when the rats are handled more by their keepers, and also when they are given more stimulating intellectual tasks – which for the rats took the form of negotiating more complicated mazes. It is quite possible that human information-processing is similarly affected. If we transfer these findings to children, it would follow that intelligence – or at least speed of thought – could be nurtured through both physical affection and a stimulating learning environment.

To some extent, the brain can also be thought of as a computer, since it seems to operate largely on programmes: bright children can cope with more complicated programmes than others. The information which the nerve cells store can either be in individual bits or in chains. A simple body action, such as raising a little finger, simultaneously triggers off millions of circuits. Whatever we learn is stored in programmes for further use, but as we are human beings and not computers, our brains tend to use these programmes in an emotional way. For example, we are reluctant to take in new learning unless it seems interesting or rewarding. In other words, we learn best what we want to learn.

Brain action is influenced by hormones; these are body chemicals, made by the glands, which affect body functions, especially the emotions. For example, if a child has a negative attitude to what he is supposed to be learning, or is bored, frightened or tired, the glands give off hormones which can actually block the penetration of new information into the highest processing levels in the brain. For example, when exam 'nerves' become real fear and panic, they can extinguish all productive study. Many individuals who have faced examination papers have found that they could not remember a thing, and in spite of every effort to put something down, even answers which were known perfectly the day before seem to have vanished. One way of overcoming this problem in children's learning is to try to keep it interesting and tension-free, and to give plenty of praise, so that they feel good about it.

Right brain and left brain. For centuries, philosophers have written about the split between thinking based on reason and thinking influenced by emotion. It is only since the late 1950s, however, that psychologists, have discovered that this differentiation is caused by the different influences of the two physical halves of the brain (Sperry, 1961; Ornstein, 1972). The research began with observation of epileptics and patients who had suffered brain injuries, where either the two halves of the brain had become separated or there was damage to specific parts of it. People who are dominated in their thinking by the right half of their brain tend to see things as a whole. They are concerned with patterns, shapes and sizes, and are more imaginative and intuitive. Their ideas can seem vague to left-brain dominated people, who are often better at more logical and academic work such as mathematics and word skills. Whereas the right side will help hum a tune, write a poem, or see a painting as a whole, the left side will help write grammatically, mend an engine or admire the brush technique of the artist. Most people have a bias to one side, giving them their special style, which can interfere with aspects of their learning. For example, poor spellers may be biased to use their right brain more than their left, relying too much on intuition, without paying enough attention to the details of the letters in a word. But somehow most people manage to work the two halves together in some kind of harmony. The brain is not so much one computer, but two, working together for better effect.

It seems that the basic building blocks of knowledge are first absorbed in large amounts by the more spontaneous right-hand brain, then sorted out and brought to consciousness by the left-hand brain. Each half can do the other's work to some extent, but each functions better when the incoming information fits into its style of processing. It is not always the appropriate half, however, which tackles incoming information.

Babies and toddlers do not usually have a dominant half to their brains, but traditional teaching in schools has emphasized the more rigid left-brain activity, sometimes to the detriment of the right. Indeed, school and intelligence quotient (IQ) tests seem designed more for the left brain than the right. It is possible that if certain right- or left-brain activities fail to be exercised regularly in a person, they will never develop properly. This bias is possibly a problem of industrialized countries, because in Asian countries, such as China and India, there is traditionally a greater concern with balance of both mind and body. Since the greatest creative achievements require the use of both halves of the brain, an overly academic education can cut down a child's creative potential, and so many teachers have begun to cultivate the more intuitive and creative

---

LEFT AND RIGHT BRAIN INFLUENCES

Left brain	Right brain
Likes formal teaching	Likes low lights and warmth
Is persistent	Not keen to sit and learn
Is responsible	
Is happy learning alone	Likes learning in company
Stays still while learning and doing things	Likes moving around, touching
Does well at school	Does not excel at school

right brain by thinking exercises which avoid assessment of ideas, such as brainstorming or dramatic activities.

It is possible that there are gender differences in right- and left-brain use. Girls, being intuitive, are usually said to be dominated by the right brain, whereas boys are said to be left-brain dominated, and so better at mathematics and engineering. But, since babies do not show any signs of this specialization, which increases as children get older, it is more likely that their style of thinking is influenced by the way each sex is brought up. Evidence from the former communist countries, where girls were given equal mathematical teaching and expectations of performance, and became mathematicians in equal numbers to boys, provides a clear example of this. Any child can fall into thinking habits that are dominated by one side. Adults can watch out for this, try to correct the balance, and help the child stay mentally agile.

Cognitive style

Another way of looking at this division of thinking styles is to group children as 'divergent' or 'convergent' thinkers. This corresponds fairly well with right- and left-brain thinkers respectively. A convergent thinker goes by the rules, will probably reach conclusions quite logically and generally does well in scientific or mathematical activities. Divergent thinkers are more creative, coming up with new and maybe crazy-sounding ideas and approaches, and often leaning towards artistic activities. Convergent-minded children do better with straightforward question-and-answer type tests, while divergent people prefer essays, where they can use their imagination. A typical test of convergent/divergent thinking is to ask a child what uses can be made of a brick, with which the converger will build houses and walls, prop up shelves, etc., the diverger will use it as a paperweight, crumble it to make cement, or throw it through a window. It is not that a child is completely one or the other kind of thinker, but the dominant style of thinking can make a real difference in learning.

Most research on learning and thinking is carried out in an experimental way, usually in classroom settings. Such studies are concerned with how children interact with the very specially ordered physical world of the researcher that follows clear rules. This is not always what happens in the normal classroom, however, and certainly not at home. Experimental designs of this kind are supposed to keep the measurement 'pure', to avoid the influence of the child's personality and social environment. It is considerably easier for a researcher to carry out experiments in which interactions between people are largely controllable, than to study the endless complexity in normal life.

Mental skills do not exist in isolation; they are a part of the whole child, reflecting actual life circumstances. This can be seen in each one's 'cognitive style' – the way each person approaches experiences, whether emotional or intellectual, practical or academic – their personal manner of learning. Cognitive style includes personal preferences for the learning set-up, such as working alone or with others, learning by listening or by reading, choice of subject area, persistence, and the rhythm and length of concentration. It also includes the way that such aspects of learning are combined – what are the preferred 'mental strategies'.

Cognitive style can partly be explained in terms of the relative use of the two sides of the brain. Given enough time, pupils have been found to reach equally deep levels of learning via many different styles, though the more creative aspects of putting that learning into action call for both sides of the brain to be used.

Concentration. The ability to concentrate depends upon whether the learning environment suits one's cognitive style. For example, concentration is affected both by the amount of distraction around and by how much one can resist its intrusion – 'redundancy control'. The most successful achievers appear to be better able than other people to adjust their learning environments for maximum effectiveness, using the type of redundancy control which suits their style. On the other hand, the academically less successful seem to be less aware both of the variety of options that are available and of which ones would best suit them. Some will use quiet background noises, for example, like traffic or soft music, to absorb emotional responses and leave the mind free for study. Others need absolute silence to do their best. Some know that anxiety about approaching examinations can help them concentrate, and so let it accumulate by leaving study to the last minute; others work better without it, and so plan well ahead.

Competition. Competing is a way of finding out and defining one's own capabilities, and the way it is used is part of one's cognitive style. But, to be effective, the comparison which comes from competition must be meaningful, which is why 'self-validation', or assessing one's own progress, is much more effective than aiming for the approval of authority. Self-validation involves personal commitment to the task, and can promote independence of action and a sense of competence – of power in oneself. That is different from neurotic competitiveness, where the thrill of winning is all and the experience itself means little. Very young mathematicians seem particularly keen to compete with themselves. They may spend more time on their own than other exceptionally able children, practising calculations and thinking about their mathematical interest (Radford, 1990).

HUMAN INTELLIGENCE

Human beings have the highest form of intelligence in the animal world. Among all the warm-blooded creatures, only humans have the ability to be self-reflexive, that is to think and to use words. Although animals do communicate, their language is decidedly restricted; words are the key to intellectual development because intelligence is an interactive phenomenon.

In its broadest sense, intelligence is the individual's power to cope with his or her personal world. It is about reaching goals, whether basic, like getting enough to eat, or more distant, like passing an exam. Intelligence works by assessing what choices are available and then deciding on the best possible actions. It can be thought of in the same terms as physical ability, in the way that practice makes a big difference to performance. Even so, some people find that they can win races relatively easily, while others trail along behind no matter how hard they try. Psychologists would be overjoyed to find the key to increasing the power of people's inherent mental abilities, but none has yet come up with the magic formula.

Though intelligence cannot be boosted dramatically, it can certainly be inhibited from reaching its full power. Physical conditions, such as brain damage at birth or early starvation, can damage its growth, as does poor psychological nourishment. Evidence comes from the accounts of children who have been severely deprived of interaction with other people, such as those housed in large orphanages, or when isolated by mentally abnormal adults. With special care, such children can improve, but if they cannot talk when they are found, they never reach a normal level of functioning. Children with lower intelligence scores from intellectually poor homes who have been fostered in mentally livelier homes have notably improved their scores (Clarke & Clarke, 1976).

In many developed countries, according to the tests, the intelligence of children is going up, increasing the numbers of those with high potential. For example, in the United Kingdom in 1935, Raymond Cattell tested all the 10 year olds in a city and found their average IQ to be 100. In 1948 he carried out the same test and found no difference. Yet a third measurement in 1985 found that the overall IQ had gone up very significantly to 112.5 (Lynn & Hampson, 1986). The researchers concluded that the second, unchanged result was due to the intellectually depressing effects of the Second World War, and that the later rise was due to improved nutrition, general health, smaller families and improved family education. It is important to note, though, that in that last measurement it was abstract reasoning and visuo-spatial abilities which had improved, while vocabulary, general knowledge and education-based skills remained the same.

The rise in measured intelligence has taken place at about the same rate in the United States and in some European countries, but at a steeper rate in Japan (Lynn & Shigehisa, 1991), to the extent that the average Japanese child's IQ is now claimed to be about 3 points higher than elsewhere. Illiteracy is virtually unknown there, compared with 10% of functional illiterates in some industrialized countries and more than 40% of pure illiterates in one or two Latin American countries.

In measuring intelligence, it is important to be aware of the influence of cultural factors, and also to include 'everyday' abilities, because intelligence always refers to the real world and what is valued in it. Whatever components go to make up this most tantalizing of human abilities, it has to be considered in its natural habitat, and how it can be enhanced there. At the turn of the century, when the serious study of intelligence first took shape, the fashion was for scientific measurement which meant that the personal aspects of mental life were seen as somewhat marginal. Not until very recently has there been a positive resurgence of interest in the way people use their minds in real life.

Intelligence tests

An intelligence test is designed to predict how well a child will achieve at school, and most tests can do this rather well. Consequently, if a child scores highly on a test, yet badly at school, it is a clear indication that this child is underachieving. On the other hand, a poor score on a test can be used as an excuse by teachers, relieving them from making greater efforts to help the pupil do better on the grounds that, 'after all, there's no point when his IQ score is so low'. The question of whether intelligence is fixed for life needs some understanding. For example, IQ testing under the age of 5 is not entirely reliable, and only when intelligence becomes more stable do tests provide a good basis for prediction.

Performance on a test of intelligence can be thought of as the end-result of the interaction of numerous distinct mental activities. In theory, then, if you alter this 'orchestration', you can alter the performance. Jean Piaget, a Swiss psychologist working in middle decades of this century (see below), proposed that there is indeed change in the style and levels of performance as children grow up. He described this qualitative alteration in terms of different stages of mental development which are associated with different ages. Although these developmental stages are testable, they are no longer as popular as they were among educational psychologists, since there is now considerable doubt about the precise ages at which Piaget's stages occur.

On the assumption that intelligence changes in its style of operation as it develops, as Piaget suggested, it should be possible to find out what types of instruction would most benefit a particular child, and which experiences would allow a youngster to grasp a new concept and make use of it. Although this is a vital role for education, there is a large gap where this knowledge should be. Teachers are less in need of an IQ as a predictor of an individual child's performance, than more specific help towards knowing the type of education which best suits their pupils. The ideal test should not only give a 'diagnosis', but should incorporate a decision about what to do next in teaching that particular child.

How does one intervene to obtain a more favourable effect from teaching? To start with, just as in business, improving the outcome depends on knowing the current status of assets and liabilities – the child's abilities. But abilities are not static entities and their measurement is not enough. Conventional tests, which provide a measure of a child's intelligence relative to his age-group, are not very useful as a basis for designing educational techniques; they work like a thermometer which tells you whether you have a temperature or not, but not what to do about it. Diagnostic tests, however, such as those for reading problems, aim to discover the child's strengths and weaknesses, and to help teachers fine-tune their teaching to individual children. A typical test might be a graded progression of series completions, such as completing the sequence 2 . . . 4 . . . 6 . . . 8, which could be used at different ages. Although these activities appear in conventional tests too (also with letters, numbers, pictures or geometric figures), diagnostic tests are designed to show how the child's progression shows up where learning or reasoning needs particular help.

Present-day intelligence tests are scientific instruments, and when used in the way they were intended and for the purposes for which they were designed, they are efficient and reliable. The results, however, apply to school learning and one could draw conclusions neither about learning outside the classroom nor whether the style of instruction is the best for a child. Additional human problems, such as being ill on the day of the test, can of course lower the score, but such effects can be recognized and accounted for. Until recently, developments in intelligence tests have been cosmetic, such as remoulding the same ideas into computer format, but newer tests, based on broader theories of intelligence, offer promise of more fundamental changes, such as the British Intelligence Scale, which produced a fine profile of a child's abilities, or Robert Sternberg's ideas of breaking intelligence into its component parts and testing how each one functions (Sternberg, 1991). It is possible that as newer, more sophisticated tests become more widely available, we may be able to improve the procedures used to identify abilities outside school-learning, although no one test is ever likely to entirely account for the mental processes of every person.

Some psychologists, such as Eysenck (1985), have taken a biological approach, arguing that intelligence can be measured by an individual's speed, either by the electro-encephalographic traces of brain action, or by discrimination between similar test signals. It is, indeed, true that a high proportion of very highly intelligent young people can think very rapidly, and great efforts are being made to associate speed of action with measured IQ. Although there is reasonable evidence of moderate statistical relationships, these may simply reflect differences in the children's level of concentration, and we need more sophisticated tests to see if there is a real biological basis for measuring intelligence (Mackintosh, 1986).

Not all quick thinking is good, however, as it can affect the accuracy of the decisions. Children who answer impulsively may simply offer the first idea which occurs to them, and in making mistakes, provide themselves with negative reinforcement. Although it can be a sign of high ability, quick responses are also found in children with learning problems, boys more than girls, and poor children more than the better-off. It may be a habit learned early in life. Impulsive children need help in being more reflective, by encouraging them to take their time, although fear of failure can slow them down too much.

Some major theories of intellectual functioning

The nature and structures of human abilities have exercised the minds of philosophers for many centuries. Psychologists, however, have only been experimenting and theorizing about them for 150 years, and until the 1950s, assumed that most abilities were relatively unchanging characteristics of an individual.

In 1904, Spearman outlined a simple, elegant theory of intelligence – the 'two-factor' theory. A general ability factor ('g') was considered to be fixed, but specific ability factors ('s' factors) were open to environmental influence. He suggested that abilities had a hierarchical structure, the 'g' factor being at the top, related to a variety of lesser factors, which in their turn contained the more specific ability factors. Even today, psychologists sometimes still use 'g' to describe children. Thurstone, in the mid-1920s, further refined the early testing and data, producing a model with seven 'primary' abilities; the first attempt to provide a profile of abilities. But his 'primary' abilities were found to overlap, and his tests proved to be relatively inaccurate in prediction.

There were two basic problems with the factor approach. Firstly, as with all research, the outcome depends on the means used to gather the data, and secondly, since a statistical factor does not describe a psychological process, its interpretation is always somewhat subjective. While these theories have had relatively little effect on teaching, they had a strong influence on the investigation and descriptions of intelligence that are widely used today, particularly on the construction of intelligence tests. These limitations do not mean that the early theories and models are now regarded as worthless, but rather that they are mathematical concepts which fail to do justice to the richness and variety of human potential.

Guilford (1967) put forward a more detailed model of the intellect in action, which included: the type of content (e.g. words, numbers); the mental operation performed (e.g. deductive reasoning); and the nature of the end-product of the mental operations (e.g. a conclusion). By combining these types of feature in every possible way, he collected no less than 120 distinguishable abilities, including convergent and divergent intelligence, the first attempts at testing for creativity. Cattell (1965) also broadened the scope of intelligence tests, and tried to avoid questions which required the subject to arrive at the answer that the psychologist had already decided on. In addition to the familiar deductive and inductive reasoning tests, he included questions to which there was no correct answer, seeking novel, creative answers.

Alfred Binet

Modern intelligence testing began in France at the turn of the century when Alfred Binet devised a means of identifying children who were likely to have learning difficulties at school (Binet & Simon, 1908). He did this by comparing their achievements with those of their age-peers. Now, nearly a hundred years later, the two most popular measures of intelligence are still versions of Binet's original scale, notably the Stanford-Binet (Terman & Merrill, 1961) and the several Wechsler Intelligence Scales designed for different age groups, including adults (e.g. Wechsler, 1949). The Wechsler scales are not built up item by item, like the Stanford-Binet, but the verbal and performance scales together produce the single IQ.

Although these two tests correlate highly (though with different upper IQ limits) the Wechsler scales are often preferred by psychologists, since the Stanford-Binet is not only more cumbersome to conduct, but its subtest scores, which make up the final IQ, are in different combinations for different ages, so that there may be discrepancies between them. Even so, the Stanford-Binet scale is so widely respected that new intelligence tests are often validated against it during their construction. Thus there are many IQ tests which are remarkably like it in make-up and scoring, which means that whatever they measure, it is likely to be the same as the original model.

J.C. Raven set out to tap 'observation and clear thinking' in his very popular set of Raven's Matrices for all ages (e.g. Raven, 1965). In a book of patterns, the subject is asked to select the missing part from a selection. The test does not give an IQ, but places the subject on a percentile ranking. As the tests does not ask for recall of learned information, poorly educated people and those with communication problems can do well on them. Correlations between the matrices and IQ scores are usually of the order of 0.7 to 0.9. Different population norms have been worked out for many nationalities. The test is easy to use, and suitable for research or as a screening device for general intellectual ability.

However, a test can only take a sample of intellectual behaviour at a specific time, during which the subject gives evidence of how well he has accepted and understood the processes of learning offered to him – all tests, even the non-verbal, involve experience and from that result performance is assessed.

Jean Piaget

The Swiss pioneer in child developmental research, Jean Piaget, evolved his theories from observations of his own three children. He was originally a biologist, who brought ideas of biological maturation into psychology with his theory of progressive learning stages leading to the eventual 'fruiting' of formal reasoning, although this ordering was never seen as static models or patterns. Rather, his view of intellectual activity took up the biological principle of homeostasis (balance) in which children have to balance the demands of the environment with their own ways of thinking about it. He saw children as actively building their own intelligences, constantly reconstructing their ideas of reality, rather than merely acquiring and storing information (Piaget, 1971). But he was more interested in the structure of the mind, than the processes which were used.

In spite of Piaget's lack of interest in the processes of learning, it was his influence which was largely responsible for changing the style of education of many primary schools all over the world. Perhaps because of that gap, his theory has now lost its dominance, even being largely abandoned in the education systems of some Western countries, although teacher training is taking time to catch up. As with any once-dominant ideology, though, traces of it are likely to remain, because it has changed people's way of thinking. Piaget was not the only psychologist to insist that a child is active in the learning situation, but he brought about the concept and practice of education as 'child-centred', rather than 'teacher-centred'. He saw that children's abilities are flexible and alterable, and that abilities take shape in the way children cope with their experiences.

Egocentrism. There is now adequate evidence to show that strong emphasis on Piaget's stages of mental development may even act as a barrier to their progress. Consider, for example, Piaget's concept of egocentrism. In their early years, he described children as 'egocentric', believing that the world revolves round them – e.g. that the moon 'follows them' as they walk. Yet not only can newborns turn towards a sound, but from the age of two months, a baby can follow a pointing finger, and can soon even look to where someone else is looking (Butterworth, 1984). This provides considerable counter-evidence to Piaget's theory that the baby is entirely self-centred, since it shows that even very tiny babies can alter their own viewpoint to that of someone else.

The same is true for Piaget as for any other experimental psychological situation: it is not true to life because the investigator has had to make some assumptions about the child's knowledge in order to set up the experiment. In normal life children have more control over the knowledge they use. This being so, when they are asked either to give an explanation or to do things for which they are quite capable of responding correctly, the children may fail the experimenter's task because they are unsure of exactly what is wanted of them.

If we believe that children cannot learn beyond their recognized stage of development, we will not provide teaching that is more advanced than this – a particular problem for the highly able who develop very fast and so can benefit from teaching at a much higher level. If school education is geared to no more than what children are expected to be able to accomplish, rather then what they could actually do, they will be educationally under-supplied and so limited in possibilities for learning.

The limitation of 'egocentrism' is also seen in children's drawing, in which the final effect is influenced by many other factors. Taking the child's, rather than the researcher's point of view – listening to and understanding what the child is trying to do – throws a different light on, for example, the development of visual perspective. Experiments show that a normal baby is quite capable of receiving and sorting visual information, to recognize and understand the position of objects in space, and later small children try to represent objects in realistic ways in their drawings.

The absence of 'egocentrism' is also seen in little children's speech, and their understanding of other people's ideas and feelings. Children soon develop the capacity for verbal description through interaction with adults, and adapt themselves to different levels of conversation relatively early; they can mentally change places from speaker to listener and back.

This is also true of their understanding of other people's mental states, as well as for their needs and feelings. Very early on children have intuition, what is called a child's 'theory of mind', i.e. how they believe other people think, which later becomes conscious. Contrary to what Piaget believed, even young children can see a variety of points of view – along with their own (Cox, 1991).

The Russians

Current theoretical focus rests on the work of Vigotsky and his student Luria, work which was long repressed within the Soviet system, and thus very late in reaching the rest of the world. Many of their ideas are concerned with the parallel development of language and intellect (see below).

Vigotsky's ideas on 'zones of proximal development' are now seen as crucial to maintaining intellectual abilities successfully, whether for playing the violin or thinking. These zones denote what is available for further development relative to the age of the individual, as well as expectations for the future, given their existing knowledge base. The zones thus determine the level at which teaching should be pitched to improve children's learning. Vigotsky also formed the concept of 'grasping' for knowledge – an intellectual hunger which all children have. He said it diminished with age because other concerns, such as earning a living, occupy energy and time. This explained, he said, some of the differences between men and women's achievements, in that boys are usually 'grasping' as part of their career development, whereas girls make less effort because career development is not seen to be so important for them (Vigotsky, 1962, 1978).

The essential difference between Piaget's views and those of Vigotsky, is that whereas Piaget saw mental development as taking place almost independently of learning, Vigotsky insisted that it was rather more dependent on learning. Accordingly, should a child be in a situation where stimulation and learning is poor, boredom follows. The best stimulation, he said, came from the distinction between what a child could do unaided and what a child could do with some help, working in 'the zone of proximal development'. If this is so, instead of encouraging more of what a child can already do, the teacher should help the child to grasp concepts which are just out of reach, as well as introducing new 'zones', i.e. concepts which are not yet to hand. Exploring new areas should also eliminate the boredom of learning, as long as it is done within a social context, so that group learning is often more effective than individual learning.

Feuerstein

Reuven Feuerstein, a former pupil of Piaget, developed ideas about intelligence and learning during the 1950s, while dealing with the assessment and education of orphaned, traumatized immigrants coming to Israel after the Holocaust. Over many years he came to believe in the enormous plasticity and modifiability of the human intellect, and the crucial role which significant adults can play in mediating the child's cognitive development, always within a social context (Feuerstein, 1980, and see Chapter VI).

Feuerstein worked from the basis that children need information to build with, but that without certain key learning skills, acquired early in life, they are less open to learning from experience; they are closed and, in his terms, less 'modifiable' than those who have them. It is while they are picking up information that children also learn to reason, that is, to use mental skills for inducing new relationships, and generating hypotheses that can be examined and tested. These reasoning abilities are pulled along by teaching which demands that children examine what they know, re-structure it, and develop it further to construct new knowledge and understanding. They can only do that if they know enough to start with. The teacher can put pupils in a position to build on what they know by providing a principle for them to work with, and then implementing it, based on the teacher's understanding of what the pupils already know. This means that the teacher must then keep track of the pupils' knowledge, further their explorations, and observe their progress.

Feuerstein's Instrumental Enrichment (IE) programme, which needs 40 to 60 hours of training, has been adopted not only by schools in Israel but by educators in many countries. Evaluation of the programmes shows that the approach can improve problem-solving for children who are below average performance for their age. Feuerstein says the effects become greater over time; the more education a child receives, the greater the development of general intelligence.

Along with Vigotsky's ideas of 'zones of proximal development', IE does bring the possibility of teaching cognitive skills within sight, at least in terms of a promising way forward rather than a static end product. It encourages teachers to think about their role in fostering pupils, and suggests ways of going about it as well as novel materials to enhance that role (Blagg, 1991).

The current state

Recent psychological understanding presents an ever more flexible picture of the human intellect. This is more frequently described in terms of a personal 'profile' – a single numerical score being scarcely adequate to describe intelligence, any more than a number could describe someone's personality. Intelligence itself is now regarded as a way of behaving, and one which has to be developed. When teachers think of intelligence as capable of being developed, it improves both their own and their pupils' motivation for learning. In all forms of education, there are always general gains in learning, problem-solving and thinking, yet there are also biases. For example, pupils in school situations which emphasize verbal aspects gain most in the verbal dimension and those in technical schools most in spatial ability.

It is now recognized that aspects of intelligence such as reasoning or learning ability owe much to past experience, i.e. to what has already been learned, especially in the early years. Conventional intelligence tests are increasingly regarded as a measure of achievement in school-work, and useful tools in education; but like any other tools, they need skilled handling.

Increasingly, psychologists have turned to studying the relationship between emotion and intelligence. Indeed, there is evidence that emotional disturbance can alter information-processing, notably in the selection and recall of information, slowing it down or distorting it. Emotion has been shown to provide a heavy influence in decision-making and problem-solving (Hoffman, 1986). So far, theories of intelligence have varied from Spearman's general 'g' factor, through a profile of specific skills numbering from 3 to 120, to the idea that the entire concept of intelligence is an illusion (Howe, 1990; Ceci, 1990). Nevertheless, it is still generally believed that babies are born with a variety of abilities, and with varied upper limits to their potentials.

THE DEVELOPMENT OF INTELLECTUAL SKILLS

Good intellectual skills have to be learned, although basic sensory awareness matures naturally in normal conditions. The intellectual ability to cope with incoming information, store it in flexible categories in the memory, retrieve it for application to different situations, and adapt new information, all have to be refined to reach levels of competence. This needs directed teaching, such as in learning to distinguish between shapes, recognizing forms and estimating distances. All the senses are teachable to develop them into intellectual skills.

Perceptual learning

Once a baby is in the world, every sense is active – sight, taste, smell, touch and hearing, even sensitivity to the pitch, loudness and direction of sounds. Eye movements are well enough organized to track a moving object, distinguish colours, and look for interesting lights; newborn babies are attracted by sharp contrasts. Refinement of these early efforts is rapid, so that by five months, some can even distinguish between strangers in photographs. They soon learn the practical advantages from responsiveness, and by the second month of life can vocalize whatever sounds are more likely to gain attention: some being more successful at this than others.

When babies see a bright flash of light or hear a sudden loud noise, they turn their heads towards it before they can identify what it is; indeed, adults do the same. This paying attention to any novel stimulus is called the 'orienting reflex'. It helps people react quickly, taking their attention away from other objects.

Even in their first days of life, infants do not passively orient only to attention-grabbing objects that appear in their visual fields; they actively seek out what interests them. There are certain qualities which will hold an infant's attention, one of which seems to be a preference for situations that are neither under- or over-stimulating. Babies also try to control the amount of incoming stimulation, and if it is too much, they will simply go to sleep to cut it off. The complexity of the stimulus also affects how much attention it receives; brighter children prefer more complex situations, though what is moderately complex to a two month-old baby may seem simple to a six month-old.

Language development. The infant's keen ability to identify sounds, such as musical tones, affects perception of speech, which includes identifying the voices of different speakers. Infants as young as three days-old not only seem able to identify their mothers' voices, but prefer them. It is possible that this preference is based on a familiarity with the voice that begins before birth, because infants suck more vigorously when tape recordings of their mother's voice are played to them.

Skill in communication can be regarded as the cradle of intelligence. Even by two months, a baby will have learned something of the structure of language, and evidence of a built-in ability to interact with others at birth has been clearly demonstrated. Early communication has a significant effect on intelligence – Tulkin (1977) found that children under 3 years old who were assessed as having a high quality of both verbal and non-verbal communication with their mothers from birth showed better intellectual progress than those who had received neither that amount nor that quality of interaction. The fortunate toddlers played for longer periods with the toys he gave them, were less easily distracted, more easily soothed, had better perceptual discrimination, and – eventually – higher IQ scores.

Adults, men as well as women, talk to infants and young children in a style known as 'motherese', which is characterized by a high pitch and exaggerated intonations. Infants as young as four months-old turn more towards statements in 'motherese' than towards speech delivered in adult intonations, and they seem to prefer it. This also helps infants to discriminate speech sounds more effectively, since the slower cadence and more marked intonations of 'motherese' both attract infants' attention and help them understand what they are hearing.

Advanced language is probably the first thing to look for in assessing potentially high ability; it has an enduring quality and underpins many other later competencies, including mathematics. In a summary of research on very early verbal ability and its outcomes, Fowler (1990) concluded that an advanced level of language in infants depends heavily on stimulation and practice from adults, such as being read to and talked with from the time of birth. Looking at the early lives of recognized gifted adults, he found that they had enjoyed an enormous amount of verbal stimulation, both spoken and written. Radford, too, in his survey of exceptional early achievers, found that although some appeared to come from homes of low socio-economic status, further investigation showed that these homes were all lively, stimulating and often highly verbal (Radford, 1990).

Skill development. The processes of intellectual development are not confined to the simple acquisition of skills; each new skill adds to and changes what has already been tried out. The first step in walking, for instance, enables a vast expanse of life to be sampled, from touching and tasting to being able to actively seek affection when it is needed by smiling or crying. The baby's social and personal image is also changed. By the age of 1 year, an infant has developed at a pace which it will never match again. Each new baby learns by trial and error within the limits of its inborn capacities.

From the beginning, the urge to learn is tempered by opportunity. The responses of even tiny babies to shapes and noises can be related to the type of care they receive, which in turn reflects that of what their mothers were given and are passing on to them. Harlow's (1958) observations of

---

PERCEPTUAL SKILLS AT SIX MONTHS OLD
* Attending – judging what is worthy of closer attention;
* Identifying – working out perceptual patterns, by comparing them with images in one's memory;
* Locating – sorting out the distance and direction of an object.

monkeys are among many which have shown how behaviour patterns are learned and transmitted over generations. But of course, the baby's own responses are also important. For example, girl babies seem to have more sensitive skins than boy babies, and respond more positively to stroking, which reinforces the parent's pleasure in doing this, and so baby girls may receive more attention of this kind: heavy babies often respond less quickly than thin ones, and seem to continue in this way.

Each of the skills mentioned in the box is different, but also dependent on the other two. For example, if you are in the jungle and a tiger is charging, you need to orient your attention towards the tiger, to identify it as a tiger, and to locate how far away it is, so that you can decide whether to climb a tree, shoot a gun or pray (Siegler, 1991). Improved performance unquestionably requires great amounts of practice, and so the best children's toys are those which provide physical characteristics to be explored, problems to be solved and the possibility of classifying things. The classic form-board, in which shaped rods have to be fitted into matching holes, is an excellent example.

American research has found that certain aspects of very early learning, measured in the first three years of life, provide reliable indicators of lifelong attributes, such as advanced physical control predicting gymnastic talent (Lewis & Louis, 1991). The strongest early indicator, which can be traced from the age of three months, is verbal ability, but spatial and non-verbal signs are also valuable indications for future talents. The researchers found the greatest overall intellectual stability to be at the extremes of the IQ range – both gifted and low – and suggest that this intellectual development is qualitatively different from that of individuals with more average scores. Indeed, the parents of the exceptionally high IQ children in the follow-up study by Freeman (1991a, and see Chapter V), compared with those of more average IQ children, reported very early signs of exceptional concentration, memory and talking.

Perception is learned from experience and it affects reasoning: good reasoning based on mistaken perceptions will produce faulty conclusions. Good quality education is largely concerned with correcting misconception and by broadening a child's view, in such a way that the child can reach personal conclusions from what he or she has observed.

In his wide survey of intelligence around the world, Vernon (1969), found that people learned to perceive differently. He looked beneath the 'trappings of civilization', at the different opportunities children had for building up their cognitive schemata, and concluded that learning ability is not identical with intelligence as measured by conventional tests, that one could not say which mental faculties underlay performance in a variety of situations, nor is there a general learning ability common to all tasks. People may use a restricted form of language which limits their conceptual development, or in a non-literate society find it difficult to distinguish pictorial images of two or three dimensions. In the Kohs Blocks test, in which children have to match patterns painted on wooden blocks, for example, children from Malawi found it difficult to attend to the tops of the blocks and to disregard the sides. Yet with some tuition from the researchers, children were able to catch on to what they were expected to do very quickly.

The teacher's job is largely to help children distinguish and make judgements on what they have differentiated. For example, in geometry, children learn to perceive and distinguish shapes correctly, and find out how they are related; in language studies they must learn to perceive subtle differences of meaning between similar words; in football they must learn to perceive and estimate distances and the strength of their own response. This is the basis of Feuerstein's programmes; acquiring knowledge from the perception of experience in order to boost intellectual skills.

Aesthetic preference. It is generally accepted by psychologists that humans are biologically prepared to discover the world in certain ways, most particularly with a bias towards vision and hearing. It shows in babies' tastes because, from the day of birth, they will look at some objects and events more than others. These preferences may be crucial to development, because intellectual growth is nourished by informative rather then uninformative aspects of the environment.

Their aesthetic preferences show that babies can discriminate between sensations soon after birth, reaching a reasonably permanent stage of reliability at about eight months-old. New-borns show clear tastes for, say, green over red, or different foods. By their first or second year, potentially creative children can already be seen to behave somewhat like creative adults. They are enthusiastic in the time and effort they put into their chosen activities, with an uncensored openness to their experiences.

There are two major differences between the creative child and adult. Firstly, what is novel in the child's experience, is not necessarily so for an adult, which means that the child is much more tied to the here and now, with a limited knowledge base from which to work. Secondly, the child has not acquired the technical skills to carry out its intentions. Because of these two constraints, children's work is not exactly like that of adults – even for such childhood geniuses as Mozart or Picasso, although it is prodigious for a child (Radford, 1990).

Piaget emphasized that early childhood is life's most creative period in curiosity, candidness and openness – until society squeezes it into conformity. Understandably, parents usually teach their children school-type skills like numbers and letters, to encourage school success, and so their natural creative interests are not always recognized. Both the creative and academic aspects of intelligence are promoted by the same general environmental influences – encouragement, example and educational facilities. But at their mature levels, the emotional aspects of those influences may diverge, and may even be contradictory: creativity draws on personality factors and needs emotional freedom to flower, whereas successful academic achievement is more emotionally controlled.

Before the second birthday, the range of mental skills shown in the box are well developed, each affecting the growth of the others (Rosenblith & Sims-Knight, 1989)

MENTAL SKILLS APPEARING AT 18-24 MONTHS
* Understanding of ideas;
* Understanding that objects will stay the same, even when they are out of sight (object permanence);
* Ability to solve problems using combined mental manœuvres
* Ability to categorize two sets of attributes at the same time – such as length and colour;
* Much of the language to be used in basic conversation, including the understanding of about a thousand words, even if they cannot use them, and primary grammatical elements;
* Some lifelong attitudes towards learning;
* A full array of social skills;
* A basic awareness of the self.

Memory

We are what we remember ourselves to be; if we lose our memories, we lose our identities. The workings of the memory depend on two broad classes of process – encoding and retrieval. The human being is neither a tape-recorder nor a movie-camera, and the brain has a limited processing capacity at any one time, so it has to simplify what it processes. The events in the outside world which a child sees or hears are not perceived in their literal, physical form. Instead, the brain makes sense of information, transforming it into a simplified, coded version to store in memory. Adults have thousands of well-learned codes, such as judging distance by using the perspective cues learned from life experiences. In retrieval, an individual has to bring to mind material that was presented earlier. For example, a person trying to retrieve a list might use category names as cues and think, 'Let's see, there were three categories. What were they?'

How does the child acquire these codes? It starts with the ability to co-ordinate impressions received from the different senses – for example, when the baby learns to co-ordinate touch and sight, so as to see and manipulate an object. Experience of this sort enables the child to transform crude sense impressions into the more abstract, symbolic representations of objects and events – the codes. These codes will contain certain characteristics of the objects which have been abstracted, such as the roundness of a ball and the way it rolls. Hence, the baby can distinguish between something round and something not quite round, since roundness is a feature with which it soon becomes familiar. A baby learns to discriminate in various ways, such as in hearing that people pay particular attention to certain things by naming them, or by being rewarded for making discriminations successfully – calling mother and father by their names is thoroughly rewarding to all three. But good perceptual skills do not just happen, they must be learned: there are, in fact, commercial courses which can help people who have difficulty in remembering.

Even in infants, intellectual development can be thought of in terms of problem-solving skills, the level of which will vary with the knowledge they have accumulated and with the way they have organized it in their memory to find what they need quickly and easily. But most of all, it is the quality of their mental representations of the problem, the clarity and meaning of their images, which help them.

Newborns are capable of remembering for a few moments – providing their first intellectual learning. From the first moment their attention is strongly drawn to moving objects, although their ability to follow the movement is limited by eye control. Typically, they focus on the place where the object was for a second or two after it has moved away, then turn their eyes forward to a position that is roughly, but not precisely, in line with the object's new location. But not until two or three months can they follow moving objects smoothly, and even then only when the movements are slow, although by then they remember new learning for days or even weeks, and from that form expectations about where interesting events might occur, and look for them. But it is only when they use their memories to plan ahead in a controlled way, about two years later, that they are really on the way to acquiring more knowledge and the ability to use it competently.

All humans organize their experiences in memory, but it may be that infants who are especially sensitive and aware have to manage an exceptional amount of incoming information. In order to reach the highest levels of thought and performance of which they are capable, they would then need a system of organization that is appropriately more complex or advanced than their baby age-peers. Should the maturation of the central nervous system be advanced, it could produce precocity in learning.

Remembering is a selective process. Things may be forgotten by an individual who finds them offensive or boring. Taken to an extreme,

> ## WHY OLDER CHILDREN REMEMBER BETTER THAN YOUNGER CHILDREN
>
> 1. They have superior basic capacities, both in absolute terms and in speed of operation of the memorising procedures.
> 2. They know a greater variety of ways of remembering and use them more often, more efficiently, and more flexibly.
> 3. They choose strategies and allocate memory resources more effectively, because they understand better how memory works. Metacognition (knowledge about one's own cognitive activities) is a major source of memory development.
> 4. They have greater content knowledge, i.e. they know more about the type of material they need to remember, so that the information is not isolated, but 'falls into place' with what is already there.

however, this emotional aspect of forgetting becomes a process of *repression*, when the memory is unconsciously denied. When a task is completed, such as passing a final exam, the learning involved may be largely forgotten unless it is to be used soon. On the other hand, an unfinished task has a 'hangover' and is more easily remembered, so that leaving a task unfinished at the end of the day helps in restarting it the next morning.

Measuring a child's power of retention is important to an educator. Three simple methods are available:

1. *Recall*: the most frequent method, as when the child is asked to repeat what he has learned, and exact reproduction may be required.
2. *Recognition*: easier than recall, calling for only familiarity and identification, but nonetheless valuable. Multiple-choice examinations work on this principle,
3. *Learning traces*: when there is no obvious evidence that learning has taken place, but relearning takes place much more quickly than could be expected, traces of the first learning having been retained. Recall and recognition may well miss these traces, which, although small, are still valuable in learning.

CHAPTER III

Thinking

The most important sign of competence in individuals is their clear and effective thinking, the way they deal with information. Competent people can take an overview of the best way for them to work, and command their intellectual powers with flexibility and speed for the greatest effect, whether examinations in school or projects in adult life. All children, however potentially able they are, need assistance to be at their most effective in thinking. A child's ability to deal with information can be judged by the degree of abstraction each one makes of perceptions – symbolic representation. An important stage of development has been reached, for example, when a child no longer abstracts and stores objects in memory in terms of their surface characteristics, such as colour, but starts to look at them in terms of their function, for instance, that they are all items of clothing.

At a more advanced level, increasing complexity in abstracting and storing impressions permits accordingly more complex mental operations. For example, by around 6 to 8 years-of-age, a child can probably reverse a mental operation – knowing not only that $2 + 2 = 4$, but also that $4 - 2 = 2$. Or he can see a class of objects as being subordinate to another class (roses are subordinate to flowers), as well as the superordinate class as continuing smaller classes (some flowers are roses). It becomes continually easier to perform more complex operations with increasingly more abstract symbols, so that such mental operations as reversal and subordination develop together. As another example, a very young child cannot see that a sausage-shaped piece of plasticine can be rolled back again into the round ball it once was. This is because he is only aware of the superficial length of the sausage; later the child can perceptually override such obvious clues as length and conceptualize the quantity of plasticine as remaining the same, regardless of its outward shape.

The development of children's thinking grows in complexity by such mental operations, each being a necessary precondition for the next to occur. To develop them, it is essential for a child to have experiences which are both appropriate to the stage of development and which can extend his thinking. If any of these foundation experiences are missing, subsequent development may suffer. That earliest perceptual learning is thus of vital importance to future competence.

Schemas

Even babies have to organize their mental experiences in memory in order to cope with them. But some, who are more sensitive to experience, possibly the highly able, may have to manage and select from an exceptional amount of incoming information. They would then need a system of mental organization that is more complex or advanced than that of other babies to cope with it and reach the levels of thought and performance of which they are capable, perhaps to become highly able children.

For everyone, the process starts with the accumulation of 'bits' of unconnected experience. As this collection expands, it is sorted into more manageable 'chunks' of connected knowledge. With growing expertise and associations between the chunks, knowledge is further clustered into wider relationships, which are stored in memory as schemas. These active bundles – schemas – can then be used as a whole for reference, without each bit having to be considered separately. A schema represents the information available from experiences, the inter-relationships between objects, situations, events and sequences of events that normally occur: it is used to interpret new situations and observations.

This is how individual accumulations of knowledge are stored, in active, constantly changing schemas. They might be either general ideas which are abstracted from experience and specific memories. The more intricate the degree of understanding required, such as a mathematical concept, the further it has to be classified into more and more detailed memory arrangements. Schemas guide the way both children and adults see and think; thus they affect decisions and are the blueprints for action. With practice, children use their accumulated knowledge more smoothly because of the improved ability to perceive relationships between the chunks, which is not necessarily conscious, and so can reason their moves towards a solution without having to consider each chunk separately. If the situation is intricate, such as architectural drawings, then the knowledge is further organized into embedded sets or hierarchical structures.

For the most efficient learning, schemas need to stay flexible, so that new experiences can be fitted in and the old learning adapted to them. This is the active way in which understanding grows, as Piaget first described (Piaget, 1971). But this intellectual processing is not confined within children's heads, because they live in a social world and are involved with the people around. Each child interprets experience through the framework of the way he lives at home, within his culture (Wertsch, 1990; Nisbet, 1991). A flexible outlook enables information to be used creatively in a wide variety of places and problems. It also helps in working with others, for instance, in the way children cope with differences between individual teachers and their methods.

Schemas which were once useful can become too rigid to be changed by new learning. Little children, for example, usually understand all women in terms of their mothers. Should the child's schemas in this respect become rigid, either for lack of any alternative experience in a strictly gender divided society, or from fear of change, they may continue to see women's role as stereotyped in those ways. Another example of an emotional schema is one of obedience, which may be useful in some early childhood situations. If it is prevented from developing, however, and becomes fixed, personal development may become so limited that thinking a situation through and making independent decisions is almost impossible. This happens to little children who must work to live, maybe as indentured labour, and they may grow up with little sense of self-direction.

During the middle years of childhood (about 6 to 12 years-of-age) some of the most powerful and enduring self-schemas that make up a child's self-concept begin to take shape. Much research now supports the view that children's perceptions of their own ability mediate their aim for achievement. For example, girls are more likely to attribute their success to luck than ability, and they over-rate the difficulty of the work; such maladaptive schema towards their own attainments lower their expectations for success (Blatchford, 1992).

How well new situations can be smoothly interpreted and integrated depends on a solid and growing knowledge-base represented in schemas and the networks between them. Should either be limited, learning is less easy. This can happen when a child whose early education has been minimal starts school in a situation where the teaching does not take this into consideration; because the lessons are set at a level too far above the child's understanding they may not be properly absorbed. Exactly the same kind of thing can happen when a highly achieving child is accelerated by a year or two in school, and so misses a vital part of the coursework.

Strategies

Further complexity in the organization of mental operations is the formation of 'strategies'. These are active sequences of schemas which are aimed at a goal; the more efficient their design, the more effective that person's effort to reach the goal will be. Whether a strategy is in the form of thought only or is actual physical behaviour, it is always active and under the control of that individual. Strategies make it easier to use experiences which are stored in memory, and so they are concerned with the encoding, storage and retrieval of these memories. Memory gets better as children get older, because they are constantly improving old strategies, both by extending them to cope with new situations, and by adding new ones.

STRATEGIES USED BY YOUNGER CHILDREN

* *Searching for objects.* In experiments, toddlers try a variety of strategic activities to remember where the researcher hid the toy. They look at the hiding place, point to it, and name it, much more often than when the object is in view.
* *Rehearsing.* Repeating information many times to rehearse it is a great help in remembering. At first, this rehearsal is very simple – each word to be remembered is repeated over and over again. This occurs by the age of 9, but 13-year-old youngsters are able to remember lists of words without memorizing each one and rehearsing them specifically (Palinscar & Brown, 1984).
* *Organizing.* When people need to recall material, but not necessarily in the original order, they often reorganize it into categories that make it easier to remember, for example, by organizing lists into furniture, fruit or animals. Children as young as 4 or 5 years old can be taught to organize things in this way. The strategic process of organizing associations can be either voluntary, or involuntary as in the Gestalt theory of the innate organization of the field of perception. Yet the Gestalt idea is passive psychology, whereas 'active' learning and teaching of organization is not. This active organization grows with age, as children develop more control over their environments and are thus less affected by them.
* *Elaborating.* Elaboration is a 'memory aid', which involves remembering by thinking or imagining connections between items. For example, a girl who needed to remember her schoolbook, her lunch and her arithmetic assignment might form an image of two pieces of bread, sandwiching the book, with the book's pages holding the assignment.
* *Systematic scanning.* As they get older children's visual scanning becomes increasingly systematic. They have learnt how to use the systems and strategies which they have developed, and can focus attention on relevant features, being less at the mercy of random attention-grabbers.

There are specific features which all strategies have in common. When small children first devise a memory strategy, they only use it in a few of the situations where it could be suitable; this will be where it is most obvious and easy. They are also quite rigid in applying the strategy, and often fail to adapt to the changing demands of the situation. Older children, as well as those who have had good educational practice and so are more experienced in using their mental strategies, are more likely to use them in a wider variety of circumstances. These include times when there are difficulties in carrying them out, elaborating higher-level versions of old strategies, or becoming more flexible in adapting any strategy to the special needs of a particular situation.

Neither training children to use such strategies is any guarantee of their continued use, nor their application to new situations – transfer. Unless they are given explicit instructions to use this strategy in later situations, they often do not do so. Yet, they will transfer their strategies more often and in more sophisticated ways when they see that the benefits to them increase, such as by earning praise or money for successful recall. Alternatively the difficulty of using the strategy can be reduced, for example, by presenting material that is relatively easy for them to rehearse. Children's use of any particular strategy is therefore sensitive to its value in the situation. The more worthwhile strategies are more frequently used as children get older because individuals appreciate the benefits, especially as they become progressively easier to put into practice.

Thinking habits: Once mental strategies have been found useful, people often find it quicker and less consuming of mental energy to stick to well-used, familiar paths of thinking. A typical example is using a tired old reply in conversation, instead of really considering what has been said, which many people find useful because they can follow their own thoughts while responding politely. The intellectually able, though, who are much better at following more than one idea at the same time, may be tempted to over-use this habit which distances them from other people – possibly the root of the absent-minded professor syndrome.

On the other hand, the intellectually able may be sometimes faced with the temptation of frenetic mental activity, which may not appear to serve any productive purpose. It seems to happen when the emotional part of a person is either neglected or actually crippled, as though it were irrelevant to the individual's thinking and creativity; almost as though that person had become no more than a brain physically supported by the rest of the body. Such a person can enter a maze of ideas, developing theories and sub-theories which have no useful function other than intellectual exercise. William Sidis, the American genius who was supposed to have had one of the highest IQs ever measured, found himself trapped by such mental convolutions. His upbringing had led him to believe that he was only valued for his intellect. This, in addition to the intense media attention for being brilliant, eventually brought about his mental breakdown. He produced relatively little work, and it has not withstood the test of time (Wallace, 1986). The effect of emotional inhibition on clear thinking can be observed in many individuals who were good learners at school: as they go through life they are keen to show how much they know by answering other people's questions, on quiz shows for example, rather than exploring new ideas.

Metacognition

The most valuable and sophisticated strategy for all mental purposes is 'metacognition' – thinking about thinking. This is the overall awareness of one's intellectual assets, such as thought processes, concentration and memory, as well as how they work best and most productively. If learners can become more aware of their own thought processes and learning strategies, they could not only widen their repertoire of such strategies, but also gain conscious control over them, by knowing when to select and apply them. This could provide the key to transfer and generalization. As yet there is no generally recognized taxonomy or even a list of such skills, although there is much agreement in research.

Lower-order processes are referred to as 'mediational skills', 'control processes', and 'micro-strategies': higher-order processes are termed 'general strategies', 'executive functions', and 'macro-strategies'. The higher level control processes are seen as being responsible for the selection, co-ordination and sequencing of many lower-order skills, in order to create purposeful cognitive strategies. Robert Sternberg (1985) devised a theoretical model to encompass these ideas, analyzing intelligent performance into a number of component processes at two levels of cognitive processing. He refers to 'metacomponents' or executive skills, which are used for decision making, planning, evaluating, etc., and 'lower-order components' (sub-divided into types), which carry out the procedures selected by the metacomponents.

Metacognition can be used for two types of knowledge:
-   conscious, factual knowledge – even pre-schoolers can explain that it is easier to remember a smaller number of items than a larger number;
-   unconscious behavioural knowledge – much metacognitive knowledge influences behaviour in an unconscious way, e.g. when children read difficult passages more slowly without realizing that they are doing so.

The ability to monitor one's own comprehension seems to be one of the key differences between good readers and poor ones. Older and better readers slow down and often return to the place in the text where comprehension difficulties began. In contrast, younger and poorer readers rarely return to problem spots. Self-monitoring skills are especially critical for choosing what and how much to study; for instance older children often use more active strategies, such as turning away from the material and testing themselves, so that they are more effective students. They also focus more of their attention on material they have not yet mastered. Allocating time between different tasks, for example, is a strategy which takes some practice before it is acquired well.

Not surprisingly, children who are still learning how to study have difficulties making these choices. Metacognition can be taught, but even then, children do not always recognize its value. For example, children who have to organize their material better may attribute their success to paying more attention to the work, or looking at it longer, or just slowing down. Research by Freeman (1991a, and see Chapter V) found that the intellectually able have a high degree of such awareness, and are often able to function nearer their best for longer than the others. The brightest in the sample could sometimes describe in detail how they managed their mental learning resources, and what they did to improve their learning strategies. The most successful examinees also knew about the importance of involving the whole self – intellect, emotion and body – in their learning.

All children ought to – but rarely do – acquire the level of insight of a gifted mathematics student at university, who said:

The secret of my learning is that I've got to understand what I'm doing. For me, there are two approaches to work. If it's a subject that bores me, or a problem I find difficult to understand, I know I have to work through it, referring to my notes and back again, just learning by heart. But if it's something I enjoy, like maths, I look for the important points, and then I can do it.

Good strategies, like the schemas they are made of, must stay flexible and open to changing circumstances. Competent planning for learning involves choosing from different possible strategies, and perhaps even rehearsing them mentally to test their appropriateness for a particular task. Indeed, the highest level of planning starts out in a broad and generalized way, but includes a variety of sub-plans for trial. The strategy used most frequently by the successful young people in the study by Freeman was to look for the principles in their work first, and then fill in the details appropriately. To do that calls for the confidence to take an overview of both the subject under consideration and of one's own mental approach.

Intuitive and analytical thinking – the 'Figaro factor'

In Rossini's opera *The Barber of Seville*, Figaro the barber made great and successful efforts to attend to the demands of his many customers at once – obviously a competent man – though he found it difficult at times.

Freeman (1991a) called this ability to react to many superficial clues the 'Figaro effect'. She was working at the 'intuitive' end of the thinking spectrum, which has 'analytical' thinking at the other end. At each of these extremes, information is processed differently: most intellectual activity uses an amalgam of both kinds, along with all the varieties of schemas and strategies that are available (Schofield & Ashman, 1987).

Analytical thinking. This is sometimes called successive processing, which uses information in a time sequence. One thought must follow another, each link in the chain of reasoning being dependent on the last. It is slow, because although it uses only a limited amount of information, the thinker has to keep all of it in mind while working with it. It can also produce serious errors, because a contradicting detail or a missing link can break the thread of an argument. An example might be working out a bus route (with connections) quite accurately, and yet failing to find the quickest route, because the train service (which is direct) was not considered.

Intuitive thinking. Sometimes called simultaneous or parallel processing, this is when all the parts and relationships between the elements and alternative possibilities are worked with together – e.g. the city's entire transport system. This includes planning and decision-making, and implies the ability to take an overview of one's own thinking – metacognition. Truly intuitive thinking works like perception, fast and impressionistic, without the person being conscious of all the details of what is going on. In processing information simultaneously, there is no limit to the amount that can be called upon. Indeed, it demands a bird's-eye view of all the ideas on the subject that could be relevant, including one's own feelings about it. Luria (1959), the Russian psychologist, suggested that it is a powerful sign of intellectual maturity in children, because it is more like the mental processing of adults. The brighter one is, the better one will be at taking the bird's-eye view, and also paying attention and processing more than one input at the same time.

In the first phase of Freeman's research, children in the IQ range of 97-170 were asked whether they could follow and cope with two or more things at once – that is, whether they could process them simultaneously. Of those with an extremely high IQ, 43% said they could – almost twice the proportion claimed by those with IQs in the middle range (24%). Ten years later, when they were asked the same question, the results were much the same. The higher the IQ of the young people, the more likely they were to say that they were able, not only to give attention to more than one thing at a time, but to process them together. This was, however, sometimes frustrating for them, such as when they were listening to several people, as it was not physically possible to answer them all at the same time – the Figaro factor.

Not only did the youngsters of very high IQ appear to be distinctly better at simultaneous processing than the others, but in the whole sample, significantly more of the girls (86%) claimed this Figaro gift than the boys (66%). Although females' ability to do many things at once has been acknowledged in many studies, it is probably a learned ability to some extent. Among these young people, for example, the education of the brightest boys was often in selective, academic, single-sex schools, which usually have a more funnelled, achievement-orientated approach to learning. The education which the bright girls received was much less specialized, enabling them to range more broadly. In the same way, children from homes which encourage intellectual growth and experiment would be expected to be better at processing ideas together than children from poor or rigid cultural backgrounds.

The efficiency of how one uses available mental resources shows up best in a novel situation. That is where the highly able are most likely to shine in their capacity to combine a speedy overview, and go on to form an effective strategy, as well the ability to monitor their own performance. Indeed, Sternberg & Davidson (1986) suggest that the main difference between the intellectually gifted and other children is in the way each approaches and carries out a new task. The adult-like planning competencies of the highly able are often noticed by teachers and parents, and are probably the major reason for their greater speed in problem-solving. But this exceptional facility may not work for all kinds of planning. It is important for teachers to understand how an individual learns and thinks so that, in an educational situation, each learner can be encouraged to improve their strategic learning skills, and evolve improved ways of thinking. It is not that a teacher has to adapt to each pupil's personal style, which would be impossible in a classroom, but that within reasonable limits, pupils should have enough freedom to learn in their own way.

Concepts

A concept is an idea of objects or events which, unlike a schema, is not active and changing. In order to form a concept, different aspects of what is perceived are grouped together on the basis of some similarity, which can vary from the concrete (a concept of chairs) to the abstract (a concept of pity). Concepts save mental effort by permitting inferences to be drawn, using existing knowledge in new situations of which the person had no direct experience. If told that peewees (lapwings) are birds, for example, a child immediately also knows that they have feathers and wings and that they can fly. Concepts have different levels of complexity, and are related to each other to a large extent embedded in 'networks' of concepts sometimes called 'scientific concepts'.

Conceptual understanding influences and is influenced by perception, language, memory, problem-solving and reasoning – in short, by every aspect of our thinking. Our concepts reflect our perceptions, and our perceptions are influenced by our concepts; we remember in terms of known concepts, and we use memory to build new concepts, and so on. This tendency to form concepts is a basic part of human beings: infants form them even during their first few months.

Concepts are remembered in terms of representations or images, which are very complex and may even have relationships which affect conceptual understanding. Young children rely more on defining features of these representations than adults do. Often, both children's and adult's representations work on the basis of what is likely, rather than sticking strictly to the essentials. Even infants abstract possible forms, cues, and correlations among features. And then there are subordinate and superordinate concepts, and abstract, increasingly complex, correlational patterns.

In teaching, the development of examples of concepts plays an important role in developing conceptual representations. Because of the complexity of many concepts and the difficulty of deciding what to encode, examples may play an especially important role when a new concept is being formed. There are certain concepts – time, space and number – which are special. These are worthy of unusual attention because they represent a vast range of experiences available in some form from infancy to old age, in all cultures. Our thinking about the world would be drastically different without them.

Prior knowledge

Learning is not like filling a bucket, but rather like lighting a fire (Dochy, 1992). Prior knowledge is the fuel which can be ignited by new information, and it influences memory in several ways – how much and what children recall, their execution of basic processes and strategies, their metacognitive knowledge, and their acquisition of new strategies.

In some circumstances, prior knowledge can exert a greater influence on learning than all the other skills and abilities combined, which makes it extremely important for teachers to know what a child has before starting further teaching, and to take continued assessments as the course progresses. This means that testing is an essential and integral part of the instruction, continually providing individual profiles of knowledge.

Prior knowledge is so important in learning that it can even overwhelm differences in IQ. When children of a normal spread of IQ levels of intelligence have about equal amounts of knowledge, they appear to be about equally able to take in new information. The more knowledge children acquire, the more accurate their memories for an event, even over time; the need to remember a great deal of information improves children's ability to do so, even without direct instruction in how to remember (Flynn, 1987). It provides the context within which children can place new information, serves as a check on the plausibility of their memories for particular events, facilitates their drawing of inferences, and helps them encode distinctive features. It also contributes to the development of other competencies which are part of memory development, such as strategies and metacognition. In older people, their accumulation of knowledge can compensate for the speed of a younger mind.

SOCIAL INFLUENCES ON CHILDREN'S THINKING

Children of potential gifted ability do seem to have an outstanding capacity for acquiring knowledge, remembering it, and relating it to what they already know.

In any social group, individuals have to adjust their behaviour according to the people that they live amongst. Assessing the capacities and predicting the behaviour of other people is an important part of human adaptation. This need for managing inter-personal relationships is vital in intellectual development, and it begins at birth. To complicate things further, each family group is affected by the social group in which it is set, as well as by physical effects from the environment. The way an individual tackles an intellectual problem may change radically with the social context. For example, a child may be affected by the teacher's expectations in school, which in turn are affected by the teacher's own sense of identity, as well as by the organization of the institution.

But there is thinking in the head and thinking in situations – children can develop their abilities for real life circumstances, rather than for passing exams and solving intellectual puzzles. Behaviour in the real social world provides evidence about an individual's cognitive capacities, and the outside factors which may affect them. Although it may not be possible to prove causal links, it is possible to point to them and draw conclusions. It could be said that human social and cognitive abilities must have evolved through the agency of natural selection, though this assumes that the same opportunities were available to all. In fact, particularly over recent generations, there have been enormous differences in the opportunities open to the world's various peoples, because of the variation in information to which they have access via the mass media.

The more complex a society, the more intelligent its people must be to exploit their opportunities, and to adjust their own behaviour to others. This requires a continuous calculation of the balance of profit and loss offered by any activity. Social skills and cognitive skills are likely to have evolved together.

HOW THE DEVELOPMENT OF THINKING IS AFFECTED BY RELATIONSHIPS

1. Context shapes basic thinking competencies, such as use of language, impulse regulation, self-esteem, and a range of choices for co-ordinating one's actions with those of others.
2. Resources – both emotional and cognitive – provide security and the skills to strike out into a new territory. Relationships are resources which protect the individual from stress, as well as being problem-solving aids, and a help towards reaching goals.
3. Existing or long-established relationships provide blueprints for the construction of new ones, and so on.

Partners in a relationship need both the relevant ability to understand the needs of the other, as well as the capacity to apply this understanding to social interaction. For example, 4-year-old children are able to assess the cognitive level of their listeners, and adjust their speech accordingly. They can talk to 2-year-olds more simply than to other 4-year-olds or to adults. Even 3-year-olds can use more sophisticated messages when interacting with 5-year-olds than with other 3-year-olds. Children get better at this, obviously, as they get older, but there can be a gap between the level of understanding a child has reached and the skills needed to put it into practice.

Things that parents do together with their child have a far-reaching effect on the child's understanding. Yet games, chit-chat, stories, walks in the park, even arguments and downright confrontations are not only stimulating but a means of fostering the child's intellectual growth. The problem for research is how to establish what results in what, because the interaction works both ways. For example, a highly verbal and demanding child can affect parents' behaviour by stimulating them to more conversation and reading more stories. On the other hand, parents who talk to children a lot are themselves verbal people. Both children and parents are affected by the social context, which may mean, for example, that a child who fails at a task in one situation (school) can be very successful in another (home).

An important aspect of learning to read, for example, is the child's ability to detect rhyme and alliteration. When children are trained to listen better, they also learn to read better. A child's awareness of the sounds in words, acquired before he begins to read, goes some way to determining how well he will read. Rhymes, word games and verbal routine in everyday life at home are important; they may lay the basis for a specific educational skill, such as one's ability to pursue ideas which the parent has implanted.

What makes for success depends on the context. Neither development nor performance can be looked at separately from the context in which they function – good performance in one context may be poor in another. Flexibility according to context is crucial to success because the more complex the context, the more difficult the thinking is likely to be. Yet good thinkers will operate well whatever the context. Furthermore, there are certain skills and tools which can be used in a variety of contexts, such as language or scientific theory. While these skills increase scope and efficiency, they may also constrain vision, because they can become habitual and unthinking.

It has often been observed that situations of conflict encourage cognitive growth – a simple conflict between different points of view can be productive. But cognitive growth is also more likely to take place in the context of a continuing relationship than in a series of disconnected encounters. Then again, cognitive growth can also lead to the destruction of relationships; for example, the success of the teacher/pupil relationship means that it must come to an end as the child learns more. Some relationships may actually inhibit cognitive growth. Perhaps the sequence of attachment followed by the stimulus of contradiction is more effective.

GOOD INTELLECTUAL PARENT/CHILD INTERACTION

1. **The absence of confusing noise and sound which is not meaningful to the child; loud clashing noises and screaming are detrimental to intellectual growth.**
2. **Provision of a variety of activities and experiences.**
3. **Ample parent/child play and conversation.**
4. **Responsivity to the child.**
5. **Nurturing parents.**
6. **Teaching of specific skills.**
7. **Opportunities for the child to explore and try out new skills and activities.**

There is not only one single type of critical parent/child interaction. It would be very helpful to know which aspects of the psycho-social environment have the strongest effect on cognitive growth and performance, what processes are involved, to what extent the effects are seen across the range of ordinary environments, and to what extent they are restricted to extremes of disadvantage. Direct stimulation does not itself promote cognitive growth, but rather, it is the reciprocity of interactions, the variety and meaningfulness of their context that are effective. Both parent and child must be involved and active for the best results with considerable parental teaching by way of gentle feedback and introduction of new ideas and discussion.

We are unsure about particularly critical periods for cognitive development in human beings, although these do seem to affect foreign-language learning. Attempts to learn another tongue after 15 years of age are very much less successful than earlier learning, so it is important to start teaching as early as possible. In general, however, the benefits of good learning experiences in the early years can be lost if subsequent experiences are bad, and conversely, there can be substantial recovery if early bad experiences are followed by good ones in middle childhood. There is evidence that children's needs change with age, such as physical contact which is most important in the first year, while conversation and responsiveness are particularly important in the second year of life. Responsiveness to the child's talk is important in the third year, but after the age of three, more variety of contacts is needed with a range of other adults. From the age of 5, maternal responsivity is less important, but parental encouragement and the availability of a range of play materials and experiences remain important. For example, it was found in a London study that as children were learning to read, those who read out loud to their parents at home had markedly higher reading attainments than those who did not. This could not be explained by any factor than their reading aloud (Tizard, 1985).

At school, Tizard found there were very few 'passages of intellectual search', because the children asked very few questions. Another problem at school is that when the teacher does ask a question, she already has an answer in mind, and until the child gives that particular answer other answers will not be accepted. Used in this way, the question is in fact a form of evaluation, rather than as a stimulus to thinking processes. Such questioning, of the 'Guess-what-I-have-in-mind' variety, may cause children to lose some confidence, causing them to doubt the knowledge they already have. The child may also be confused by the teacher's questioning, particularly when working-class children are taught by middle-class teachers. Teachers who do not respond to children's questions, or question them so hard that the child is not allowed to think out loud, are not making proper use of the educational situation. The very fact of teachers taking on the role of questioner may inhibit some children from asking questions themselves.

The mother also has an advantage in that she and her child share a common life, stretching back into the past, and forward into the future, which makes it easier for her to understand what her child is trying to say and enables her to relate the past to the present. The parent/child relationship therefore has some distinct advantages over the nursery-school relationship, but nursery schools have the very important functions of socializing the child into a wider world than the family, liberating the parents, and providing opportunities to run and climb which are not available in many urban homes.

Intense close relationships between young children and their friends seem to improve cognitive development, given that children normally choose friends of similar academic achievement. Consequently, it is the quality of conversational interchanges and their friends' attitudes to education, as well as the effect of these on self-esteem, which improves thinking.

SOCIAL COMPETENCE

Psychologists have been trying to measure social ability for about a century. Even the earliest measure of intelligence, the 1905 Binet-Simon Scale, introduced rudimentary social measures to assess children's perception of people, which are still present in the latest version. For example, at the age of 5, children are presented with paired drawings of faces, and are asked, 'Which is the prettier?'. Freud used the term *Menschenkenner* for people who were notably good at the perception of people, but was not specific about what constituted this ability. The ability to deal competently with people is looked at here in terms of social cognition, pro-social behaviour, moral reasoning and leadership (Abroms, 1985).

Social cognition

Social cognition is the way an individual perceives other people and comes to understand their thoughts, emotions, intentions and viewpoints. There is currently agreement among many psychologists as to the processes by which children manage to represent mental states in schematic form, such as beliefs, desires and intentions. It comes from a form of social role-taking, also tied up with personality formation, concerning the ability to 'stand in another's shoes'. It is described in the theory of 'personal constructs' (Kelly, 1955), in which people are seen as scientists, in the sense that we can all be seen as placing our own interpretations (theories) on the world of events confronting us, and from these personal theories, derive hypotheses and make predictions about future events. The way we behave is the 'experiment' which with feedback from the environment determines how we behave in future. It is also described in the 'theory of mind' (Wellman, 1990); Gardner (1991) calls it 'intuitive understandings', the ways in which children use their emerging intelligences to think of the objects, events and persons around them in a coherent way.

The basic idea is that children's experiences are used to develop a system of inferences from the way they see others, which they then use to make predictions about them, especially in relation to themselves. The development is part of every infant's learning, coming from the earliest social relationships, and is essential to people's understanding of each other's behaviour, and consequently how they think and behave themselves.

The theory of mind is used, for example, to make sense of the following scenario: a man comes out of a house, hesitates, then turns back into it. One might infer from his actions that he *remembered* leaving something inside, *wanted* to retrieve it, and *believed* he left it there. Indeed, all human communication requires individuals to share some understanding and suppositions, as well as wanting to communicate. Children who grow up in conditions of severe neglect, and so fail to develop an adequate, flexible theory of mind, can be disadvantaged in human relationships, self-awareness, and feelings of competence.

To explore their awareness of other people's feelings, children of 3- to 6-years-old were asked to predict what someone else would like as a birthday present, rather than what they themselves would have liked to receive (Flavell et al., 1968). Each child was presented with an array of objects, and asked to select a birthday present for each of his or her parents, siblings and teachers. Choices were judged as role-appropriate on the basis of age and gender. The 3-year-olds disregarded both the age and gender of the intended recipient, while 4- and 5-year-olds' choices represented a type of transitional level, and all the 6-year-olds made appropriate role responses. Age seemed to improve social cognition, which was more advanced for the brightest children in each age group.

Studies of social cognition have been carried out to investigate pro-social behaviour, voluntary acts, such as helping, sharing, donating, reacting to distress, and showing physical affection for the benefit of others, which are done without expecting an external reward. This behaviour is affected by circumstances, such as the individual's mood, the presence of others, compliance with previous requests, familiarity with the person in need, and the amount of freedom the helper has in deciding whether to attempt to help or not, as well as the degree of urgency of the situation. It is learned from family experiences, added to personal characteristics such as aggression, expressiveness, and social and emotional adjustment. From the available research, it does not seem that there is a recognizable relationship between social cognition and actual behaviour towards others, whether intellectual or emotional.

The same seems to be true for moral reasoning. Much research on it is derived from Piaget's ideas, further developed by Kohlberg (1978), who described the stages of moral development as hierarchical, each higher stage subsuming the lower ones. To measure it, he constructed a 'moral judgment scale' of nine hypothetical human dilemmas, the responses to which are analysed for their form rather than actual content. Other researchers, though, suggest that moral reasoning is positively related to cognitive maturity. There is some evidence that gifted children differ from their peers from an early age by their extreme social sensitivity to attitudes, values and morals. Modelling, internalizing one's behaviour with that of another, is an aspect of inductive reasoning which is closely associated with the development of moral reasoning. For example, if parents explain their actions to their children, pointing out the 'rights' and 'wrongs', they are modelling consideration for others, and, at the same time, stressing the social implications of their own behaviour. Unfortunately, current understanding of the relationship between moral cognition and moral action is less than reliable.

Leadership is usually considered as an outcome of superior social cognition and moral reasoning, combined with pro-social behaviour. A sign of it is when a child has many friends. It is a process which changes other people through influence and control on a consistent basis, but it is not dependent on an exceptionally high level of intelligence, since personality characteristics and situations play a major part in it. These, which are commonly found in leaders who do good to others include enthusiasm, easy communication skills, problem-solving skills, humour, self-control and conscientiousness. Such people should be able to reason at a highly principled level, and show personal and group behaviour which induces change of a universally acceptable nature. It may seem reasonable for leaders to have a high level of social cognition, because to effect change, they must understand the perspective of others, but it has to be recognized that leaders can be removed from normal life, being both brilliant and evil, such as Hitler and Stalin, who dramatically influenced, controlled and led millions of people to disaster without any apparent social-cognition.

Friendship comes from social cognition, and is a vital aspect of emotional and therefore intellectual development. It is through friendships that we learn about how to behave and cope with life. They begin with detachment from the family in the first few years, followed by a rapid increase during adolescence (Hartup, 1978). These friendships have a significant influence on the regulation and integration of such developing forms of behaviour as social competence, aggression and sexuality. This increasing number of friendships in early adolescence in almost all cultures, together with conformity to peer influence, can appear to be at the expense of the quality of the parent/child relationship, an influence sometimes seen by parents as against their values.

In work with delinquent adolescent boys, poor ability to make friends was seen as an indication of emotional problems. Whilst the boys would give an impression of forming close friendships, any depth of commitment within a relationship was usually lacking. Thus, if one of a pair of friends who appeared to be inseparable left a therapeutic group, the other showed little concern. An emotional outburst seemed all that was likely to mark the ending of the relationship. Their relationships within the therapeutic unit seemed to reflect those which existed within their homes, where there was usually a lack of real bonding between the members of the family (Brooks, 1985).

It is strange that highly intelligent children are often thought of as having poor social cognition, and so few friends, but in fact they tend to have sympathy, adaptability and compassion in abundance, and do not usually choose to be without friends. They can expect to have the same number and depths of friendships as all the other children at school, but are sometimes less eager to spend time playing with them at home. The reason is often that there is so much that they want to do after school, such as hobbies or practising a musical instrument. There may be a problem of lack of friends, though, when a child is very much in advance of his age-group. If highly able children do not seem to want to make friends with others of their own age, it can be for two reasons. The first may be a high level of self-sufficiency, which means that they are happier on their own for longer periods of time than other children. The other reason is that they may have been discouraged from playing with other children by their parents' unspoken, but understood, disapproval.

Younger children often enjoy playing with older children and usually imitate them, so older children can be very good teachers for younger ones. Some schools take advantage of this, especially when children start school, by putting the older ones in charge of showing the newcomers how to behave.

Social skills – how to get on with other people – are not usually taught specifically to children, but their commercial value has been recognized in improving the sales, management and efficiency in an organization. In his theory of multiple intelligences, Gardner (1985) recognized that the 'personal intelligences', i.e. knowledge of self and others, are an important part of the sensitization of young people to moral and ethical issues, and to the major problems facing society. Among others, he has suggested that they be an integral part of education, especially for the highly able who may become leaders; the emphasis would thus be shifted from psychological 'adjustment' to positively recognizing and developing emotional and social sensitivity as abilities in their own right.

Although social cognition is related to intelligence, actual social behaviour comes from involvement in a variety of social situations, and does benefit from adult guidance. Socially positive attitudes, such as being sensitive to the feelings of other people, are more often shown by confident young children, especially if they are highly intelligent, who are also better at making use of adults as resources, and play more imaginatively (White, 1985). This being so, both home and school must be concerned and actively involved if children are to develop pro-social behaviour.

EVERY-DAY PROBLEM-SOLVING THINKING

* *Alternative solution thinking.* An example of this technique is trying to get somewhere when the approach is blocked, so that it is necessary to think of a way around the situation. This method of problem solving is as appropriate to a young child as to an adult: the more alternatives, the better the chances of success, and the fewer alternatives, the more the frustration, to the extent of withdrawing or acting without thinking. A child who has broken a pot, for example, may simply deny it if he hasn't got the social skills to know how to respond differently, while a more competent problem-solver may think of ways to avert his mother's anger, such as offering to clean up the mess or explaining how it happened. A skilful 4-year-old will think of a variety of ways of getting a toy from another child – by argument or trading – while the less-skilful child will simply try to grab it.
* *Consequential thinking.* This involves thinking through the consequences of any action. If one child takes a toy from another, the first may simply hit out to get it back, or may realize that this will only make the first child cling harder. While impulsive children do not consider what may happen next, reflexive children do try and can therefore choose to take another course of action. One reason for the impulsivity is that the child may have experienced so much failure that it has given up the effort of trying to reason and empathize. Yet, even little children can be trained to be resourceful and to think things through for themselves.
* *Means-end thinking.* This involves careful planning, step by step, in order to reach a stated goal. It involves insight and forethought to forestall potential obstacles or get round them, as well as having an alternative means of getting there. It implies an awareness that goals are not always reached immediately, and that sometimes it may be better to act one way or another way. A less-skilled child typically thinks of the end-goal, rather than the means to obtain it.

Interpersonal cognitive problem-solving skills

Thinking through and solving typical everyday problems between friends or figures of authority can be detected from as early as 4 years old. The ability to find solutions to everyday problems can enhance social adjustment, interpersonal competence and peer relationships.

Interpersonal sensitivity is another skill which involves the cognitive ability to perceive a problem when it exists – an ability to find how the problem affects the individuals involved. These interpersonal skills are usually learned initially from the mother, who guides and encourages her child to think of solutions to problems and of the consequences of each action. On the other hand, learning is inhibited by the mother always telling the child what to do, belittling the child's own suggestions, so that she is thinking for her child, rather than stimulating the child's own thinking.

Girls are more likely to acquire good interpersonal skills than boys, which is also seen in monkeys reared in different family arrangements (Hinde, 1991). No one is quite sure why, though it may be to do with modelling, because boys brought up by mothers without fathers acquire better interpersonal cognitive skills. It is not so much what children think, as whether they think at all which is more important. Both parents and teachers can help children learn cognitive skills by taking a counselling approach – asking children why they behave as they do, and getting more talk out of them in their everyday interactions.

Adults have considerable influence on children's thinking. This is evident from the way children think: for instance, in Japan and China most children learn to operate abacuses, whereas in the Western world very few do; how they acquire knowledge; for instance, parents in Western societies encourage their children to learn by asking questions, whereas parents in many parts of Africa do not; and their motivation to think, which is also affected by peers societal attitudes.

HOW ADULTS CAN HELP CHILDREN'S THINKING

* By increasing their own sensitivity to the fact that the child's point of view may differ from theirs.
* Helping children recognize that there is more than one way to solve a problem.
* Teaching children to think about what is happening in, say, a quarrel, which may in the long run be more beneficial than immediate action to stop it.
* Providing a model of problem-solving thinking – which might inspire a child to think. Learning these skills means reducing over-emotionality in the face of frustration and aggression, and keeping one's thinking free of the limitation of the here and now. These attitudes are evident in expressions such as: 'I'll think of another way' or 'I won't give up too soon'.

CHAPTER IV

Literacy and numeracy skills

Babies have to learn to make sense of what adults say, not only to understand the direct meanings of their speech, but also the unspoken implications of their gestures and body movements. Learning to speak correctly requires yet further effort: pronouncing the individual sounds, ordering words correctly into sentences, and sentences into groups that communicate comprehensible thoughts. To accomplish all this, babies use various means, such as paying special attention, and remembering particular phrases, while searching for generally applicable grammatical rules.

Conversation involves getting one's own meanings across as well as interpreting what other people are saying, which means sharing some assumptions about the way in which language is used in the society. Sentences that do not express intended meanings will not be socially adaptive, even if their grammar and pronunciation are perfect. Part of the reason why children acquire language so quickly and with such apparent ease is from their keen desire to communicate.

At about eight months-old, before they can speak, babies begin to understand language, and by about 1 year have developed sufficiently to listen and respond reliably to words and signs, and will also have learned to produce some words. Generally, future high attainers at school speak earlier and are more talkative; the highly intelligent child aged under 5 often demands and receives more stimulation from the family, and so in this sense alters his own learning environment. Girls normally develop language skills earlier than boys.

At first infants cry, then they coo, then they babble and then they produce words. All languages reflect those first sounds by making them the names of caretakers – mama, papa, abba, ima, etc. – so that the first words and word-meanings of children throughout the world are similar. The first words refer to people, animals, toys and other relatively concrete objects that both interest and attract children. Learning names for objects facilitates grouping them into categories, while categorizing objects makes it easier to learn more new names, which is how, by the end of the first year, language and thought become bound up together, each affecting the other's development. Language continues to influence thought by firming-up the growing sets of categories of words, while thought influences language by making it easier to learn words that fit into the existing categories.

Language development is a form of symbolic behaviour in which words are symbols representing concepts, with an accepted meaning. Its very early development is the clearest single indicator of intellectual growth, vocabulary being easily measurable, though this varies so much that it is not an entirely reliable guide. Learning to speak, read and write are affected by a number of factors, such as the child's emotional security and the need for communication by verbal routes. As words are learned, almost all of them carry emotional meanings from the situation in which they were learned, which can change as the experiences associated with them change, because language is both informative and emotional.

The linguist Noam Chomsky argued that people are born with an innate knowledge of a universal grammar – a system of principles, conditions and rules that are elements or properties of all human languages (Chomsky, 1968). He pointed out the characteristics common to the grammars of the world's languages, and assumed that variability among the grammars comes from variations in just a few basic properties. Children, he said, form grammatical rules, which can be seen when they try to apply the rules of regular verbs to irregular ones, where they do not always apply. Chomsky said that it was this innate knowledge of universal grammar which enabled toddlers to grasp any particular grammar so quickly, despite its inherent complexity and the minimal teaching babies receive, which mostly happens only by hearing other people use it. Compared with language, the acquisition of other complex cognitive skills seems more dependent on favourable circumstances.

The Russian psychologist, Vigotsky, in his 'socio-historical' approach (see Chapter II), described every child as capable of taking on 'ready made' parcels of culture as tools of thought, as part of the cultural birthright. The system works because adults have learned it and share the cultural assumptions, as described by Vigotsky's student, A.R. Luria:

Children develop language – a ready-made product of socio-historical development – and use it to analyze, generalize and encode experience. They name things, denoting them with expressions established earlier in human history, and thus assign them to certain categories and acquire knowledge. Language mediates human perception, resulting in extremely complex operations: the analysis and synthesis of incoming information, the perceptual ordering of the world, and the encoding of impressions into systems . . . and thus serves as a basis for highly complex creative processes (quoted by Pickering & Skinner, 1991, p. 184).

The development of language

Competent language development is helped considerably by verbal interaction – not just in passing – but systematically with adults. This is an aspect of the wider intellectual development, which includes acquiring knowledge and thinking skills. Children who emerge from infancy with exceptional verbal ability, for example, reading well by the ages of 3 to 5, are well prepared for exploring broader educational fields on their own. Early verbal mastery is not only the precursor of eventual excellence at school and in life, but is associated with the necessary curiosity and drive for the child to reach the heights of excellence.

Language is developed with feedback – being heard, corrected, using words to demand – the rate and breadth being clearly related to that of the adults who look after them. Under-privileged children can miss this necessary feedback from parents, and the gap in communication ability between them and better-off children usually grows over time (Bernstein, 1972). Developing spontaneous complex speech in children who are not used to conversing in this way is not easy, because children with poor verbal ability are often also impoverished in their perceptual and other intellectual abilities.

In most homes, conversation between adults and children is more evenly balanced than at school. Even in nursery schools, teachers tend to dominate children's thinking by constantly asking questions with an answer already in mind, which can actually inhibit the child from thinking up questions (Tizard & Hughes, 1984). The teacher's well-educated style of speech can also be confusing to young children from less well-educated backgrounds. It is important for teachers to encourage children's questioning and listen to them, allowing them almost to think out loud and use all their powers of imagination.

Linguistic and intellectual understanding are interdependent and yet distinct, for example, memory and language depend on each other in the ever-improving shorthand for concepts, and thus for reasoning, although both memory and language are distinct. Using langauge and concepts, 3 year-olds can provide reasons for why things happen, using connecting words appropriately to express relationships, such as 'because' and 'so', and by the age of 5 can distinguish quite clearly between intentions and results (Donaldson, 1986). Such understanding and the ability to reason out the differences between causes and effects, actions and intentions, or a conclusion and the evidence for it, comes from experience contained in concepts and guided by language. Teachers can help by encouraging the child's explanations of cause and effect further and further until the child becomes well practised at using language in explaining things, as an excellent intellectual exercise.

READING

Literacy is probably the most important foundation stone of lifelong learning. Even so, millions of people all over the world leave school never having acquired the ability to read or write – a real social and intellectual disablement which is not normally due to any deficiency in themselves. Given enough time and suitable help, most normal children should be able to read.

School teaching, however, may only account for about 10 per cent of the variability in learning to read (Boekaerts, 1987). Looking at 5,600 Australian children, Rowe and his team (1991) found that their age, gender and socio-economic status had neither direct nor indirect effects on their reading levels: the significant differences were due to reading at home, which also had a positive effect on their general attentiveness and achievement. Indeed, parental involvement is consistently found to increase reading skills, as shown in the study of London primary school-children, where children whose parents listened to them learning to read were more advanced than those who only learned at school (Tizard & Hughes, 1984). Not only do little ones need to be taught specific reading skills, but they have to be given the chance and the encouragement to practise them, a situation which is considerably helped by the involvement of parents in their play and conversation. The same appears to be true for learning to write (Blatchford, 1992).

Language and reading. In order to read, a child must have sufficient command of words and the way they are used, including understanding the cultural assumptions in the text. This means that immigrant children learning to read in a new culture may experience difficulties with it, and need extra help. Adults can help to enrich children's language by providing experiences such as day trips or other activities and talking about them afterwards. Constructive listening with reasoned responses, as practised in educationally supportive homes and good primary schools, is a vital preliminary to reading.

Reading cannot be identical for each language, although it will be very similar with all of them. In French, for example, one cannot distinguish between 'one' book or 'a' book – they are both 'un livre'. Yet children have to learn both to distinguish the meaning and to make it clear when they speak. In fact, French-speaking children go through a stage where they positively question the difference.

Reading readiness. This concept, at one time prevalent in Western countries, deprived children of reading tuition and frightened parents into withholding reading help until a child was of an 'official' age to begin.

One 'pre-reading' skill which has been dropped, for example, is the ability to distinguish letters, because learning the letter names does not facilitate learning to read. We now know that it is probably more harmful for children to delay reading, whether or not 'readiness' is present, by neglecting their valuable enthusiasm. There is also evidence that very early reading is beneficial for many other areas of learning.

Current concern is with finding the appropriate method to suit the individual. Children seem to develop their own strategies to a large extent. The sensitive educator takes her clues about readiness and progress from the child's sensory and intellectual development, so that readiness is a matter of being able to meet the demands of the task, and to relate it to previous learning.

INTELLECTUAL SKILLS NEEDED FOR READING MEANS BEING ABLE TO:
1. **Follow oral instructions;**
2. **Retell the main points in a story in the correct sequence;**
3. **Describe pictures in some detail;**
4. **Anticipate what will happen in the story;**
5. **Describe what the child has done and heard himself;**
6. **Be aware of phonemes – recognition of the sounds that are to be blended to form words.**

Does the child show interest in trying to read signs or advertisements, to construct and use complete sentences, to play with sounds and words? Efficient reading necessitates keeping a whole word or phrase in mind, while attention is paid to particular parts of the word or phrase; it is a complex process. As a basis for reading, a child should have a vocabulary of about 700 words, an ability to discriminate between sounds in sequence, and to blend them smoothly and rhythmically in words. Simple children's rhymes are good practice for reading.

Teaching reading

There are many reading schemes in use today, each having its devotees. While available evidence reveals merits and shortcomings in each, combinations of systems often seem to be the best. Reading is dependent on development processes, and should be taught in relation to speaking, listening and writing. If a specific reading scheme is to be adopted, it should be relevant to the individual child. Any printed material that the child learns from should be well illustrated and use large letters. As the scheme progresses, so too should variation in the type of story presented and the breadth of interest. Supplementary reading should also be carefully chosen to complement the scheme.

There are many different pathways to the goal of becoming a skilled and efficient reader; the use of one method alone is unlikely to be adequate for every child and, in fact, can prove damaging to children. For example, the 'apprenticeship approach', in which the teacher acts as a guiding friend, is not as good for children with difficulties, but works well for children who find reading easy. It is no more possible to teach reading in a sequence than it is to teach speaking in that way. Yet, because the written language is not as natural as speech, its teaching can be structured to a much greater extent.

'Sound-skills' is a reading programme in which children match rhyming words, and break words down into individual sounds, such as saying how a word would sound if the first letter were removed. Children who are taught by this method alone become very good at it, but fall behind in later reading. On the other hand, when children's reading efforts are corrected by the teacher, they are not as good at reading as those who have had both sound-skills and listening-skills. Seven year-olds, given practice in both sound-skills and helped reading, make far faster progress than children of a similar age who are taught one or the other.

Very early readers can be spotted before starting school: they are the ones who are best at identifying rhymes or breaking words down into sounds. Fluent readers do not skip the details of words and letters, as was once thought, although they often work by deduction, actually 'reading' only a few words in each sentence, and filling in the rest by guesswork, logic or relying on clues from the context for meaning. In an American research project, adult readers were given special goggles using infra-red light to measure where their eyes rested on text. These showed that not only do good readers read almost every word of a text, but they take in individual groups of letters as well. The words that normal readers skip over are those like 'and' and 'if' which are not context words at all. Good readers are careful readers; when they do not understand what they have been reading, they go back and read it again (Siegler, 1991).

'Real' books versus the learning of sounds. It has been suggested that only 'real' books, as distinct from books designed as a learning-to-read aid, can produce real children who read, although there is no evidence for this. In spite of this lack of evidence, it seems likely that if books are less attractive to a child than competing attractions, then the child will be less likely to read, and real books are usually more attractive than a learning-to-read book.

The real-books approach to teaching reading is not so much a single theory as a collection of interlinked ideas about the development of written and spoken language. Its strength lies in its use of interesting litera-ture and reading material, which is more likely to capture children's interest, and to lead to increased motivation and improved reading abil-ity. Children do, however, have to be helped to learn letter-sound combi-nations (phonics) as well as other approaches and skills in reading, such as spelling. The issue, therefore, is not real books versus phonics, but finding the appropriate balance between approaches for each child, and the adequacy of the teaching.

It is a question of degree as to whether different types of teaching read-ing, such as multi-sensory approaches, are better, since individual chil-dren succeed best by different routes. Recognizing this, the vast majority of primary school teachers try to give their pupils a range of reading instruction, rather than concentrating on one method. The better their training in how to balance a judicious contribution of developing practi-cal skills and critical reflection, the better their teaching of reading will be.

Reading resources. The development of reading relies as much on appro-priate teaching methods as on the level of resources necessary for the methods to be allowed to work. Simply providing more money is not enough – the right methods must also be found. It is also essential that every school has a policy for literacy as well as providing appropriate resources, such as: teacher time; non-teacher time (parents, peers); books and reading materials; support (e.g. initial and in-service education); detailed assessment of children with reading disabilities.

Reading problems

Even the most intelligent children can have difficulty in learning to read and write. The word which is often used to cover the whole range of such problems is 'dyslexia' or word blindness. Interpretations of this condition range from the mildest reading difficulty to very specific problems, such as a child's inability to translate the visual symbols on the paper – the letters of the alphabet – into words. It confuses and sometimes irritates teachers when they can see that a child is intellectually bright but not producing the expected level of work. Both Thomas Edison and Leonar-do da Vinci had literacy difficulties that today would be called dyslexia.

Of all children with reading problems, those with dyslexia are only a small minority. To be dyslexic, a child must not only have difficulty in reading, but must also have an average or superior intelligence and nor-mally functioning senses. Other members of a dyslexic child's family are often found to have the same problem, and the disorder is most frequent-ly found in boys. It is possible that 12.5 per cent of all children are dyslexic to some extent, although diagnosis of dyslexia is sometimes used as an overall term for children's reading problems, some of which may come from other sources.

There are some fairly clear signs which indicate dyslexia. The earlier they are spotted, the better are the chances of improvement. Though children who learn to read normally can also show similar problems, they will get over these and eventually make good progress, but the dyslexic child cannot go forward without special help.

Many sufferers seem to have difficulty in interpreting the letters of a word in the right order, or may write as though looking in a mirror. By sheer hard work, a dyslexic child may learn the correct way, only to forget it all the next (if not the same) day. Sometimes a dyslexic child's spelling can be so bizarre that even the most empathetic reader cannot make it

---

SOURCES OF READING PROBLEMS

* *Poor language learning.* Having to read and memorize unfamiliar words. Dialect variations, particularly in vowel sounds, may mean that the spoken word does not match what is written. Speech handicaps may arise when reading out loud, such as lisping or stuttering.
* *Poor feelings about the self and insecurity.* Reading calls for some confidence, and such circumstances as a lack of friends, etc., are associated with poor reading.
* *Perceptual problems.* If minor problems, such as slight deafness resulting in poor language ability, are not detected early on, they will obstruct reading, though major difficulties, such as the inability to distinguish letters, needs specialist help. Reading different language scripts can present specific problems, such as reading from left to right for left-handed children. Learning to read depends heavily on visual memory; the script must be recognized and reproducible in different forms, such as capitals, joined-up writing, printing etc. Children are better at remembering words that have more meaning for them, or which they like the sound of. Memory games and activities can be devised to make the learning easier, more meaningful and longer lasting. Spectacles with tinted lenses have been found to help some dyslexic children (Evans & Drasdo, 1991).
* *Poor environment.* Poor circumstances have a depressing effect on both the starting age and the extent of reading ability. Lack of books in the home, large families, lack of parental interest, poor health, and so on are all detrimental. Poor educational means for learning to read, including teaching.
* *Motivation.* As with all learning, success breeds success. First reading experiences should always be successful and exciting. Later reading can be reinforced by talking about what has been read, as well as by acting, art work, films and visits. The genuine desire to read comes from the child's recognition of its importance, which begins at home.
* *Dyslexia* (see above).

out. Such mistakes can carry on into adult life, even when the person has learned to read usefully. Dyslexic children usually have difficulty in working out laterality – left/right and up/down – and they cannot re-find their place on the page, if their attention is lost for a moment. They may have very poor short-term memories, forgetting what they have just been told. Some seem unable to keep still, to fasten buttons and put their clothes on properly.

Unfortunately, whatever the reason, poor reading skills can spill over to affect a child's learning in other specific areas, such as arithmetic, or even all round, so that he feels low about his general ability to learn. The child may also take to misbehaving, possibly opting out of classroom projects, which isolates him even further from the others. Bright children are particularly good at hiding their basic reading problem. It is important to help a dyslexic child realize that this difficulty is not a stigma – but there are no easy cures available.

Any child with normal hearing and seeing faculties can learn to read reasonably well, even though development may be slow or uneven. Bright dyslexic children are usually helped by a good capacity for comprehension. Some children, with great spirit and determination, go on to undertake prolonged study for professions such as medicine or dentistry. This problem does not necessarily inhibit creative writing – the Irish poet W.B. Yeats, and Hans Christian Andersen, the Danish storyteller, were both dyslexic.

WRITING

Writing is more difficult than reading. Reading and writing skills, although they are clearly related, do not necessarily develop together, because they make use of different psychological procedures. Some very young, and undeniably gifted children may even be able to read fluently by 3 years old, but they will not be able to write at that age. A 5-year-old girl may read fluently, but still find difficulty in tying a bow in her hair. Many schools try to co-ordinate the learning of reading and writing, but this can make life difficult for a child who is expected to pull his writing level up to that of reading; so the child struggles with writing, but cannot get it right because the reading is so much more advanced. As a result, he can become unhappy at school and all-round progress suffers.

The beginnings of writing come from painting and drawing. As soon as a child can grasp a crayon or draw with a stick in the sand, parents can show how pleasant it is to draw and then print the name of what the drawing represents, encouraging the child to copy and practice going over these letters. Children should be encouraged, not pressured, to write as clearly and carefully as they can, so that they can see the words they usually know – in their own writing. Teachers sometimes insist that mistakes which have been crossed out are kept in for inspection, and they also teach the children to cross-out in an approved manner; but for keen children it is a mark of shame to keep their mistakes on view.

In writing, the breaking up of words into their different sounds is physically reinforced by the movements of the hand, and then they are re-blended to put the sense back. The physical component of writing does, however, add some extra difficulties to its learning, and so is often the despair not only of teachers, but especially of their boy pupils. Producing a piece of written work is also a very complicated intellectual process. It involves keeping several ideas in mind at the same time, and working them together into a narrative, while attending to the physical aspect of forming the letters legibly. The essence of successful writing, as in mathematics and reading, is the ability to co-ordinate different types of knowledge, and to shift attention flexibly among them.

Composition. Composition is the most difficult kind of writing, but also a superb mental exercise. It imposes demands that neither speaking nor reading does in three main respects:

1. *Unfamiliar topics.* Most school essays are on topics that children do not often discuss – certainly not in a school-like way, such as 'My best friend'. To make a sensible whole, it obliges children to search in their memories and produce a coherent and co-ordinated whole piece of writing.

2. *Multiple goals.* Writing is complex and the goals can vary widely: whether to amuse, intrigue and arouse interest – as well as satisfying the teacher. The intonations and non-verbal gestures which punctuate speaking have to be produced in symbolic form, and without the immediacy of response from the listener which provides clues as to how to continue. The strategy that many children employ is to keep a single goal in mind at any one time. That is why a child's early compositions appear more as a kind of listing until, with maturity, they are better able to organize their way to finding the appropriate memories, as and when they need them. A good way of improving the writing of young children is to ask them to consider two or more goals simultaneously, and to relate these goals to each other.

    As children develop their writing strategies, they learn to compare what they would like to say with what they have actually written – a knowledge-transforming strategy. It means recognizing the problems of expression, and trying out ways of describing the points they want to make. In writing, children move backwards and forwards mentally between the subject goals and their knowledge of verbal devices that could be used to translate these on to paper. This effort to communicate reveals gaps or inadequacies in their thinking. To fill the gaps often deepens understanding; that is why essay writing for children is an extremely useful mental exercise. Older students take more time before they start writing than younger school-children; during this time they decide what they will say and organize their thoughts into a coherent form.

3. *Mechanical requirements.* Lower-order writing skills include the actual formation of letters, ordering them into correctly spelled words, adding the grammar, and putting capital letters and punctuation marks in the right places. They pose such major challenges for children that some may have to proceed so slowly that they lose track of what they wanted to say.

The trend in teaching children to write has been to encourage them to use their imagination, interests and experiences – to be creative – with little regard for spelling and punctuation. Although this is a welcome change from the drudgery of hours of copying that children used to undergo, current feeling in many countries is for the return of the discipline of some grammar in children's writing. It is unrealistic to expect every child to be a creative genius or have a free-flowing mind. Most children's work, even that of bright children, is fairly conventional.

NUMERACY

New ideas are reshaping the teaching of numeracy skills. The style of calculations that parents learned as children has fallen into disuse, because the focus has been redirected away from numbers and towards logical relationships and mathematical language. Instead of doing arithmetic in school, children are now likely to measure rooms and desks, and consider and compare many aspects of what they have discovered for themselves. A child cannot grasp the mathematical basics – which it took great thinkers centuries to work out – all alone. Children need guidance and help in understanding these ideas.

What really matters, right from the beginning, is the child's attitude to calculation. It should be seen as a pleasant thing to do – fun, and not too difficult. Bright children have a real capacity to enjoy exercising their mathematical ability and feel good about it, even before they fully understand what they are doing. What puts many children off is the old-fashioned grind of arithmetical exercises.

The effects of context

Babies start to learn numbers by listening to parents counting things, such as fingers or steps, over and over again. Many children's rhymes have counting in them. The language of mathematics can emerge quite naturally in a lively home. Professor Seymour Papert (1980), the American mathematician, says that a home should be mathematically literate, by which he means that in the same way as children are expected to learn their letters, so they should learn to use numbers. Papert views the child as a builder who needs materials to build with. Children who fail at mathematics usually come from environments which are poor in 'maths-speaking' adults, so they arrive at school lacking the basic learning necessary for the easy continuance with school mathematics, and the school cannot usually supply the missing material.

Papert refers to 'cultural toxins', which contaminate people's images of themselves as learners and lead children to define themselves as incompetent in any subject area. Thus their deficiency becomes their identity, and learning deteriorates from being the child's free early exploration of the world to become a chore, limited by insecurities and self-imposed restrictions. Many children who grow up with a love and aptitude for mathematics owe this positive feeling, at least in part, to picking up 'germs' of their 'maths culture' from adults who, one might say, know how to speak mathematics. It's not that they know how to solve equations, but rather that they are marked by a turn of mind that shows up in the logic of their arguments. For such fortunate children their preferred play is often puzzles, puns and paradoxes.

Maths phobia is a mental block which is endemic in Western culture, especially affecting girls. It prevents people from learning anything which they perceive as mathematics, although, if they do not recognize it as such, they may not have any trouble with it. Such phobic children are forced into school-learning situations where they are doomed in advance to generate powerful negative feelings about numbers, and perhaps even about learning in general, setting up a vicious self-perpetuating cycle. Then, when they become parents, they will not only fail to pass on mathematical 'germs', but will certainly infect their children with the opposing and intellectually destructive germs of 'mathsophobia'. This self-perpetuating cycle has to be broken, and should be done at the very earliest in a child's life, although it could also be done by a good teacher in the child's first school. There is no need to force early arithmetical understanding, it exists in everyday conversation. Every time someone says 'more than' or 'less than', it is part of numeracy. Parents can bargain with children by saying things such as: 'If you eat up two more spoonfuls of dinner, you can have one sweet'. It should be remembered that since children can tackle mathematical tasks without understanding the concepts behind them, parents sometimes think their children are cleverer than they really are, and may expect too much from them.

Even a simple sum requires consideration. Firstly, children must understand the meaning of adding up. Secondly, they have to be able to carry it out mentally. Thirdly, they have to cope with the symbolic notation of '+' and '=', and finally, they must understand the essentially confusing wording of '2 and 2 are 4'. The child needs help in each of these steps.

The context within which school mathematical questions are presented exercises a substantial influence on children's ability to answer them. For example, the tangled wording of many arithmetic problems burdens working memory capacity and increases the difficulty of the problems, in a way which has nothing to do with the arithmetic. Even when wordings are not over-complex, unfamiliar contexts often strain children's competence, and thus prevent them from applying procedures that they use successfully in other contexts.

This is illustrated in a study of 9- to 15-year-old Brazilian street children, the sons and daughters of poor migrant workers who had moved to a large city. The children contributed to the family financially by working as street vendors selling coconuts, popcorn, corn-on-the-cob and other foods. Their work required them to add, subtract, multiply, and, occasionally, to divide in their heads. (One coconut costs x cruzeiros; five coconuts will cost . . . ?). Despite little formal education, the children could tell customers how much purchases cost and how much change they should get.

In an experiment, the children were asked to solve three types of problems. Some were problems that could arise in the context of buying and selling transactions, while others involved similar problem-solving situations but not with the goods the child was used to. Another type were arithmetically identical problems presented without a problem-solving context, such as how much is $85 + 63$. The children were able to solve 98% of questions that could arise at their food stall, 74% of the items that involved selling unfamiliar goods, but only 37% of those outside a problem-solving context. The children clearly knew how to add, but did not always know when to do so (Karraher, Karraher & Schliemann, 1985).

The children were not, in fact, understanding the fundamental laws of mathematics, but a very limited selection of techniques. There was almost no insight or reflection involved in what they were doing, such that it made it difficult if not impossible for them to transfer their techniques to other mathematical situations or subjects. What they were using were coping skills using numbers, rather than exercising genuine competence in numeracy.

Space and weight

The idea of shapes is communicated most easily by puzzles, or sorting things, such as the matching involved in fitting lids on containers and some games. Matching a shape to a hole in a board teaches children about up and down, across, sizes and relationships between parts. Circles are easier to insert than squares, and squares easier than triangles. If the toy has all three, it might take time and much frustration for a very young child to master the whole pattern. Separate shapes on each block are easier and better to start with. The 'rightness' of the successful move, when the shape fits the hole, is very satisfying, and makes a useful balance for more open-ended kinds of play.

Toddlers can manage puzzles of two kinds, though some are more interested in this activity than others. One kind is an Island Puzzle, where each piece is complete. It may be an animal, for example, which fits into its own shaped hole in the board. The other kind is the jigsaw, where the pieces must slot together correctly to make a whole picture. Bright infants can start using a three-piece jigsaw from about eighteen months-old.

USING JIGSAW PUZZLES WITH INFANTS
* Make sure the pieces are big enough to be handled by the child; they should not be so small that they could be swallowed or poked into an ear or nose.
* Colours should be bright and clear.
* The pieces should fit into the holes easily.
* Stories should be told along with pictures of familiar scenes.
* The puzzle should not be completed for the child by an adult, but merely suggestions made, so that the child believes he has done it.
  The attempt should be rewarded with praise.

Little children need plenty of practice at comparing sizes and shapes. Practical exercises include seeing how much water from one jar fills up another, or how many beans can be put in different pots; children can measure with parts of their bodies, such as the number of hand-spans, thumb-widths, or foot-lengths that make up a table or anything else. As soon as they want to, they can move on to using rulers, measuring tapes, etc. They can then make a diagram of what they have found, and draw simple block graphs which can be coloured. It gives great satisfaction to see one's work pinned up on the wall.

Weighing things is rather more complicated. Children have to get the idea of weight and balance first. For this, they need practice at feeling the heaviness of things, and then weighing them to compare them more accurately. Start by using some simple balance scales to show first the idea of heavier and lighter, and then the idea of equilibrium. When a child seems to understand these concepts, it is time to move on to a spring balance to see how weights are measured on a linear scale. Even bright children have usually been at school some time before they understand about standard-ized weights.

Basic arithmetic

Learning to use numbers successfully means that a child has to develop and co-ordinate three types of competencies: (a) understanding how to solve problems: (b) understanding why they can be solved in that way; and (c) deciding when a particular technique should be used.

As early as 2 years old, children show some natural understanding of addition and subtraction which they can demonstrate with small sets of objects. By the time they reach the age of 4, bright children have often learned to solve most addition and subtraction problems with numbers below ten.

Back-up strategies. One of the most striking characteristics of children's arithmetic is how adaptable they are, since they choose among the differ-ent strategies they have available to them. They often devise back-up strategies which do not rely on simple memory, such as counting on one's fingers. Even among 4 and 5 year olds, the harder the problem, the more likely children are to use a back-up strategy to solve it. It is not the use of back-up strategies which causes errors; those are more likely to happen when children are forbidden to use them.

These back-up strategies work similarly with subtraction and multipli-cation. For example, consider a 5 year old's choice between solving a problem of addition by stating a remembered answer or by counting from one onwards. Remembering may be faster, but simply counting from one onwards tends to be more accurate for young children, especially on diffi-cult problems. Most 5 year olds reconcile these goals by using memory primarily on relatively easy problems, and by using back-up strategies on the more difficult problems. This allows fast and accurate performance on easy problems, and slower but accurate performance on harder ones. In general, children tend to choose the fastest approach that they can execute accurately.

CHAPTER V

Exceptional children

SLOW LEARNERS

Children who have difficulty in learning pose great problems, both at home and in the classroom. From the child's point of view, the learning situation can become very depressing, if not intolerable, but then, maybe, progress is made and life looks rosier again. The teacher has good reason to be confused with these changes of mood and behaviour. How is it that the child can learn well sometimes and appear to be a complete blank at others? The answer lies in three things: in the nature of the learning problem; the way in which the disability shows itself; and how the individual child reacts to that difficulty.

Investigating a slow learner is like being a detective following up a number of clues. The difference is that not only do the causes of the learning disruption have to be identified, but one must also try to alleviate them. Although ordinary parents and teachers are often able to understand and be of some help, they are limited by their lack of knowledge and experience. It may be necessary to call in someone else, either an educational psychologist or a specially qualified teacher, to address the problem situation. Slow learning can have many causes, which are rarely found singly, but tend to come in clusters.

It may seem obvious to say that children cannot learn any task if they lack the appropriate ability to do so. Nevertheless, this is only one of many possibilities to be considered with a slow-learning child. It is not unknown for a child to be labelled 'stupid' or 'clumsy' when, for instance, the fault lies with some form of poor hand/eye co-ordination that could be improved. Until fairly recently, children suffering from cerebral palsy were assumed to be of very low intelligence, but we now recognize the condition as one of brain damage affecting only muscular control. It merely gives the impression of abnormal intellectual functioning.

Some children's rate of intellectual development is not only extremely slow, even though it may approximate to a normal pattern, but it is also limited in the upper level it can reach. Such children will not benefit from the normal classroom situation unless they are recognized and special provision made. Unfortunately, unless it obvious that they are severely handicapped, it may be some time before they are identified as such by the teacher and transferred to a special school.

If slow learners are left to fend for themselves, without a special curriculum, they will simply wait around for many hours each day – uncomprehending and without learning – while the rest of the class makes progress. They may be just docile watchers, but they can also be a considerable source of disruption in the class: aggression or, at the very least, some activity to break the tedium, is a well-known outcome of frustration. The same condition of non-comprehension will apply to other children, with the required abilities but who, for various reasons (as described in this chapter), might reasonably be called slow learners and in need of special attention. Without this intervention, children with neurological or developmental faults will certainly suffer in their eventual intellectual growth.

Developmental disabilities

Sequential development. All meaningful learning is related to previous learning and activities. If a child's developmental growth misses a part of that sequence, he may only acquire a form of unrelated, non-meaningful learning, such as simple memorising.

A normal classroom containing thirty to forty primary schoolchildren is likely to include several who show evidence of isolated bits of learning. For instance, a child is quite happy to say the word 'cat' when he recognizes the picture of a cat on the presented card, with 'CAT' written above it. The child may not have the faintest idea what those marks above the picture mean, but teacher seems pleased, so he must have done well! You can try this with small children and, say, present them with a picture of a fox with the letters 'FOX' written above it; some will 'read' it as 'DOG'.

Making the child's hand move to form letters comes into the same category. A teacher can make a child grasp a pencil and draw lines, which to the teacher form letters but to the pupil are meaningless: it is not really learning, but rather a form of conditioned response. In this case, there has been a gap during what should have been the stage of learning to co-ordinate physical movement and sight. Communication between hand and eye, which is a sequence of normal developmental learning, is missing.

Sensory development. During the time that normal infants learn to make distinctions between the different things they perceive, they come to select and control their own reactions to them. Depending on the amount of early stimulation they have received, they build up a repertoire of perceptual skills which vary, but are usually of a sufficient level for the normal classroom. Where early stimulation, such as conversation has been severely deficient, a child will be limited in auditory skills and can only make clumsy perceptual choices. This means that he will probably have communication problems, and appear more stupid than he really is. Reading, too, depends on the ability to make fine discrimination between written or printed letters; for instance, mixing up 'd' and 'b' is a frequent problem.

Co-ordinating perception. As the development of sensory discrimination becomes more precise, so should the individual's response to it, so that behaviour is more closely related to incoming information. Motor information comes from physical movement and has an immediate feedback – when you pick up a ball you are immediately aware of its properties. But visual and auditory information does not offer this reassurance. When a child cannot co-ordinate what he feels, sees, and hears, he is not able to understand. As a result, children may receive instructions and not be able to carry them out: and teachers can repeat the spoken instructions to them without effect. What is needed is a form of bridging communication, so that both motor and sensory information are on the same wavelength and can be reinforced simultaneously. Co-ordination is a very complicated neural process and even in a normal child its completion takes many years; how much more difficult it must be for those who are slow at learning.

Sensory perception must be matched to motor action, and not the other way round: there is only one direction for the matching process. In other words, the sequence of development must be kept in the natural order. Motor information is also the more reliable: when children match objects the wrong way round, the perceptual response becomes dominant. For example, in copying a triangle, a perceptually dominant child can be seen tightly clutching his pencil, making sure it moves as requested, but perceiving only the tiniest fraction of a line at a time – the perception of the triangle as a whole form is not seen, and cannot be reproduced from memory. In fact, learning visual perception is largely a matter of learning to accept distortion; such as the interpretation of two drawn lines running closer together as the perspective of railway lines viewed into a distance. The interpretation of pictures in books and maps is almost entirely a learned process. Some primitive peoples or newly sighted people have problems in learning how to interpret two-dimensional representations of perspective.

Co-ordinating feedback. Children learn to monitor their own responses by exploring their worlds, using sensory feedback to co-ordinate the information they have perceived. In order to transform information into effective learning, the different kinds of impressions which reach the brain have to be co-ordinated and translated into meaning. Children who have problems co-ordinating their many perceptions often let one perceptual mode take the upper hand. It saves time and effort. For example, a child without the ability to co-ordinate could perhaps read silently (visual behaviour), and then be able to tell the story of what he has read (verbal behaviour), but he cannot read aloud and comprehend together (using visual and verbal behaviour at the same time). Educationalists have long recognized differences in learning styles between individuals,

---

CHARACTERISTICS OF THE MBD CHILD

1. He has a short span of concentration, so that he does not watch television or read a book for long. He only hears half an adult's instructions or sentences, with the result that he cannot remember even simple directions or is unable to complete school learning tasks.

2. He has difficulties in perceptual and intellectual functioning: orientating objects in space, distinguishing right from left, auditory discrimination, short-term memory, arranging items in a sequence, or generalizing from one sense perception to another. Reading and writing problems are also not uncommon.

3. He has problems with personal relationships. Such children tend to be impulsive, difficult to discipline and poor socialisers. They cause damage and are difficult to toilet-train. Although outgoing, they have few friends, tending to insist on their own rules.

4. He is more often a boy.

5. Most MBD children are moody, 'short-fused' and prone to tears. Relationships between themselves and others, whether adults or other children in the family, tend to slide into negativity, because of irritation on the part of the others as well as feelings of low-esteem on the part of the child. Groups of age-peers and families both tend to pick on the child, and school performance is often detrimentally affected as a result. Teacher's comments such as 'You're really quite bright, but you just aren't doing your best' are deflating, particularly if he is really trying hard. One American study showed that MBD children made up about a half of adolescent under-achievers.

---

such as the auditory learner or the visual learner. Extreme dominance in any perceptual mode slows down learning considerably.

The clumsy child. The medical term used for this common cluster of problems is minimal brain dysfunction (MBD). It may affect as much as 5 to 10 per cent of the population, depending on definition, but is not related to intelligence. Among normally active children playing outdoors, the clumsy child may not even be noticeable. But on a rainy day, when they are confined indoors or in the classroom, their lack of movement control creates difficulties and emotional problems for both themselves and others.

Research on behaviour modification with MBD children has been carried out in the United Kingdom, but with little benefit to report so far: perhaps bio-feedback techniques will be found to be effective one day. Remarkable results have been claimed for drug therapy, although it has been recorded as being inappropriately used and over-used in the United States. Psychotherapy may help, but is not often available. The understanding, sympathetic school-teacher can be the problem-child's main source of comfort.

LEARNING HANDICAPS
* **Extreme poverty.**
* **Unfavourable social or cultural attitudes.**
* **Neglect or maltreatment of the child.**
* **Personal problems, such as emotional deprivation in the child, probably arising from the three preceding obstacles.**
* **Extreme lack of stimulation.**
* **Specific physical handicaps, such as poor sight or hearing, which remain either undiscovered or neglected.**

The teacher of young children is always in a key position. It is her responsibility, and it should be within her ability, to bring to the notice of the appropriate authorities any abnormalities in her charges which she feels need attention.

Reading problems. 'Dyslexia' is a term which is often used to describe the many varieties of reading disability, which can be due to many causes, both physical and psychological. For many of the reasons described in this book, reading problems start early and, equally, the earlier they are identified the better the prognosis. Slow learning in other subjects at school can affect the motivation and facility to read, and vice versa. Reading ability is adversely affected by a high level of anxiety, which is also detrimental to other school attainment.

The treatment of reading disability and the inevitable psychological problems that accompany it (before and after) is best carried out after a full professional investigation. Ideally, every child should be screened for physical defects before reaching school, so that a child with, say, visual problems could be given glasses and a seat at the front of the class. Different methods of teaching reading could be selected for the individual child. Where a blanket method, such as 'look and say', which teaches children to see words as wholes, is applied to all the class, children with visual perception problems will be disadvantaged. Auditory dyslexics, who cannot distinguish between short vowel sounds, and might write 'cit' instead of 'cat', will be confused by the 'phonic' method, which breaks up words to learn them.

Simple visual and auditory tests can be used by all teachers to screen new schoolchildren for possible learning problems. This is particularly important for the at-risk groups, such as those with learning problems or those born into dyslexic families. If children were to be screened early on for possible reading/learning difficulties, they could receive remedial teaching from the start. This teaching puts considerable emphasis on repetition, which children with these difficulties often need.

Behaviour therapy has been used successfully in some cases of reading difficulty: another approach is to minimize distractions, keeping the teaching atmosphere calm and prohibiting interruptions. The remedial teacher always has the difficult task of combining 'therapy' with an attack on the child's specific learning problems. In California, work with children of very low intelligence showed that they could make up sentences with plastic symbols – as indeed can chimpanzees if trained long enough. Perhaps similar 'concrete' methods of writing and reading could be devised for children with dyslexic problems from other causes. A coloured letter-learning scheme obviously has drawbacks for the colour-blind, but is nevertheless an effective method of teaching reading to those who have difficulty.

Help for the slow learner

Teaching the slow learner is a prime example of teaching to learn – in particularly difficult circumstances. The important parts of a slow learner's education (as is the case with other children) are not so much what is achieved as how to set about the task, and the means of getting there.

The type of dysfunction from which a child suffers is revealed in his learning behaviour. Normally, classrooms or learning groups function at a recognizable level, and if a child fails to reach the minimum goal of the lesson, the teacher should be the first to notice this. For example, a child asked to colour in a picture may not be able to colour the apple red, because he cannot find the apple. The reason he cannot find the apple is because he is unable to differentiate the conflicting maze of lines he sees on the paper. The task is meaningless to him, and this will be clear to the observant teacher.

Tests for learning problems. Various tests can be used by teachers, but only when signs of learning problems have already been noted, and only as an indication of what is wrong. They can provide a clearer picture of the child's problems, but at our present level of knowledge, tests cannot predict future performance with accuracy.

Slow development. As always, children should be educated according to their developmental level and not their chronological age, because they often vary in their developmental levels for different abilities. The teacher is often obliged to 'play it by ear'.

Disrupted development. Sometimes, stages in development can either be partially completed or else missed entirely, and children will show this in their learning behaviour. Since the teacher's problem is to try to fill in the missing stages, the first move is to identify these. As each stage depends on the completion of the one before, a useful procedure is to go back through all the stages until the incomplete or missing one is reached. The teacher's task is then to mend the gap – to teach the missing development. If the processes of learning are not mastered first, then the subject matter will never be understood.

Teaching such a child is extremely difficult and calls for particular teaching techniques, which may have to be evolved for the individual child. Children do not skip stages without good reason, and it is not always possible for a teacher to find out what has gone wrong or how she can put it right.

Although the child may be out of step and struggling, he is nevertheless getting older, continuing his development, and both home and school continue to make more complex demands on him. Thus, even when it is possible to fill a gap which appeared at age 3, the child may by now be 6, so that the new teaching/learning techniques must be changed to accord with the needs of the present 6 year old. To take away his current learning props and ask him to perform at an obviously 3-year-old level carries the danger of lowering morale and inviting consequent deterioration in performance. Lateness in learning to read poses many such problems, since the available reading material is so often meant for 5-year-old minds. But new, simplified reading books are now being written for teenagers and for adults who have missed out on earlier learning.

Cases of extensive interference with development, spotted by the class teacher, are normally passed on to a specialist, such as a trained remedial teacher in the regular school, or a staff member of a child-guidance clinic. Be that as it may, there are limitations to what a normal school is able to cope with, and a child may be better suited to being in a special school, if one is available.

MALADJUSTED CHILDREN

Psychological adjustment is not a static condition; the relationship between an individual and his environment varies, even from day to day. All adjustment is a learned behaviour, which is governed by the same principles that affect other forms of learning, although the degree of adjustment itself affects other learning, such as school progress. A child is termed 'maladjusted' when his adjustment is so poor that the resulting unhappiness deflects his development from its expected route. Such children can show their condition in many ways – not necessarily in overtly disturbed behaviour.

When a teacher is aware of the normal range of children's development and the various influences upon it, she will also be aware of the variations from it that may be expected. For example, teachers should recognize the problems of the withdrawn child as much as they do those of the disruptive child. Maladjusted behaviour is to some extent relative to the life-situation in which the pupil finds himself, so that the same behaviour tolerated in one situation may be thought worthy of referral to a psychologist in another. Teachers, parents and doctors, sometimes in co-operation, are most often the people who define certain qualities as 'maladjustment'.

Disturbed behaviour is not confined to children: adults in charge of children can cause terrible damage by their own maladjustment. Immaturity, neuroticism and certain psychiatric disturbances in teachers can bring distress to both children and other school staff, though stress and conflict in the classroom will affect each child differently. It is difficult for education authorities, even if they are fully aware of an unhealthy situation of this kind, to do anything about it, except in extreme cases, when deputations of parents have sometimes resulted in a teacher's removal.

Identifying maladjustment

What is considered 'normal' and what is 'abnormal' behaviour depends on: (a) the individual concerned; (b) the situation he is in; and (c) the consistency of the behaviour.

Everyone has moments of maladjustment, such as depression after 'flu, or aggression due to fatigue or frustration. On the whole, they pass by without interference from others, so that potential maladjustment should be carefully watched before any action is taken. Many behaviour disorders, such as bed wetting or temper tantrums, are very common and, to that extent, 'normal'. 'Difficult' children who are insolent, break the rules, bully other children, withdraw to unresponsiveness or lie may really be crying for help. But they may also be behaving according to another set of rules – that of their world outside school; and with their socially orientated, middle-class values, teachers may have difficulty in understanding that different set of rules.

With knowledge about the problem, and with some screening, maladjustment is detectable and should be largely manageable, if addressed before a child becomes actively delinquent. The recent development of quick questionnaires which teachers can use, either with suspect children or entire school populations, provides some reliable evidence to use in this work. As with many other aspects of child care, however, tests alone are insufficient. It is the sensitivity of the educator to spoken and unspoken communication between her and the child which makes the difference.

Problem behaviour. A child's behaviour is considered to be a problem, not only when it is different from the normal pattern, but when it offends people's idea of what is right and appropriate. Both adults and children judge each other; it is part of daily social interaction, but some are less tolerant than others and some have more power to act. The gang of bullies in the playground has power over one small boy, which would be considered a problem – if adults ever found out. The teacher can also be a destructive bully in the classroom, of course, but her behaviour would probably be called 'strict' or 'eccentric'.

Children's behaviour must be individually evaluated in the context of the eternal triangle of home/school/child. Then, what is and what is not 'maladjusted' behaviour may become clearer.

The homes of maladjusted children

The sad list of unpleasant circumstances in which many children are brought up summarizes the origins of what may result in maladjusted behaviour. Even in less dire circumstances, children can miss out on the basic psychological necessities, and remain stunted or distorted in their development.

Research work over decades has shown that children raised in situations such as old-style orphanages very often do not receive sufficient affection to become loving, responsive and emotionally well balanced. It is clear that emotional deprivation in infants is followed by long-lasting and, perhaps, permanent ill-effects on personality – in particular, the ability to build relationships. The mother/baby bond in normal family life has been given considerable attention. It should be noted that the father's relationship to his baby, and the relationship in the extended family, have only begun to be investigated over the last few years.

Parental demands, rigorously enforced, leave the child with the choice of complete compliance or rebellion. For instance, excessive insistence on toilet-training in infancy can result in the child withholding his faeces, and so becoming constipated. The child then finds it even more difficult to perform, the mother is even more exasperated, and a psychological impasse has resulted which could have been avoided. The same type of parenting can result in extremes of outcome – either in varieties of childhood rebellion, at any time of life – or in an over-obedient individual. Children put under such pressures may experience difficulties while growing up, such as making friends of either sex, and eventually in taking on the responsibility of marriage and parenthood. Children under excessive pressure endure excessive anxiety, often building up personal psychological defence mechanisms in order to cope with their lives. Other people who inadvertently breach these defences may be surprised by the violence of the reaction.

Although socially acceptable (and thus 'adjusted') behaviour varies between families, there is often a vast discrepancy between the ways of a minority sub-culture and those of the outside world. The child torn between a strongly enforced home culture and that of his school-mates can become emotionally disturbed. The 'generation gap' – that clash between the values of different age-groups – is a well-known cause of problems of this kind.

Socially deprived children are handicapped in many ways, such as nutrition and intellectual stimulation. They also have a higher than normal likelihood of physical and mental abnormality and, in addition, particularly in economically and culturally poor homes, they may be brought up on a regime of punishment. They may feel that school and teachers are not on the same wavelength as their outside experience, and their education suffers as a result. It is from this stratum of poor, educationally limited and discouraged children that most, although not all, maladjusted and delinquent behaviour comes.

Schools and maladjusted children

Schools may themselves contribute to maladjustment in pupils; they are institutions which deliver values along with the information. As a general rule, the stricter the control a school exerts, the less concern is usually shown for the individual pupil and for his developing self-concept. On the surface, strict control exists to promote learning, but over-strict controls can actually inhibit learning. Although a child must submit to the rules of the school in order to be a good pupil, schools vary in the expected levels of subordination and initiative, so that the same behaviour may or may not be punished in different schools. Children who cannot accept the values of their school as relevant to their life experience may 'drop out', either mentally or physically, and will show their feelings in maladjusted behaviour.

Teachers are not angels – favouritism and dislike are familiar in the classroom: but their effects on children's self-image are less well known. One child may be picked on by most of the staff in their different lessons, each teacher unaware that the others are doing it. Probably no teacher has ever been to the child's home, so no one is likely to know about any mental battering he gets there too. Teachers can be deliberately and constantly unkind to pupils, with little regard for them as people, subjecting children to classroom ridicule, or deflating their imaginative efforts with sarcasm. If the learning experience is unpleasant, incomprehensible, boring or biased, children will (not unreasonably) both under-achieve and, hating this daily torment, misbehave.

Growing up and the maladjusted

Growing up always brings its own stresses, but some children are born with extra difficulties. For example, minimal brain dysfunction, while difficult to detect, is likely to cause considerable disturbance. Similarly, many genetic disorders are still poorly understood and behavioural problems tend to occur at different times in the process of development. What were once considered to be symptoms of maladjustment, such as occasional regression into an earlier stage of emotion, for instance, when the intellectual pressure is increased at examination time, are now accepted as a fairly normal part of growing up.

Although in the Western world adolescence is often regarded as a turbulent time, much of the apparent distress is probably caused by adults expecting adolescents to be both troubled and troublesome. Now that full-time education continues longer, the extension of the period of dependence creates an unnatural and strained relationship between young adults and older ones. Apart from these cultural factors, distinct emotional changes are to be found in adolescents around the world. For example, old, familiar emotions become notably more intense and spontaneous, and emotions can swing relatively easily to extremes such as over-control, as in sulking.

Sexual behaviour also changes, not only as an individual matures, but because society has certain expectations of a young person's behaviour. For example, in preparations for the future, parents of a 17-year-old girl may not demand as high a level of school achievement of her as they would of a boy of the same age. Adolescent group conformity, such as the one-sex clique, is well known, although this again depends on what society expects of social learning, and is less apparent among better educated teenagers. However, the relative democracy of the adolescent friendship group is important to each one's changing and sensitive self-esteem and sense of identity.

As with other age-groups, maladjustment in adolescents is a relative term. Often, what adults consider to be maladjustment is normal behaviour to the adolescent, or perhaps a readjustment to the spoken and unspoken demands of adult society.

Help with maladjusted children

Understanding the causes of maladjustment goes a long way towards understanding how it may be prevented. The logical measures which would follow from such insight call for deep-seated changes in administrative thinking, from the level of government downwards. Home conditions are the responsibility of the social welfare services in most countries, though voluntary groups also often play an essential part.

Some school conditions can be changed at grass-roots level more easily than others. For instance, reduction in the size of the teaching group can sometimes be a matter of rearranging staff responsibilities, so that needs of individual children can be responded to better. Teaching attitudes and ways of teaching *can* be changed enabling the school to render support where the home has failed. Respect for children as people should always be a priority.

Teachers are a kind of parent substitute. Most teachers take this aspect of their task seriously, since education is also a social activity and the teacher its mediator. The greater liberalization of much teacher training means that more teachers are coming into schools who see their work as considerably extended into a complex of social and intellectual skills. Some qualify in school-counselling or extend their role by taking children for out-of-school activities, by being a father-figure, and so on. For example, teachers may have to positively seek communication with parents, building a bridge between home and school.

Training in social skills would be of particular value to teachers working in difficult conditions. Carrying through observations means knowing where to get things done and how to understand and communicate with the social services or other people whose help may be needed.

The kind of morality presented by schools may be irrelevant to their pupils – 'Thou shalt not steal', for example, to a child in a family of thieves. In Western schools, the teaching of morality was once part of the prevailing religious (Christian) ethos. Today, unless the school is either specifically religious, or the country makes religious demands on the curriculum, moral education is minimal at many schools. The aesthetically satisfying side of education, the teaching of art and music, is also given very little attention in many primary and most secondary schools – these subjects are the first to be dropped when money is short. In fact, planning for leisure activities should figure significantly in education where circumstances merit it, primarily in the more developed countries.

When outside services are inadequate to deal with maladjusted children, it can help to isolate a small group of such pupils from the rest of the class for part of the day. Even one disturbed child in a class can harass the teacher and considerably disrupt school life; his removal can be a surprising relief to both the teacher and an improvement to the classroom atmosphere. Small children in particular, can find it easier to make contact with an adult and to adjust to school if in a smaller group. The happiness of a potentially or already mildly maladjusted child in school may depend on the attitudes of the headteacher – whether she sees her obligation as helping the child to understand and adapt to the rules, or of forcing him to conform.

GIFTED CHILDREN

To some extent giftedness is what you choose it to be. Some American research has claimed that as much as the top 30% of the population is gifted; but most international concern is with the top 10% of children in any population.

Every child needs mental and physical nourishment in order for ability to flourish: where the appropriate facilities for learning are missing, so too are recognizably gifted children. The prevalence of noted giftedness is related to the educational situation in different regions or countries. Assuming a roughly equal proportion of ability levels between children in different education authorities, one might ask why there are so few mathematicians in one, musicians in another, and so on. The availability of nursery school or other early education seems to be a most important influence on later school achievement.

Children who are gifted in any way are normally conscious of their difference from those who are not. In an unaccepting school atmosphere, some children may hide their abilities and perform at the same level as the rest, because, on the whole, children prefer to conform to the average. Giftedness helps them to be very good at this disguise, but the price of anonymity is high – frustration, boredom and disenchantment with school. The important role of the professional in explaining high ability to parents and teachers involves sensitive handling to help prevent isolation of the child.

Gifts

An individual's gifts may be single, in groups or widely spread. Studies of gifted adults are virtually all retrospective; they are often subject to social forces and anecdotal vagaries about individual scientists or generals, or the like, and how they arrived at the top of their professions. Although non-verbal talents, e.g. music and art, are not normally considered to mature until adolescence, some individuals, such as Mozart or Picasso, gave evidence of very early development, although others – such as Van Gogh – developed late. If identifying giftedness was based on an idea of early maturation of the sequence of growth, the late developers would be missed out. We do not know whether their particular abilities in child-hood were different from those of their peers, nor why some precocious children have failed to carry their promise into adulthood.

For convenience, five main types of giftedness in children are suggested here:

Intellectual. This is the easiest to measure, both in terms of infant development and with intelligence tests, although high intelligence test scores (say IQ 145) are not always on a par with high achievement in school. It is sometimes only when parents protest about low or high achievement levels that children of high potential ability are discovered. The gifted children who are better performers at conforming socially will remain 'average' at school, although they sometimes find their way to high-level achievement when they leave.

Technical. Primary school-teachers can become dependent on the technically bright child in the class – the one who dominates group craft-work, whose understanding of how machines work is outstanding. They will often look for a boy to do such tasks, and so not encourage the girls in that role.

Aesthetic. In order to play a musical instrument, it is necessary to have access to one, in order to paint, one must have paper, paints and brushes. For all we know, there may be brilliant sculptors around who have never seen a chisel. Around the world, the teaching of the arts in schools is very varied in its availability; most aesthetically gifted children receive encouragement and opportunities for creative work mainly at home.

Social. The socially gifted are particularly sensitive to other people and tend to be popular. They may act as confidantes for their classmates, and teachers will also find themselves talking at a more intimate level to such children.

Physical. The popularity of gymnastics, recently fostered by brilliant displays in the Olympic Games has brought to light many young girls who are highly talented, where none were apparent before, the lead being taken by the formerly communist countries. Some physical gifts which could be used vocationally, such as football, have always been recognized in boys. Fortunately for these gifted children, sport and athletics are currently enjoying a vogue with the result that provision of the extra tuition and practice needed to develop their abilities is better than it has ever been.

The Gulbenkian Research Project and follow-up

The nation-wide Gulbenkian Research Project in the United Kingdom compared how gifted and non-gifted children experienced their education and relationships, and how this affected the development of their abilities and satisfaction in life. It was designed to investigate the environmental influences which could have shaped the children's behaviour – in particular, those of parents and teachers. The uniqueness of this study was in the long, deep, counselling-style interviews, with both the young people and their parents, about the fabric of their lives. Sometimes the same story – told by children and parents – took on quite a different aspect. The follow-up study made use of multiple sources and techniques, seeking to find whether the gifted children's behaviour was the same as that of other children, and where it differed (Freeman, 1991a).

The original project took place between 1974 and 1979 and involved 210 children, who were then aged 5 to 14; the sample began with children who had been presented as gifted by their parents. Each of those *target* children was then matched with two *control* children for age, sex, socioeconomic status and the same school-class, but only one control child was matched for intelligence, the other being taken at random in that respect. All the children and their families were visited in their homes, and their sixty class-teachers and sixty headteachers were interviewed. An important finding was that the development of children's abilities was inhibited, at whatever level, by lack of appropriate provision – whether material to learn with, appropriate examples to follow, or tuition.

The follow-up study. Ten years after the original study, 81 per cent of the original sample (169 individuals) and their parents were interviewed; the work took place between 1984 and 1988. The follow-up sample was statistically valid, with almost identical ratios of the original groupings, such as the proportions of the sexes, and the IQ range. They were a highly intelligent group of young people; two-thirds of them scored at the ninety-fifth percentile or above on the Raven's Matrices, and the remaining third at the ninety-ninth. In Stanford-Binet IQ terms, over a quarter were at IQ 150 or above.

The uniqueness of the study lay in the personal, in-depth investigation of the (by then) young people's experiences. The approximately 400 semi open-ended interviews, lasting at least four hours, were carried out in each one's home, but as many of the young people were by then living away from their parents, they were seen in their own homes, and the parents in theirs. The recorded and transcribed texts were scored and analysed statistically, the data being thus a mixture of both interviewer judgement and objective measurement.

The young people were then aged 14 to 23 – 60 girls and 109 boys – with a mean Stanford-Binet IQ of 135.438 (SD 19.877), spread throughout the United Kingdom: 14 per cent had attended selective grammar schools, while the others were about equally divided between comprehensive and private schools. Although the sample did have some middle-class bias, it included the full spread of economic levels.

Results. A continuation of earlier environmental influences was found in the behaviour of the young people; in particular, their style of upbringing and education was seen to be related to their academic achievements and creativity. Although most of them, both gifted and non-gifted, had fulfilled their earlier promise in a wide variety of schools, a significant number had not. The reasons for the relative failure of these young people were connected with the psychological effects of both their home circumstances and those of the communities they lived in. For example, the expectations of their community sometimes made them alter what they felt they could hope for from life, and if the effects were negative, it lowered their aims. On the whole, most schools coped well with their gifted pupils, but there were notable problems of communication between teachers and pupils, and sometimes lack of both teaching material and teachers.

A major block seemed to exist in British education preventing people from saying that one child was considerably brighter than another. Allied to this was a fear of closeness with pupils, which denied teachers the information about children's strengths and weaknesses which they needed to teach them better. What the gifted were in special need of were teachers who would work *with* them, rather than *for* them; teachers who were as concerned with the structure of learning and the pupil's ability to cope as with the passing on of information. Such matters as self-confidence and satisfactory personal relationships can be as important for achievement as the mastery of skills and knowledge.

The gifted spoke of special pressures, such as feeling obliged to conform to the average through being 'put down' by teachers, and of being influenced to do less well by their classmates. But on the other hand, even greater pressure came from parents and teachers who, perhaps for their own vicarious satisfaction, pushed them very hard to achieve. Some youngsters did their best to respond to this, subduing their personalities in a single-minded striving for academic excellence. For them, healthy emotional development, including the freedom to play and be creative, was severely curtailed; the glazed look in their eyes, as they worked doggedly on to achieve their top grades, revealed the pressure they were under.

The message for those who are likely to cause that stress – teachers and parents – is that such pressure often has the opposite effect from what was intended. In the end the children might in fact achieve less well. Far better results in terms of both human and examination results were found when children, whether they were below average or gifted, were treated with respect, allowing them enough responsibility to make many of their own discoveries and decisions. Some, especially those talented in the arts, seemed to have a natural impetus, a unique spark which could light up their personalities, bringing them great inspiration and success.

**SPECIFIC CHANGES OF DIRECTION
SUGGESTED BY THE RESEARCH**
* All children, including the gifted, need adequate material to work with, and physical or tutorial help in schools. But, of all children, the gifted are often the least likely to have access to what they need for their educational fulfilment.
* Parents should be involved as much as possible. Parents as well as teachers teach, providing living examples for children to follow, especially in the children's early years.
* Teachers should also be concerned with the children's emotional development, so that both sides can learn respect for each other.
* The children's own values and interests are the basis of their enthusiasm, and should be carefully sought out.

Milestones of giftedness

Although gifted children often reach their developmental milestones more rapidly than other children, these signs are not entirely reliable as an indication of future giftedness.

Walking. Gifted children appear to walk at an earlier age than the average, but there are socio-economic influences on physical growth, which must be taken into account. Poorer children are generally less well developed.

Talking. Although most gifted children speak earlier and more fluently than their age-peers, it is not a sure sign of giftedness. Girls are usually more advanced than boys, socio-economic influences being minimal on this particular gender difference.

Reading. Some gifted children teach themselves to read at 3 years old, but others may be prevented from doing so – even though they are intellectually ready – by parents who may feel that it should be taught at school, or by lack of reading matter, or for emotional reasons. Girls tend to read earlier than boys.

Cognitive development. Logical thinking, reasoning, mathematics and memory are considered together here. Many researchers have concluded that the gifted child is advanced in generalizing from what he has learned, in seeing relationships between objects and ideas, and in applying them to new situations. The gifted child is not only likely to be in advance of other children in the stages of intellectual development, but sometimes seems to jump whole stages. Such behaviour is confusing to teachers when, for instance, a child gets his arithmetic right but cannot explain how he did it. The child may also be aware of ambiguities in questions which the rest of the class cannot discern, causing him to pause before attempting the answer. This can even gain a gifted child a reputation for slowness or awkwardness.

Arithmetical development is difficult to compare in children, because schools use different methods, some drilling their pupils to memorize tables and techniques, others helping them with individual discovery methods. Gifted child mathematicians often devise methods of their own, sometimes before they have reached school age.

The gifted child seems to have an exceptionally good memory from a very early age, and brings it into use when gathering his store of knowledge. Teachers are more often able to accept good memory as a guide to giftedness than other qualities.

Other developmental indications of giftedness

Sleep. 'Problems' of children's sleep often depend on what is expected by the parents. If a child is permitted to read until he falls asleep, for example, there are less likely to be 'problems' than if lights are put out too early for a child who needs less than twelve hours' sleep. The Gulbenkian research (Freeman, 1991a) found that a child's sleep pattern is related to his age at the time, and to the style of upbringing. But there is no evidence that gifted children sleep less than other children.

Physique. Every study on gifted children has concluded that they are above average height, weight, strength and so on. However, these physical indications of superiority are also tied to socio-economic attributes. Children discovered to be gifted frequently come from the economically better-off sections of society.

Health. Apart from the surprising fact that gifted children are more likely to be short-sighted, they are notably healthy. It is possible that they have a higher incidence of 'sensitivity' diseases, such as allergy or asthma, but again, identification of these troubles is more frequently encountered in children from the higher social classes.

Friends. Gifted children are still children. Although some seek friends older than themselves, especially when this is expected, most are happiest in their own age group.

Curiosity. Parents and teachers often agree that genuine curiosity is a sign of giftedness, but there are distinct cultural variations in the amount of curiosity and questioning which is expected of children. The quality of their questioning is important, because much asking of questions may merely be attention-seeking. Educators find this constant 'in-depth' questioning very wearing, but the gifted questioner really wants good, honest answers and solid facts. Teachers may be surprised to find that they have a tendency to answer some questions or questioners more readily than others. A monitoring check-guide, which they can devise themselves, would be useful in such circumstances.

Slow, yet gifted, learners. Children with the potential to be gifted can suffer from the same difficulties as slow learners, giving the impression of stupidity. They may also be impatient with the slow communication of writing, since their thoughts flow on too fast for a child's hand to keep up with. So their writing and spelling can, as a result, be below average, especially in boys. Whether this is because of poor co-ordination or impatience is hard to decide, but in either case, factors such as writing and spelling and exam conditions will mitigate against a child's success in some schools. On the other hand, given access to a typewriter or a computer, many gifted children learn to use it with great happiness and at speed, even though their spelling may still remain poor.

Perception. Keen powers of perception, especially aesthetic perception, are associated with giftedness. But teachers are not always aware of this ability in children, perhaps because of their own perceptions of what characterizes a 'normal' child.

Energy. Gifted children can be more intensely energetic than other children, which might present problems to the adults around, and may even be diagnosed as 'hyper-activity'. Extreme physical energy certainly makes it difficult to sit still for long at school, and learning in the formal school situation may suffer. Boys have this 'problem' more than girls.

Creativity. The creatively gifted child is as difficult to describe as creativity itself but, by the use of expert judgements, such children can be identified in some subject areas, such as art or poetry. Even so, almost all the research on the early behaviour of the creatively gifted has come under considerable criticism because of its inherent methodological difficulty. Some creative gifts may take years to mature into recognition, while others may fade with childhood. Highly creative children are often said to have a well-developed and 'dry' sense of humour.

Adjustment

Maladjustment in gifted children is sometimes caused by an unbalanced growth of abilities. They can be unpopular and misbehave in class if their brilliance becomes overly dominant in their lives, at the expense of their consideration for others and some attempts to fit in. As part of her long follow-up study, the psychologist Mia Kellmer Pringle (1970) found that among 'able misfits', too high or too low parental expectations often contributed to the child's maladjustment. These could result from a typical family situations, unhappy homes, illogical parental discipline, or 'inconsistent handling', which occurred more in this group than in the population at large. She suggested that good intellectual ability by itself is insufficient to compensate for inadequate parental support and interest. Set against this is the fact that extraordinary initiative, independence of mind and self-confidence have been identified by most researchers as important facets of the gifted child's personality.

Parents and teachers can feel threatened by a child who seems to know far more than they do. On the other hand, they may allow the child to 'take over' the family or class, so that he is presented with situations with which he may not be emotionally able to cope, and his relationships with everyone concerned will then be likely to suffer. Although gifted children usually perceive themselves as different from others with respect to their abilities, most can cope. Because such children can occupy themselves alone for hours, however, they appear to be introverted and are labelled 'unhappy'. Their apparent fondness for daydreaming and dislike of large groups adds to this often misleading image of a sad and lonely child.

Some children face terrible events, which would be expected to be destructive to them, but instead show a high level of adaptation and competence. Research in the United States has found that highly able young children are more competent, confident, humorous, flexible in their approach, and believe more in the accessibility of adults in their environment than normally able children (Lewis & Louis, 1991). Evidence of the relationship of vulnerability and intelligence level suggests that children in the gifted range of intellectual ability may be less vulnerable to major stress events than children of average or below-average ability.

There is little reliable evidence of the implications of belonging to one of the sub-populations of the highly able. Gifted girls, for example, have been found to be much like able boys in their intellectual interests and behaviour, but resemble other non-gifted girls in their social-emotional reactions. Girls tend not to be identified as gifted as often or as early as boys, and highly able women do not get studied as much by men. The follow-up research begun by Professor Terman in California in the 1920s of children gifted by IQ, showed that the gifted women's expectations and life circumstances had distinctly limited their achievements outside the home (Terman, 1925-29). However, although a study was made of the sources of life satisfactions of the gifted males in the study, no such data are available on the female cohort (Oden, 1968). There are some interesting psychosocial data from other sources, such as those on the often unfulfilled lives of the equally able sisters of 'famous men', such as Nanerl Mozart, or Mileva Einstein, the first wife of Albert Einstein (Stedtnitz & Schar, 1992).

Education of the gifted

Although gifted children may be bored at school, so are other children. Like the slow learner, the gifted child may be either doomed to hours of boredom in a formal school situation, or he will look around for relief in the form of more challenging problems and may become a ringleader in mischief.

It is hard for a teacher to keep a gifted child 'stretched' and able to achieve his potential in the normal school situation. But even with supreme effort from the teacher, a child's achievement will still be relative to the school and home conditions in which he operates. Two children with the same high IQ can perform quite differently in public examinations, depending on their circumstances, as research in schools has shown (Rutter et al., 1979). Able children who achieve less than their potential often have a high incidence of emotional difficulties, so that teachers judge them as being of no more than average ability, often making this judgement on the basis of the children's achievement. Thus, a bright under-achiever is likely to remain unrecognized, setting up a vicious circle which may possibly lead to fully developed maladjustment.

How to educate the highly gifted is the subject of endless debate. Some would separate them from other children and educate them in special schools; others would have special provision made for them in the normal school situation. Advancing children a class or two to keep up with their intellectual level has its difficulties – younger children may find themselves out of their emotional depth, teachers forget how young they are and make no allowance for this, while classmates may be jealous or cannot be bothered with the younger child. It is not easy to have an 'old' mind in a young body.

Education implies far more understanding than the acquisition of knowledge. The growing understanding of giftedness brings to schools yet another reason for 'enriching' the curriculum, which is important for all children, especially those from culturally poor homes. But it is of particular importance to children of potentially very high ability to have early access to new modes of perception and to practise their learning. Ability to play a violin, for instance, is particularly vulnerable to a late start. For all skills, the sooner the open mind and supple fingers of a young child begin to practise, the finer his perceptual and practical technique will become over time.

Though gifted children need at least as much affection and reassurance as a normal child, they often receive less because they appear to be so mature and competent. But when the violin is finally put back in its case after a three-hour session, perhaps the teddy-bear and bedtime attention by adults are even more important. Parents and teachers sometimes seem to hover between a strong desire to make the difficult child conform, and simply giving up their responsibilities to help the child structure his learning, in case they get in the way of something wonderful.

Gifted children of any kind need challenge rather than spoon-feeding. Teachers and parents may find themselves more in the position of a testing board for a child's fertile imagination, than in more conventional roles. Children of exceptionally high ability have a lot to offer the world – but too much of it is still running to waste.

PART TWO:
EDUCATION
FOR COMPETENCE

CHAPTER VI

Adaptable learning

Learning takes place when an individual adapts to experience, and is most effective when it is flexible enough to be applied to many kinds of experiences – competent behaviour. The changes in styles of learning and teaching suggested in this book have profound implications in two major aspects. The first is the change from individual to social learning, encouraging learning as a two-way process between pupil and teacher. The second is the move from passive to active learning on the part of the learner. Although these changes are not new (they were approved by both Socrates and Dewey), their practice is still rare. What is more, as pupils sit in their rows in the classroom listening to their teacher, the information they are given is not always ordered in the most logical or easiest way for it to be absorbed and applied. In fact, probably the least efficient way of stimulating the learning process is the formal college lecture, where the students try to catch the lecturer's message in their notes, without any planning and little involvement with the principles of the subject matter.

The best learning is that which can be used in other situations – termed 'transfer' – the specific use of learning strategies taken from one situation to another appropriate one. It means that the pupil is able to abstract the key operations from any task and recognize how they can be used in others, whether similar, such as calculations in physics and mathematics, or superficially different, such as language and craft. Helping the pupil to see similarities between problems and responses is essential to learning in any situation, and is most effectively built into teaching. Negative transfer happens when something previously learned gets in the way of new learning, like learning a new language which is similar to one already known.

It cannot be assumed that transfer of learning will occur automatically, because different subject areas have their own characteristics, and most teachers know they have to make sure it has taken place. Current psycho-logical thinking is that because most skills are specific to a particular subject area, they are not readily transferable between them. On the other hand, thinking strategies (the sequences of skills with a goal) *are* transferable (Nisbet, 1991).

Appropriate educational provision for any children means that each one, including the highly able, has the chance to develop their abilities fully. The educator's goal is to help pupils to learn adaptably, to use the abilities they were born with – competently – in many different situations. That is how the 'expert' works, with a high degree of competence based on a sound knowledge base; the novice, by contrast, has not only to acquire the information, but also the increasingly difficult procedures to apply it to more complex and unfamiliar problems. In general, one can think of children as novices and adults as experts.

Mediation. Virtually all learning is social, with someone carrying out the essential role of a mediator between knowledge and the learner. A mediator is not quite the same as a teacher. Mediation is a subtle process in which adults emphasize, interpret, extend and embellish the environ-ment, so that the child builds up an internal model of the world in which a variety of experiences can be meaningfully related. Because experiences are relatively random, much of their educational value may be wasted, unless they are mediated to the child's attention and recognition. Media-tion identifies the most important features of the environment, which are amplified, transformed and rescheduled, while others are blocked out so that the child is helped to systematize, select and appreciate what should be ignored and what should be noticed (Blagg, 1991). Parents are normal-ly the first mediators between their young children and their culture, introducing ideas in ways the children can understand, shielding them from unwelcome events, and helping them to formulate their own per-ceptions and thoughts. This is later carried on by some school-teachers, and others who have influence in the child's life (Vigotsky, 1978: Feuer-stein, 1980, see Chapter II).

Of course, learning does takes place without mediation and in situ-ations which are not social, such as sitting alone with a computer pro-gramme. These are not constructed to be mediators, and in fact some are made with little regard to the principles of programmed learning, so that children are badly taught by them, and a teacher may not always be at hand. If the children are too young for such isolated learning, what they absorb is not flexible and adaptable, and decidedly limited in its applica-bility elsewhere. Learning alone through reading works differently, be-cause the text is an extension of the author, who is thus a distant media-tor. Nevertheless, the book is no more than an inanimate version of the author, and then not always a good one. It is important, therefore, if the learning is to be most accessible and flexible, for the young reader to discuss and question what is in it with a living and responsive mediator.

Because children learn best on the basis of developing shared understanding, teachers have to be aware of the nature of the child's personal world. Schools could increase the effectiveness of their teaching if they provided more help with the learning process (as in the ways described in this chapter) in addition to the traditional presentation of information. This is both because new learning depends a great deal on how prior knowledge has been stored, and also because learners have to relate the new learning to the old in ways which are meaningful to them. This is something which good teachers try to do every day and, if asked, even small children are able (with some help) to describe the ways in which they feel more comfortable in learning.

Real-world problems. The ability to apply knowledge in a variety of situations depends on its being stored in the memory in a flexible way, so that it can easily be found again and put to work. The most efficient way of setting up a flexible mental storage system is to learn the material in a problem-solving way in the first place. There is much evidence that learning taught in such a way increases the potential for its transfer to other situations.

In life, finding and defining problems is both more difficult and more valuable than merely solving those with pre-set answers, as most pupils do in school. In mathematics, for example, working out the best way of spending the weekly classroom budget is a real-world problem, while working out how long it would take three men, each digging at the rate of 1 metre an hour, to make a 3.6m trench, would not be. Finding problems is the creative approach, because it obliges the learner to take an overview, comparing and contrasting possibilities and so on, while those considerations themselves provide some of the directions to the solutions.

When children have been set the task of finding and solving real-world problems, they are given the opportunity to exercise their minds with a more creative outlook. Their resulting accomplishments are products of a higher level of thinking than any which could come from problems presented in the standard paper-and-pencil tests of creativity or divergent thinking. Evidence from comparisons of standard creativity and real-world tests given to seventy-seven young teenagers, showed that the real-world problem-finding measures produced scores that were more reliable and predictive of creative extra-curricular activities than conventional measures of divergent thinking (Okuda, Runco & Berger, 1991).

Real-world situations can be used to assess divergent thinking: for example, pupils could be asked to compare the effects of TV, radio and newspapers in persuading people to stop smoking. Other situations could involve school regulations, pupils' friendship groups or homework, etc. Teaching in this way means a change of style from didactic instruction to problem-solving, at all levels and for all children. The benefits are to both the teacher, who finds the work more interesting, and to the children, who can use their minds more competently for the rest of their lives.

Behavourism. In the long-established, behaviourist view, the learning process also includes what happens afterwards, as when learning is followed by a reward (positive reinforcement) and so is more likely to occur again. In its simplest form, the encouragement of learning by reward implies that the child is already practising the desired learning, and that the reinforcement merely makes it appear more frequently. The behaviourist view is less concerned with the processes of learning than the ensuing behaviour. Yet teachers know that the same reward can affect children differently – a public word of praise meant as a reward might be an embarrassment to a rebellious adolescent. But behaviour which only remotely resembles the one the teacher is aiming for may be refined or 'shaped', by reinforcing only those features which approximate ever closer to the desired behaviour, termed 'operant conditioning' (Skinner, 1972). This is useful in showing that learning has taken place, although it does not describe the richness of the mental operations which underlie intelligent behaviour, nor fully explain why children behave as they do.

The idea of programmed learning comes from operant conditioning. For it to be effective, whether by book, video-tape, acoustic tape or computer, it must be based on sound teaching principles, the learning sequence being presented in a logical order, from simple to more complex material in an inter-related and sequential manner. The principle is that the learner makes a response to a question, and is then immediately informed whether it was correct, children moving through the 'lessons' at their own rate, which can be quicker than in the classroom, so diminishing the risk of boredom. This use of feedback brings motivating rewards to the pupil, both in the immediate information that the answer is correct, and in encouragement to move on to the next point. Just like a good teacher, programmes even have built-in praise and gentle reprimands, although without a real teacher it is inflexible.

Technological teaching aids have not always been warmly received, but they now have a place in education in industrialized countries. The language laboratory, for example, is a means of acquiring an accurate basis for a foreign language, while discussion of literature, the finer points of interpretation, and practice in speaking can take place outside the language laboratory in parallel.

Public television is not a teaching machine, because programmes are neither paced to suit each viewer, nor is a response demanded. Even so, it is highly beneficial as a form of class instruction. Professional films and other points of view can provide useful support to the solitary teacher, particularly in subjects such as geography, or physics concerned with advanced technology. Obviously, follow-up by the teacher is necessary to make sure that the children have accepted the lesson: it helps if teachers can implement a programme by good preparation, and by tape-recording all or parts of it to be played back at another time. If it were possible for the teacher to preview programmes before they were broadcast, then it would also be possible to pre-select the viewing group so that the programme content and ability level of viewers could be better matched.

FROM NOVICE TO EXPERT

Excellence in performance comes at a late stage in the development of a person's skill and knowledge, because it requires each individual to persevere through thousands of hours of hard work and learning: if one leaves the field, as most do, the prize is surrendered (Elshout, 1993). Expertise demands both a vast accumulation of knowledge and deep understanding, which must be flexibly organized for easy access, both for fast, automatic and error-free action as well as for slower, deliberate processing. It is easily recognized, at least by others who are in the same field, because whether they are tennis players or mathematicians, experts show ease and assurance in the excellence of their performance. Yet greater expertise does not always result in higher-level performance – the younger ones can produce a swifter, smoother response than an older expert.

Although expertise is clearly not only a matter merely of staying-power, in certain specific areas of learning with a mechanical aspect, such as mental calculation and memory for numbers, people can learn to perform on an extraordinary level, such as 'idiots savants', after a great many hours of training (Howe, 1990). Experiments have shown that some people have a particular aptitude for acquiring the mnemonic structures which these tasks demand, although this is not real expertise because it lacks the depth of understanding and feeling needed in artistic performance.

Expertise presupposes the availability of a vast number of patterns of information that can be recognized as 'old friends' – well-structured knowledge in active schemas of ideas and practical experience (Elshout, 1993). It also includes the possibility of switching between levels of attention and complexity, from the basic stimulus-response level to understanding and the ability to explain. All this makes the expert qualitatively different from a novice who may have the same level of intelligence and motivation.

Experts need years of experience to form the schemas that they use in making connections. In doctors, for example, schematic 'illness-scripts' connect patterns of symptoms to certain illnesses, resulting in an 'AIDS-script', a 'pancreatitis-script', or whatever. An illness-script is different from a medical syndrome, which is a scientific construct describing which symptoms go together. The illness-script is a knowledge-structure which a doctor has built up personally over years of studying and practice with real patients. This structuring of medical knowledge develops gradually, each script describing the causes and outcomes for a particular illness. Often, one patient's history can function as the nucleus around which the schema is organized.

In the later stages of gaining expertise, such scripts move smoothly into action, the chain of reasoning no longer coming fully to mind, so that the expert seems to jump to conclusions. But the short cut is only as good as the longer chain of reasoning from which it is derived. It is the deep understanding behind the actions which are typical of expertise in any field – knowing how things work, and why it is important to act in that way. Without that deep well of principled reasoning and understanding, the novice can do little but truly 'jump to conclusions'.

The advantage of looking at the lives of highly achieving individuals is that one can detect the motivational influences on their progress, which are often missed when only more limited methods of psychological tests or experiments are used in investigation. In the United Kingdom, Freeman (1991a, and see Chapter V), in her fifteen-year study of children of a wide range of ability, found that there were always powerful, personal motivating reasons why the successful young people took the paths they did. Without that drive, very little might have been achieved. For the high achievers, the most important influence in their lives was almost always support and encouragement from their parents, based on recognition of their potential to do well. The young people had enjoyed good incentives for learning from an early age, and their parents warmly acknowledged and rewarded any success. Their school-teachers too often provided appropriate positive feedback, which was particularly effective when pupil and teacher liked each other.

In the United States, Benjamin Bloom and his team (1985) spent four years putting together a retrospective picture of the processes of exceptionally high-level achievement. They telephoned 120 young men and women, who had reached 'world-class' levels of accomplishment in particular fields – pianists, sculptors, research mathematicians, Olympic swimmers and tennis champions. These respondents told them that no matter what their initial gifts, they had not reached those high levels of achievement without a long and intensive process of encouragement, nurturing, education and training. Very few of the successful people had been regarded as prodigies in childhood, so that any predictions made then would have been wrong, not least because of their unknown capacity at that point to stick out the years of hard work ahead of them.

It is hard to say why these particular children had worked so continuously for most of their growing-up years because, unfortunately, Professor Bloom does not seem to have investigated either their brothers or their sisters with the same upbringing, or any other comparison group. When they were little, these respondents often said that they had enjoyed playing at their particular interest, such as the piano or swimming, and took a great deal of pleasure from their learning. But when their early enthusiasm waned their parents had stepped in, taking them to lessons and making sure they practised and did their homework, rewarding them regularly with smiles and gold stars. And the children had often formed deep relationships with their teachers. Practice and study became a routine habit like cleaning teeth, which in the end produced their feelings of competence and mastery.

Studying

Motivation problems in getting children to study alone are common. This may be because the goals set are inappropriate to the child's ability or the content of the lessons seems irrelevant to the child. Training in the techniques of study can help, for example, directed effort is better than vague searching, just as learning in sequences is better than learning in little, unrelated bits.

COMMON INEFFICIENCIES IN STUDY PROCEDURE
(Nisbet & Shucksmith, 1986)
1. Poor ability to read textbook material.
2. Study conceived as a process of memorising.
3. Failure to organize and summarize.
4. Failure to review.
5. Lack of a regular time and place for study.

Here are some strategies for improving motivation to study.

Competition. Competition is a way of finding and defining capabilities, whether against others or one's own best, but the comparison must be meaningful or it is a waste of time and effort. Self-validation is not the same as seeking the approval of authority; it involves commitment to the experience, and it promotes independence of action. Self-mastery is liberating, because it brings with it a sense of personal power and autonomy, and thus courage for further challenge. Joy is part of it, as is a sense of power in oneself. This is not the same as neurotic competitiveness, where the thrill of winning is all and the game is nothing.

Self-monitoring. Each child should be encouraged to keep personal records, and to have access to someone who can discuss them honestly.

Concentration. Many children give as their longest time of concentration the time they spend in exams. If it is possible for them to concentrate for long periods on these occasions, it is presumably possible for them to work on extending their concentration span to their own benefit in other situations, enabling them to study to better effect.

Organization. Pupils can plan a rough timetable to see that each aspect of the subject to be learned is adequately represented, and that there is logical progress through the subjects; each then follows on from the other, and is as close as possible to the class teaching.

Physical matters. For most serious study, any noise should be quiet and constant, such as gentle music in the background. A heavy meal and alcohol act against learning, as do a chair that is too comfortable and a warm, airless room. Always having the same workplace sets the mind quickly in a working mould.

IMPROVING THE STUDY PROCEDURE
* Skim the work to map out the route to be covered.
* Relate new learning to old by conscious effort and questioning.
* Look up half-understood passages or words: incomplete understanding only encourages forgetting.
* Summarize material, including lecture notes, in one's own words, and briefly outline the principles of the subject.
* Reciting aloud will quickly bring faulty learning to light.
* Mnemonic systems are valuable, if not too complex.
* Improved reading techniques can enhance learning, including skill in scanning, avoiding vocalizing while reading (which slows it down), and being aware of unthinking reading.

INTELLECTUAL SKILLS CAN BE LEARNED

The shift of emphasis in education from methods of teaching to methods of learning aims to enable children to be more effective in a variety of problem-solving situations. For example, a repertoire of intellectual skills which enables children to adapt to differences in teaching methods puts them in an advantageous position for school learning. In general, however, the more education children receive, the more their intelligence rises, largely due to the acquisition of knowledge. This rise is not always broadly based: pupils in schools which emphasize verbal learning grow most in the verbal dimension, and those in technical schools grow more in spatial ability.

Learning how to learn

In all learning, the most important part is learning how to learn, and the way to learn is through strategies. A strategy is an integrated sequence of procedures, selected with a purpose in view (see Chapter III). Once acquired, good learning strategies are valuable for the whole of life (Nisbet & Shucksmith, 1986). The most effective learning strategy is to be aware of one's own learning and thinking processes, to be reflexive – metacognition. This ability to overview, to know how to plan and be aware of learning, is what children should – but usually do not – learn to do in school in any systematic way. Metacognition is sophisticated, and does not always come naturally, although those capable of the very highest achievements do seem to use it more readily than others (Freeman, 1991a).

Learning is interactive, but it may also be dominated by either teacher- or self-regulation, the difference being that the learning controlled by a teacher, computer or book is external, whereas that by the pupil is internal.

There is little point in putting in great effort if the strategy is poor. Rote learning, for example, is not really a strategy but rather a memory technique, and without organized procedures, learning is boring, tiring and inefficient. The better the strategies the better the learning, especially that most important learning of all – self-knowledge. There is no getting away from involvement of one's whole self in learning. Everyone has to do their own learning to learn, but it is the teachers, and of course parents, who can teach a child how to study.

Teaching learning strategies

Teaching learning strategies to children makes their expectations of their learning competence more realistic, reducing feelings of failure and increasing their motivation to learn. The teacher's task is to put children in a position in which they can reconstruct new forms of knowledge from what they already have, on the basis that they already have enough information to build on. The teacher can help pupils to do this, for example,

---

METACOGNITIVE ACTIVITIES IN LEARNING

1. *Preparation*
Deciding on goals, strategies, time.
Anticipating problems, choice of strategies.
Accessing necessary previous knowledge.

2. *Regulation*
Monitoring the process of change.
Testing and questioning.
Revision.

3. *Evaluation*
Looking for and judging feedback.
Judgement of performance.

---

by providing an initial theory – a principle – and then implementing it with an understanding of what the children already know. The teacher must then keep track of the child's previous actions and knowledge, promote their explorations, and monitor their progress.

Not only pupils, but teachers too need to be aware of their own abilities and strategies for learning and thinking. This does not mean making conscious decisions for every little task, but awareness of possible choices of action when there is a problem.

Some strategies may be effective when well learned, but destructive if poorly learned. For example, taking notes in a lecture is more effective if they are arranged in a dynamic pictorial design, rather than by writing down key-words or outlining (Buzan, 1988). But (according to Buzan), achieving effectiveness in that design method takes twelve hours or more of practice, and if it has not been well learned, attempts to use it can overload the working memory, so that students cannot concentrate on the message in the lecture while they are busy designing the notes. Alternatively, the strategies used in reading a very difficult chapter of a textbook may be quite different from those that would be appropriate for dealing with an easy storybook.

To keep pupils from overloading their cognitive capacity, they need to have plenty of practice with strategies that become organized and automatized, on the way to becoming expert, leaving time and energy for deeper considerations of new ideas. It is not enough to be told that a strategy would be effective in different situations, the learner has to have a feeling of competence from practice on varied tasks with attention to their commonalities and differences. This means assessing a learning task before attempting it, analyzing problems and judging goals, with feedback.

Self-regulation in learning

Self-regulation in learning is about the extent to which one is able to be one's own teacher. In the Netherlands, Professor Pieter Span has over-viewed the area, and summarized what procedures are involved: being able to prepare one's own learning; to take the necessary steps to learn; to regulate learning; to provide judgement of feedback and performance; and to keep oneself in a state of concentration and motivation (Span, 1993).

The highly able child appears to be better able to self-regulate learning than the less able child. Could an explanation be found in upbringing, or is this to do with the innate faculties of the individual? In Leipzig, Germany, Professor Lehwald (1990) developed the idea of a link between the input of information and the metacognition used by the highly able. He considered this link to be curiosity or, in his words, 'a quest for knowledge'. When he compared two groups of highly able young teenagers solving science problems, who differed only in level of curiosity, those with the highest levels were far more self-regulated – planning and evaluating their activities, and rarely asking for help. They were also better organized and did not try to find solutions for the several isolated problems, but instead looked for rules or laws which were valid for a category of problems.

Even with much younger children, of between 4 and 6 years, Lehwald found that the more intelligent and curious among them were better at exploring systematically, using their metacognitive resources more skil-fully. He hypothesized that the parents of these young children used metacognitive hints (in a mediating way) while they were solving prob-lems together during play, instead of simply telling them the solution.

For the older, highly able pupil, the teacher's directions can sometimes interfere with their self-regulating capacities, because their learning skills in processing relevant information are personal and efficient. This is in contrast to the processing of lower-ability pupils, when the teacher's external regulation is vital as compensation for their lack of self-regula-tion, and if there is no external regulation, they may revert to primitive, unorganized and ineffective trial-and-error learning.

All experiences are meaningful in a personal way, such as when reading a novel and identifying with some of its characters. Because of that per-sonal involvement in the humanities, the encounter alone, especially when guided by a good teacher, is enough to develop thinking. But to do it well calls for the careful seeking of the principles behind the work. When the teacher is acting as a mediator, she brings thinking into the open including access to her own thought processes, guiding the pupil with something she knows well. But then the teacher also needs a frame-

> **MAKING META-ACTIVITIES EXPLICIT (Nisbet, 1991)**
> * The teacher talks aloud while working through a problem.
> * Cognitive apprenticeship, in which the novice learns from the expert thinker by interaction.
> * Co-operative learning, which allows youngsters to explain their reasoning to each other.
> * Discussion, if it involves analysis of the processes of argument.
> * Questioning which demands thoughtful, rather than automatic, answers.

work in which to make decisions, to be reflexive and self-critical, and sometimes to provoke confrontations. Shock can act as a stimulant.

Unfortunately, what tends to happen in many secondary schools, especially where examinations are pressing, is that the processes of independent study and self-directed learning are drowned in a tidal wave of knowledge memorising by the pupils. Yet it would be unreasonable to expect teachers to diagnose the individual differences between pupils, for example, in scanning, problem-solving and actualizing memory. The situation can, however, be optimized if the learning environment is focused on the pupils' ideas and initiatives, rather than those of the teacher. The learner needs the freedom to change direction to meet new situations and use different strategies, for example, being allowed physically to move in and out of the classroom, working in different grouping arrangements within and outside the classroom, and having access to materials and equipment as needed.

Where possible, learning tasks should be open-ended to stimulate wider consideration, addressing problems which are real to the learners and can be adapted to other situations. The highly able, in particular, should be guided towards attempting more abstract concepts and generalizations in a more complex way than the regular curriculum.

LEARNING TO THINK AT A HIGH LEVEL

While it is difficult to define higher-order thinking exactly, it is not so difficult to recognize it when it occurs. It is not only the learner of high potential who can aim for a higher order of thinking, but within their own capacities, each child can reach out for advancement in its reasoning power and so improve competence.

Reading is a higher order thinking skill. In trying to understand what the author had in mind – comprehension – all readers abstract mental repre-

---

HIGHER-ORDER THINKING (Resnick, 1990)
* The path of action is not fully specified in advance.
* It is complex, the total path not being 'visible' (mentally speaking) from any single vantage point.
* Yields multiple solutions, each with costs and benefits, rather than unique solutions.
* Involves subtle judgement and interpretation, and the application of multiple criteria which sometimes conflict with one another.
* Involves uncertainty, not everything being known that bears on the task in hand.
* Means self-regulation of the thinking process.
* Imposes meaning and finds structure in apparent disorder.

---

sentations of the text using their prior knowledge, checking and organizing the information to make inferences and connections. Readers evolve selective representations which omit details that do not seem central to the message, and add information that is needed to make it intelligible.

These processes, by which individuals learn from reading, are usually so automatic that most skilled readers are unaware of them, especially with a little familiarity with the subject. The processes slow down when comprehension stumbles on even a minor modification in the textual flow, when there is a difficult point, or when deliberate strategic attention is needed as in the need to study and remember the text rather than just read and understand it, especially if the reader lacks prior knowledge for interpretation. Evidence of these mental activities can be seen in the reading of even a simple text, either from studying eye movements during silent reading, or pause-patterns when texts are read aloud.

It is true for reading at any level, that processes which have been traditionally reserved for advanced students might be taught to all readers, especially those who learn with difficulty, to extend high literacy standards to the mass education system.

Improving mathematical thinking. Like reading, successful mathematics requires learners to understand the tasks in terms of imposing meaning, that is, of doing interpretive work rather than routine manipulations. There is abundant evidence that young children – even before attending school – develop rather robust, although simple, mathematical concepts, which they apply in a variety of situations. Yet for many, mathematics is decidedly difficult to learn at school. Some of the difficulty could be avoided by teaching it in a way that draws more strongly on the children's intuitive knowledge and capabilities for imposing meaning.

This early competence can be seen in children's first and best-developed mathematical competence – counting. The short-cut procedures they invent show that they have an implicit understanding of several basic arithmetical principles. For example, starting at about the age of 7, children solve subtraction problems by either counting down from the larger number or counting up from the smaller number, whichever is the quickest, providing evidence of their understanding of the complementarity of addition and subtraction. But the formal rules of school mathematics, however, may not appear to them to be related to their own independently developed ideas.

A less routine approach to mathematics could produce substantial improvements in learning, with pupils using more metacognitive behaviour, such as checking their own understanding of procedures, monitoring for consistency, and relating new material to prior knowledge. Competent mathematics learners also work out more alternative strategies for attacking problems, as well as generating solvable sub-problems, in the same way as expert mathematicians. They do not stay at a superficial level, but interpret the problems, recasting them in terms of general scientific principles until the solutions become almost self-evident.

Similar kinds of higher-order thinking occur in many fields, involving, for example, reconstruction of the problems, a search for consistencies and inconsistencies, implications of ideas, modifying rather than seeking a quick solution from the initial idea, and reasoning by analogy to other, similar situations. This is evident in the work of expert writers who see their compositions as a complex task of shaping a communication that will appeal to and convince an intended audience, rather than simply writing down everything they know on the topic. Similarly, skilled technicians repairing equipment do not proceed through a routine checklist, but instead construct 'mental models' of complex systems, and use these to reason about observed breakdowns and potential repairs. Such smoothly working metacognitive skills appear repeatedly in the analysis of all complex task performances as characteristic of adaptable learners, being found much less frequent in younger or lower ability individuals.

Grouping as an aid to higher order thinking. Social interaction helps children to learn to reason at a higher level (see also Chapter VII). When problem-solving is tackled by pairs or small groups of pupils, or in discussion and practice sessions, it provides the opportunity for the demonstration in personal ways of problem approaches which are otherwise hidden and implicit. These may be such tasks as analyzing a text or constructing arguments, when the less skilful thinkers can model their thinking strategies on their more effective partners (not always those of the teacher). Such dynamic examples can be inspirational, although they also run the danger of being confrontational when there are disagreements with others who are perceived to be more powerful, or of not arriving at the expected answers, and above all of not always responding instantly.

In group problem-solving, whether writing a composition or building a model, the members no longer work things out in isolation; novices can participate in actually solving the problem and, if things go well, may eventually take over all or most of the work themselves with a developed appreciation of how the individual elements in the process contribute to the whole. This has been called 'reciprocal teaching' (Palincsar & Brown, 1984, and see chapter VII). It encourages children to try new, more active approaches, and normally supports even partially successful efforts. Children new to groups often find that they have thinking abilities which they did not know about before, and can persuade them to use those processes more widely and deeply.

Fostering higher-level thinking in the classroom. There are three recognized approaches to fostering higher-level thinking in pupils – stand alone, embedding and immersion (Prawat, 1991).

1. *The stand-alone approach.* In this approach, there is an attempt to teach thinking skills separately from the content of the subject matter. Generic thinking programmes, such as that of Edward de Bono's CoRT system (de Bono, 1991), claim to address a need in low-achieving populations. The rationale is that we all use basic cognitive processes, like comparing, ordering, classifying and making inferences in our daily lives, so that it must be possible to teach them to youngsters with little knowledge, or who are failing in the traditional curriculum. But experimental evidence indicates that generic thinking skills as such do not transfer, either to other parts of the curriculum or to out-of-school performances, because specific knowledge plays a central role in learning and reasoning.

2. *The embedding approach.* Embedding also emphasizes discrete thinking skills rather than conceptual understanding, but they are taught in the context of the subject matter. The information and the thinking processes are integrated and taught together, neither one being played down to promote the other. The problem is usually where to start – whether to teach skills first and then show pupils how they are used, or to teach thinking skills on a need-to-know basis – there may be some motivational advantages in waiting until pupils have struggled a bit before offering them the skills.

3. *The immersion approach.* The principle behind immersion is that ideas function like shared schemas, allowing individuals to extract information from the environment, while at the same time building on existing knowledge. It is essentially different from the embedding

approach in that the principles of good thinking are *not* made explicit, but instead the content of the pupil's thoughts is given the highest priority. Pupils are immersed in a rich, in-depth understanding of subject content, and the teacher's task is to mediate, guiding the pupils to focus on important aspects of the material to be learned, leading them to gain their own 'insights' built on their innate curiosity. Thus, rather than memorising and reproducing either information or other people's ideas, deeper understanding and thinking can arise 'naturally'.

There is a growing body of research indicating that the immersion approach leads to high levels of understanding and thoughtfulness in pupils, especially in mathematics. It is possible that classroom teaching structured on the lines of ideas rather than information will provide the stimulus for creative thinking and conceptual understanding in pupils, although it is difficult to find a starting place or sequence of lessons that is universally appropriate because one topic does not necessarily follow another. Hence, it is more important for the teacher to develop a global view, using a network of big ideas that help to define the subject area. For example, current research findings indicate that working in other areas with those parts of the traditional curriculum that are inherently 'enabling', such as reading and mathematics, is a valuable route to children's advanced and adaptable learning. Such changes could transform schooling in fundamental ways, and offer higher-order learning and thinking skills as a reachable goal for most children.

Improving teaching for learning

Teaching, as measured by tape-recorder, timed observations or film, can only be fully evaluated together with pupils' learning – a highly complex task involving many personalities and backgrounds. Nevertheless, there is sufficient evidence to show that although teachers are generally effective, they could benefit greatly from more training in social skills, as well as in skills more commonly associated with the use of psychology in advertising, or mass communication. Teaching is also a very old profession, which has acquired a considerable weight of unquestioned tradition. As teaching resources become more expensive, there is all the more reason to evaluate them more accurately, to help in planning the most effective education for the consumer, who may also be the future teacher (Shon, 1987).

Student-teachers find that their effort and achievement in school is evaluated in relation to both their techniques and the pupil's learning, but not for professionals. Regular self-evaluation does not come naturally to most, and the willingness to be voluntarily evaluated by others implies a constantly open mind, as well as positive attitudes towards change in one's own teaching. The more forward-looking teacher-training courses, it is true, attempt to treat their students as partners in their own learning, as a preliminary exercise for open future teaching attitudes, but for the older practising teacher, when researchers are 'planted' in a classroom to take samples of interactions and feed the results back to teachers, they do not always change their teaching ways.

HOW TEACHERS CAN CHANGE THEIR WAYS OF TEACHING TO IMPROVE PUPIL LEARNING

* *Explanation.* Talking, often assumed to be the most worthwhile part of the teacher's task, is not always found to be so. Often, either vital facts or the essential explanatory principle are missing. Teachers are not always quite clear at the lesson-planning stage about which methods are most appropriate to put over their points, and they may also make unjustified assumptions about their pupils' level of understanding and concept-formation. Sometimes, the syllabus asks for an intellectual skills which many pupils may not have acquired, or for levels of explanation requiring higher communication skills than those which the teacher possesses.

* *Attention.* The amount of individual attention a teacher gives to pupils in the class varies for reasons unconnected with either teaching or learning, but is to some extent a part of the teacher's own outlook. Even when some noted neglect of a child has been pointed out to teachers by researchers, they are not always able to adjust their behaviour to provide the encouragement and concern the child needs, for example, the lower attention paid to girls than to boys (Archer, 1992). Indeed, the flexibility of approach to individual needs and the sensitivity to silent cries for help from pupils may call for more counselling skills than teaching skills, which relatively few teachers have acquired in their training. Pupils too, have their individual ways of reacting to the teachers attention or drawing it to themselves by their behaviour.

* *Non-verbal communication.* Research findings, particularly from the study of primate societies, have thrown new light on the study of human non-verbal signalling. In ethnological terms, the teacher is in a dominant position by the nature of the job. The non-verbal cues which she transmits and is able to receive, recognize, and respond to are an essential part of communication in the classroom. These might be, for example, children's posture, proximity, facial expression and voice-tone. Plentiful eye-contact indicates warmth and friendliness, but dropping eyelids to focus on the desk when a pupil is present can signal dismissal or rejection. The teacher is behind the desk or 'boundary' in home 'territory' which is 'safer', but this indicates less friendliness than one who comes out to the pupils. On the other hand, too much friendliness – stepping out of one's role – by either pupil or teacher, can be distressing and detrimental to learning. The dual role of authority figure and friendly guide is difficult.

CHAPTER VII

Teaching for competence

The teacher's task is to act as a guide between knowledge and the pupil; to be most effective, he or she has to be aware of the variety of educational routes, their unevenness and the children's individuality. Children may need encouragement, for example, when they are in difficulties, or when nothing seems to be happening, and even more encouragement to keep going after a set-back, when it seems that they have to start all over again. Good teaching is both a science in its use of technique, and an art expressed in the skills, experience and personality of the teacher. Developmental psychology has little place in teaching when it is no more than a trade, a direct presentation of information from teacher – as textbook – to pupil. A good teacher is able and willing to find out and evaluate the published results of educational psychological research, and to incorporate some of the practical implications into practice. The teacher's methods govern the two basic aspects of the pupil's learning: processes, which change behaviour; and aims, which specify directions.

The variety of trends in teaching in the 1960s, 1970s and 1980s, have been confusing for teachers. There were, for example, teaching styles – either formal or progressive or informal – which were supposed to change the general achievements and attitudes of pupils. But research found that each had different specific effects. Formal teaching appeared to result in gains in mathematics and language, whereas informal teaching helped children in their social adjustment, maybe improving motivation (Bennett, 1976). But it was difficult to be exact about what, if anything, was changing pupils' learning, not least because differences within the styles could be greater than those between them. More importantly, the concept of styles assumed a direct positive relationship between teaching and pupil learning, and so implicitly denied the involvement of pupils in their own learning. The idea had outlived its usefulness.

After that period, the importance given to teaching was diminished in favour of the pupils' active learning, assuming that they were given the opportunity. In particular, the amount of time a pupil spent actively engaged on a topic was regarded as the most important determinant of achievement on that topic. Indeed, there is evidence that, across large numbers of children, the length of school day, absences and homework are all related to their achievement. But in individual cases, the tasks which teachers set may neither embody their intentions, nor do they widen understanding, particularly in languages and mathematics, which are often limited to the acquisition of knowledge or skill. It may be that the teachers themselves do not thoroughly understand their subject matter, seeing themselves more as providers of information than as stimulators of reflection and explanation. The focus on opportunity to learn, certainly in terms of time spent at a task, did not take the learning processes themselves into account, and so it too faded from sight.

All learning theorists now agree that learning is more likely to take place when pupils are mentally engaged in the pursuit of knowledge than when they are merely recipients of it. But, like any other approach, active learning can be over-used and misapplied. Many teachers, as well as their own tutors, have confused active learning with activity for its own sake, so that in practice there has been too much activity, too much noise and too much movement – a situation in which the pupils lack clear guidance and control. The quality of a lesson cannot be judged by how much apparent activity there is in the class, but on the quality of the learning which has taken place, because a silent class can be mentally active and absorbed in what a skilled teacher is saying or doing. Classroom projects, for example, can be a stimulus to learning, but pupils sometimes complain that they are too time-consuming, and at times the products are more trivial than profound. The aim is to find the best balance between activity in the mind and quietness in the classroom.

There are two opposing schools of thought on discipline in education. The first holds that, in the right conditions of provision and psychological permission to make mistakes, children will enjoy learning for its own sake and there will be no discipline problems. The second (promoted by Piaget) says that children learn when they feel uncomfortable, to right the balance of their equilibrium. The child psychologist, Bruno Bettelheim (1989), even said that discipline in the classroom should be strong enough to induce fear in some disadvantaged children; not fear of eternal damnation or corporal punishment, but a fear of losing self-respect. He said that children have to be able to accept guidance to see how work is done, until in time they can work things out for themselves. Learn first . . . creativity later. Either way, when children do not learn, the fault is seen to lie in the school.

Distraction

Distraction is the drawing away of attention, and in the educational context it can be costly in terms of learning. What causes the failure of attention? Could it be the way the educational material is being presented? How easily does a child become distracted?

Perceptual set. In attending to a particular sort of event, either in the environment or in the mind, a child can prepare his or her mind in advance for various demands that may be made, to 'set' their perception. This gives the child a head start in selecting the sort of strategy which would be appropriate for the learning, which is why psychologists always give children a trial run in psychological tests. In school, if children are perceptually set for a history lesson, and come to class only to find that it has changed to biology, they will have to make an energy consuming mental adjustment.

SOME SUGGESTIONS ABOUT ATTENTION

1. *Change attracts attention.* If a teacher were to stop talking suddenly, she would acquire the attention of the whole class.
2. *Contrast is not quite the same thing as change*; it refers to something which stands out from the background. Clapping hands is frequently used by teachers to contrast with the general classroom noise and draw attention. Contrast is particularly useful in display.
3. *Repetition*, as every teacher knows, *is a part of teaching.* A weak stimulus repeated several times can be more effective than a strong one given only once. But here lies the art; too much repetition leads to boredom or worse. One hand-clap may be ineffective, and three claps draw attention, but twenty might bring in the children from the next classroom.
4. *Intensity is an effective attention device.* Loud sounds dominate lower sounds, big pictures catch attention before small ones. But continual shouting at children is known to lose its original intensive effect.
5. *Novelty contributes to attention and recall.* But how often are the novel anecdotes remembered when the lesson is long forgotten?
6. *Social suggestion means following the actions of a group*, such as the old game children play of staring into a tree until a crowd gathers. Children working together on a theme can increase each other's attention this way.

MIXED-ABILITY TEACHING AND LEARNING

In a class of over thirty pupils with a wide range of ability, it is impossible to provide every single child with differentiated learning experiences which are just right for their development and ability. In one primary school class, for example, there may be some children reading fluently and others unable to recognize letters. If the teacher controlling the class is skilled, and the class is not too big, then mixed-ability teaching can work very well. But it requires a high level of teaching skill, and extremely good planning, because it can place great strains on unprepared teachers. The major problem is that teachers are not trained for mixed-ability teaching.

There is considerable evidence that most classroom teachers tend to pitch their level of lessons to middle-range ability, and there is not enough time in the day either to stretch the brightest ones or to deal with the specific difficulties of those at the other end of the ability scale. In fact, teachers and pupils often collude in keeping group cohesion towards the mean, which in effect provides a steering group for the class. Some teachers of mixed-ability classes use their brightest children to teach the others; although making subsidiary teachers of them in this way means that they do not get the teaching and stretching that they should, and so they can be held back in their own learning.

Mixed-ability teaching and learning is everyday teaching because, however carefully they have been composed, all classes have a variety of individuals in them with mixed aptitudes for learning. As a result, teachers must know what differentiated learning methods are, in what circumstances they flourish, and what educational principles underlie them. All pupils, of whatever ability and in whichever subject, need teaching which meets their individual learning needs. Good art lessons provide an example of individualized teaching, where it occurs as a matter of course, as do dance, drama, music and physical education in all its forms. Yet, parents usually prefer selection of some sort, as do teachers and, often, highly able pupils. It is particularly interesting that in Japan, where achievement levels are very much higher than in most of the world, the idea of selection is irrelevant; all classes are mixed-ability and everyone is expected to do well if they work hard, in the belief that with effort anything can be done.

CRITERIA FOR GOOD MIXED-ABILITY TEACHING

* Teachers should employ a range and variety of methods encompassing grouped, paired and individualized activities.
* Lessons should be planned by teams or at least pairs of teachers wherever possible.
* Mixed-ability organization should not be undertaken piecemeal by some departments and not others, but instead adopted as a whole-school policy and be carefully planned during the year preceding its introduction.

Organizing for differentiated teaching

Differentiated teaching to mixed-ability classes aims at meeting the range of pupils' abilities and building on their previous achievements, without fragmenting the class. All the pupils should be following the same theme, but to different depths, according to the nature of the task and the skills they bring to it, and each one according to his rate of progression, based on past achievements. Lessons should be planned with both short- and long-term aims, so that although pupils should have the satisfaction of short-term goals of, say, a few weeks or less, each one should be a step forward in the development of concepts and skills across three years or even five. The work should be given unity by the teacher or teaching team that plans it, and by the aims underlying it.

The main aims of differentiated approaches in teaching are concerned with developing competence in children – in order to improve their thinking, to give them practice in working collaboratively in groups and also on their own, to help them take responsibility for their work and persevere despite setbacks, to develop their potential to criticize and evaluate through discussion, and to develop their communication skills. The aims are applicable to any pupil grouping, to any subject and to any age group. The tenuous threads which bind education, teaching and personal relationships together are directly involved with the organization of teaching in a school.

Ideally, differentiated teaching should take place in a room: where tables rather than desks are used to facilitate group work; where there is a range of books on the current topic, which match the pupils' reading levels and language development (e.g. bilingual pupils should, if possible, have access to books in their first language); where there is equipment for painting, drawing and modelling to hand; where space can be made for drama, discussion and improvization; and where investigative work may be undertaken.

The principle of making a classroom arouse interest should never be overlooked. Pin-boarding for display should be on every wall, if financially and architecturally possible, and the room should show respect to pupils by being clean and attractive. Teachers have often transformed the most unpromising rooms into enticing and inspiring places by judicious use of posters, photographs, mobiles and written work, and by their own (or the school's) contribution of plants and curiosity-provoking objects.

Everything in the classroom should be designed to empower pupils, to make them feel that the room is not just at their disposal but is in many ways their own, because it is devoted to the creation and display of their work, whatever form that may take. Cupboards and stacking boxes or drawers, clearly labelled, should be near at hand and pupils should be expected to select whatever tool they need and return it later to where it belongs.

In the first year of the secondary school pupils should be taught as frequently as possible in their base classroom so that their sense of ownership in it and all it contains may be continually reinforced as new work is displayed. Even though some subjects must be taught in specialist rooms, it is possible for evidence of work there to be brought back to the base room. Later, subjects are increasingly taught in specialist rooms, but pupils of all ages should feel that they have a personal stake in as many areas of the school as possible by seeing work which they have produced around them. In such circumstances they are likely to have the confidence to undertake more responsibility for their work than in an area where they feel they have no roots.

Grouping. The idea that learning and thinking are embedded in social experience is not new, but, until recently, social relationships had been seen as energizers and motivators rather than as processes that shape the form and content of thought itself. But one is not merely the background to the other: Vigotsky and Piaget, for example (each in his way), treated social interaction as an essential aspect of the development of thinking.

The benefit to pupils of learning to work together in groups and teams of different sizes is that they will almost certainly continue to do so in their subsequent careers, both educational and occupational. There are three groupings that are most commonly used with success in differentiated learning: the whole class; clusters of four or five children; and pairs. There should also be occasions for pupils to work on their own to exercise reading, writing, computation and specialist skills.

Whole-class work is most commonly used to begin a theme or topic, to round it off upon completion, and to act as an audience to a group presenting its work to its peers for assessment and appreciation. Group work is designed for the identification of problems and decisions about methods of solving them, and solitary work will be an offshoot of this process, pairs being usually more efficient for an investigational exercise or role play.

It is essential that groups should not become isolated units, because the pupils must retain a sense of class identity. When a complete task is undertaken by a group, the teacher should decide in advance whether its composition should be dictated by the nature of the task or by friendship; task groups chosen for homogeneity by the teacher are not necessarily the most effective. Learning foreign languages, for example, can be better in mixed-ability groups if the variability is not too wide, but not all the time. Groups can be mixed and remixed for different purposes, i.e. flexible grouping. Although children and adolescents usually prefer to work with their friends, they will not always have this choice when they are adults and it is valuable for them to learn the respect that comes from working well with someone, even though the task is the only thing they have in common.

TASK GROUPS SHOULD CONSIST OF:

* At least one person who can read the language in which the information to be studied is expressed.
* One who has graphical skills.
* One who is more numerate than the others.
* Someone who can organize.
* Someone who can record.
* Friendship groups are self-selected but, provided the composition of the group is clearly matched to the nature of its task, pupils will accept nominations by the teacher to join a new one. This process of nomination should be used to break down sexist and racist barriers and assumptions. In time a task group often becomes a friendship group through the medium of the work shared together.

Exceptional pupils, such as those of considerable ability, or who have difficulties with the majority language, or who have a learning difficulty, may need exceptional teaching, which may be easier to cater for in groups. This should be discussed with the pupil, and a means of support decided on. It may be necessary for them to be withdrawn for basic-skills teaching so that they can succeed in whole-class lessons, but, as soon as possible, they should by returned to their class and given support by a teacher until they have the confidence to work with the same degree of autonomy as the others. All support teachers should be familiar with their charges' strengths, as well as their weaknesses.

Primary schools seem particularly keen to teach children in ability groups. As long as these groups remain open and flexible, they may avoid the pitfalls of the formal classroom. In primary schools, some groups even spill over chronological age boundaries, so that differences in speed of growth in individuals can be catered for in the regular school. An example of flexible education is the open-plan construction of many British primary schools. There, with the co-ordinated guidance of a team of teachers, children are able to read in the quiet, carpeted reading corner, experiment with sand and water at the other end of the building, or work with a teacher on numbers in a different section. However, although this system is seen to work well with extravert, well-brought-up children, it is less productive with the introverts and children from lower socio-economic strata (SES), who fare better in a more structured environment

(Bennett, 1976). Less internally disciplined children can be helped by teaching them coping skills and problem-solving strategies, loosening the structure as they approach autonomy. There is clearly a limit to the amount of child-centring that any system can accommodate successfully.

Use of support staff must be carefully planned so that they know when they are to attend lessons, which pupils they are required to support, and what they are aiming for. Helping bilingual children to increase their vocabulary and confidence in the majority language will be far more profitable if the support teacher feeds them the words and sentence structures they can immediately use in group work, thus reinforcing their learning, both in the majority language and within a subject (see Chapter VIII).

PROBLEMS OF LEARNING IN GROUPS

* Dependence on the teacher and reluctance to value the contribution of peers.
* The habitual dominance of one or two pupils.
* The breaking up of groups into 'potentially combative' factions that 'argue' from a fixed perspective (sometimes girls versus boys).
* Inequality in the acceptance of responsibility for the group's work.
* The acceptance of an over-easy consensus in the face of complex issues or problems.
* The maintaining of roles defined by labels derived from other classroom activities. For example, the pupil who is always laughed at, or ignored or deferred to; this habit prevents pupils from taking each other's contributions at face value.
* Uncertainty as to whether discussion is 'real work' and can lead to 'proper learning'.

Selection within school. Pupils can be streamed, setted or tracked for their ability, whether lower or higher, in classes or smaller ability groupings. A *stream* is formed by putting children into classes on the basis of perceived ability within their own age group, most frequently for the duration of their school life, and can imply the use of a different syllabus. A *set* is an ability group, which can span different ages, and is for a specific subject or group of subjects. Sets are usually more flexible than streams, and children do move about between the levels. It is a system which suits some pupils and not others. About 15 per cent of children will be assessed as being in the wrong stream by the end of the year: those in too high a stream tend to improve and those in too low a stream tend to deteriorate.

THE DISADVANTAGES OF SELECTION BY ABILITY
* Children will only come into contact with similarly selected children.
* Social experience and possibly cultural background will be reflected in the classroom situation.
* Children will only receive educational stimulus considered appropriate to their needs.
* Late-developing children will fall behind in achievement and be unable to catch up.
* Being labelled 'lower-stream' increases feelings of failure and rejection, lowers morale and distorts the self-image.

In large streamed schools in a mixed SES area, pupils in the top streams are better able to identify with their teachers, and the gap between the lower-stream pupils and theirs tends to widen over the years, not least as there is often a class where the less teachable as well as the less able are 'dumped'. The lower streams of a large school may develop clear reactions to their injured feelings in the form of poor discipline and, in addition, their teachers tend to acquire a lower status than those involved with higher streams. Those who do the selecting have made momentous decisions about the children's lives, normally without the help of any psychological tests or deep understanding of developmental psychology.

The extent to which the teacher believes a child to be more able, and the performance that is expected as a result, have been said to be self-fulfilling. This 'Pygmalion' effect, although questioned and contentious, came from an American experiment in which children chosen at random by psychologists were pointed out to their teachers as being highly able. At the end of the academic year their marks were found to be significantly higher than those of a matched control group of children who had not been singled out (Rosenthal & Jacobson, 1968). This experiment has never been satisfactorily replicated. Certainly, differing amounts of intellectual stimulation with similar groups can radically alter the children's levels of functioning, and extra attention has a well-recognized effect on outcome, so that any classroom organization is likely to have an effect on individual children's performance.

Groups within the total school can be formed and reformed for various functions other than instruction. Children with special interests may be better able to progress together. 'Family' groupings are not uncommon in primary schools, where children across a three- or four-year age-range are grouped together for at least some parts of the day. Older ones can help the younger ones with dressing and washing, and the newcomers are found to adjust much more quickly when they are assigned to a group of already settled children. This system can also be of advantage to a psychologically disturbed child.

Sizes of groups are not necessarily of great importance, but the purpose behind their formation will determine the value of their homogeneity, stability, freedom of expression, responsibility and so on. A table of four to six children in a primary school, all working on the same subject, is not uncommon, and is becoming more common at the secondary level, even in pre-streamed classes. More fluid groupings of children, based on a learning rather than a teaching approach, enables individual children to develop at their own pace. A clear example is in musical-instrument playing, where a group of, say, trumpeters of all ages will be gathered together because of their ability and interest. This is also possible in more academic subjects where children may proceed at their own pace and style. Ability groups may also be called 'sets'.

Planning for differentiated teaching and learning

Teaching should be planned as a developmental sequence, including the possibility of extension work so that exceptional pupils at either end of the achievement spectrum are provided for. Teachers plan the themes and skills with which they mean to make their pupils familiar, and estimate how and when it is appropriate to develop them. The subject matter is then broken down into units or modules so that the pupils are presented with short-term goals that will give them the satisfaction of achievement, both individually and as a whole class.

Children should never be allowed consistently to fail, but nor should they consistently find their work easy. Work should challenge and extend their whole range of abilities and skills, because all pupils, whatever their starting point, are capable of growth. When the module begins, there is usually a lead lesson with the whole class, maybe with early exercises to judge the degrees of confidence within a class. The teacher then determines the composition of the groups.

The pupils begin their work with clear criteria about what is expected of them and know that the module will end with a completed piece of work which both they and the teacher will assess and which they will share in some way with the rest of the class. The teacher's role is to initiate pupils into the skills required by the task; to assist them, by judicious use of praise and constructive criticism on progress; and to monitor progress by criteria established in advance and explained to the class. The criteria may vary from time to time according to the teacher's observations of pupils' weaknesses so that oral skills, or reading, or working successfully with someone else, may all in turn receive emphasis allowing for all the participating children to have some measure of success and some measure of failure.

There is always profit from linking with other teaching departments, whether by integration of subjects or simply by co-ordination of syllabuses and specialist vocabulary. In this way pupil success in one subject can be liberated into others and something of the fluidity of the best primary learning can be retained for all ages. Where the school has a library, for example, it is a valuable joint resource in differentiated teaching and learning. A good librarian can enrich pupils' studies with a range of fiction and reference books that has relevance to the teaching theme, catering for both children with good reading ability as well as those whose reading skills are still insecure. The librarian should be enrolled in discussions from the outset.

Styles of teaching delivery

Successful differentiated teaching and learning should not be reliant upon a teacher instructing a whole class, nor should it be characterized by the use of work-sheets given out indiscriminately to each pupil. At its best, it comes about collaboratively, involving the pupils in decisions and allowing them some negotiation about how they approach the task, as long as each child progresses in at least one area of former weakness and does not simply reiterate earlier success.

The task should be multi-dimensional and, if possible, open-ended. Since reading is essential for most educational activities, it should have a place within most lessons – as a means of furthering the task. Talking clearly and using the correct and appropriate terms for each subject must also be a skill constantly called upon. The teacher listens while groups discuss, but may supply words where necessary and insist on repetition of ideas until an explanation is clear. Where possible, tape recordings could be used by groups and then exchanged with others as a test for clarity.

There should always be some writing, and not exclusively during lessons usually labelled 'academic'. Although one person may be given the role of recorder, the whole group should assist with and decide on the final form of the report. Redrafting is normally necessary for both group and individual written work, and every pupil should have practice in doing this at some point.

Communication is at its most effective when an audience shows both receptivity and empathy. These skills are taught in drama and often in language and humanities, but are essential for education in general. For this reason, group work profits from firmly applied rules about listening to other people and from regular use of the drama techniques of improvization and role-play. The other creative arts, as well as mathematics, science and technology should all, at times, have a place in the exposition and study of any single subject, allowing for the wide range of ways in which people in general learn, sometimes aurally, sometimes through written language, often by investigation, sometimes by creating an object or through an aesthetic experience.

Comprehension and enjoyment are often linked, and in acknowledgement of this fact, differentiated learning is often characterized by games and simulations, each more challenging than the last. There is no doubt, judging by the demeanour of the pupils in such enjoyable circumstances, that they are experiencing the exhilaration of learning in the course of their games.

Co-operative teaching and learning

Co-operation itself, while a worthy curriculum objective, is not the principle aim in co-operative teaching; the objective being sought is more that ordinary school learning is considerably enhanced when children, following one or another of the co-operative learning procedures, learn in groups rather than on their own or in competition with other pupils. Co-operative teaching can take a number of forms. It is not merely placing two teachers in a room with a class; nor is it team teaching, where two or more teachers from the same discipline share responsibility for a part of the curriculum; nor is it collaborative teaching, where, while each teacher is informed of what the other is doing, the work done by each may be distinct and separate (Davidson, 1990).

Co-operative teaching provides the opportunity for two teachers with different backgrounds in training and experience to develop common understanding, shared meanings, and the will the explore and improve the quality of teaching and learning in the classroom. It provides a sound basis for systematic reflection for individuals, groups and schools which are trying to develop into self-reflective communities. In co-operative teaching the teachers share in the debate about the appropriateness of the curriculum to the range of pupil need and ability, as well as sharing their own particular perspective and expertise. They must decide on how to tackle the difficult processes of developing, monitoring and evaluating curriculum differentiation, and each must work towards understanding the outlooks of the others in the enterprise.

Teachers need to understand each other because they are helping the groups of pupils to work together in an understanding way. Co-operative teaching involves knowing about protocol, which means how the system works in terms of culture, conventions, hierarchies and constraints. The teachers who are co-operating work towards becoming reflective, bringing assumptions and understandings to the surface implicitly, laying them open to criticism, possibly restructuring them and embodying the changes in future action. This is what Shon (1987) calls 'reflection in action'. Typically, the class is divided into groups of four to six children, usually of the same age but differing in ability, ethnicity and gender. The directions that the teacher gives are designed, one way or another, to get the children to work together as a team on some learning task. The children, of course, must learn to co-operate in order to follow the teacher's instructions.

While traditional whole-classroom instruction has always entailed a degree of co-operation and competition among pupils, co-operative teaching requires pupils to work together as a team to learn. What they learn thus depends on their common effort towards the shared instructional goal: each pupil's success depends upon and is linked with every other pupil's success, and never their failure. Pupils share materials, divide up the work, help each other and share the rewards of their performance.

Reciprocal teaching (Palincsar & Brown, 1984) is a method of teaching reading in which the teacher and the pupil take turns as teacher (see Chapter VI). Each reads a passage to themselves and the teacher mediates for the pupil by demonstrating how to formulate a question based on the passage by summarizing it, clarifying it and making predictions based on the information contained in it. When the pupil takes a turn as teacher, the teacher carefully coaches the pupil in the skills of comprehension, and offers prompts and criticism until none is needed by the pupil, at which time the teacher's role becomes more passive. Both laboratory and classroom studies have demonstrated that the reciprocal teaching method is effective in significantly raising and maintaining the reading comprehension scores of poor readers.

Basically the method is thought to be successful because the pupil gradually but solidly develops a new conceptual model for the skill, practising it with specific strategies that are used by expert readers. The corroborative learning features of these expert/novice teaching procedures lead the pupil to integrate the multiple role that the successful problem-solver inevitably masters. Thus, novice writers are helped to be expert writers when they read and criticize other pupils' work, and when they have their own work read by others, and so on. By taking turns in writing and reading they acquire a wider view of the writing task and a new conceptual model for it, a model closer to that possessed by the expert writer.

Team teaching is another method of crossing the one-class/one-teacher barrier, although children of roughly the same age are normally put together. Large numbers of children – even up to sixty – can be taught by a co-ordinated group of teachers. The essential connecting factor within the teaching team is harmony of purpose, and this feeling of co-operation will be reflected in the behaviour of the pupils. Disharmony between teachers can have a devastating effect.

SOME BENEFITS OF TEAM TEACHING
* Groups of children can be varied in size and ability to suit the task of the moment.
* Specialist teachers can use their skills with appropriate groups.
* Non-specialist staff and equipment can be effective where they are needed.
* Personality clashes between individual children and teachers are diminished.
* Pupils are less likely to see their teachers in a formal role, a practical asset to education.

Teachers can use differentiated teaching methods in every subject across the curriculum. Although this might increase the volume of work, so too is the satisfaction gained by using it in the progress of the pupils. As in all educational methods, it can be used unimaginatively and lack rigour, but if the guidelines set out here are observed, the results in both intellectual and social achievement among pupils will be impressive.

Homework

Children who are set homework, complete it and have it marked, perform better at school than pupils who do none. Though there is a wide variation in the quantity of homework schools set, the amount and quality of homework a pupil does depends on parents' outlooks, which in turn are influenced by social differences. Some parents see a heavy homework load as a sign of a caring school; they are familiar with its routine from their own childhoods, and they believe it promotes self-discipline, as well as keeping their children away from pop music and television. Schools in poor areas sometimes make the classrooms available after hours to pupils whose homes are not suitable for quiet study.

Well-designed homework demonstrates a teacher's trust in the pupil's autonomy and responsibility. Its value is one of the ways in which a school insists on standards, shows value for learning, and involves parents in a partnership with the school. Effective homework is built into the original lesson-planning, aiming to make children use the skills they have learned in class by undertaking a small, individual piece of writing, research or other form of creative achievement. If appropriate, it may be done collaboratively, but as a single piece of work it enables a teacher to see how much pupils can achieve when there is no group support. This is not to say that homework should exclude parents and frustrate their wish to be involved in the topic studied, although they can provide an unfair advantage to some children as a source of knowledge in its execution.

Homework can take two routes. The 'high road' is to set problem-solving in school to be done alone at home. The teacher neither prepares the children in class with explanations of what they are to do, nor, in some cases, even offers them clues. The pupil has to do all the thinking. The 'low road' is an extension of class-work, sometimes the 'finish off what you did in class' variety, which takes away autonomy and challenge from this private work time. The child goes home with examples of lesson material to repeat at home, which the teachers hopes that everyone has understood. Children of higher ability do better with the high-road approach, which is stimulating and thought provoking, whereas less-able children prefer the low-road approach, which uses more memory skills and offers practice in their application. Unfortunately, children who follow the low-road style of work tend to stay as low-roaders, and are much less well-fitted for the skills needed for higher education.

EVALUATING TEACHING AND LEARNING

Assessment and marking are essential components of teaching and learning. Although in a face-to-face situation a pupil can be told either why work is of high quality, or offered constructive criticism, it should also be recorded in written form for future reference. Assessment must include definition of the teaching goals, and of how far the teacher expects the pupils to have travelled along the way, and so provide feedback and guidance to both teachers and learners. This record should be part of the overall view of how the pupil is progressing along the curriculum, and more specifically along the plan of lessons, of which it is a part. The pupils must know its contents and, for preference, even take part in the writing of the report, to see which aspects of his development need to be strengthened and how. Having their work recorded, and thus 'officially' recognized, can give pupils an extra sense of achievement.

The mark given to a single piece of work measures its quality in the context of the pupil's educational development, and it can also identify strengths and weaknesses in group work. Progress can be made clearer by plotting the accumulating marks on a graph, which can either result in a fairly smooth line or one which is spiked, depending on what has been learned and how it has been taught. A teacher who knows how the learning curve operates will expect learning rest-times and will be aware that progress is not always upward. She can offer knowledge and encouragement to the pupil when his continued effort seems to be producing less good results.

The teachers' assessments, recorded throughout a pupil's school life, provide a guide through educational and work choices, and are most effective when negotiated with the pupil. All subject areas will contribute to the pupil's general records so that skills and excellences of all types may be taken into account. However, in most schools assessment is normative, which means that pupils are compared with their age-peers on test and examination results, little attention being paid to their personal strengths and weaknesses. This means that they are given distinctive labels – 'failure', 'top 10%' and so on – with the result that to both teachers and pupils the curriculum is often split into two unrelated parts: what they should know; and what they need to know in order to pass their examinations.

The alternative is criteria-referenced assessment, in which the criteria used in the assessment are specified in advance, so that assessment becomes an integral part of the learning process. The alternative – criterion-based assessment – looks at achievement in different parts of the curriculum, and because it measures all levels of curriculum activity, each pupil has at least some recordable achievements. Teachers very often like criterion-referenced assessments, but parents, and employers who like to hire the best they can get, find it difficult to match their job criteria to a candidate's achievement profile, and prefer examination marks in recognizable subjects.

Testing attainment

Examinations and tests, either end-of-year exams or spot tests during the term in which specific times are set aside for a pupil to answer questions, normally with expected answers, are not usually tasks which most pupils enjoy; many feel that this kind of assessment emphasizes trivia and is not necessarily a true record of a pupil's learning. There are very many reasons for underachieving in examinations, not least that young people may have other priorities than study. On the other hand, the academically highly able often look forward to examinations as a stimulating challenge, even though, as they get older, they too must study for good results. For those who like being seen as clever, it provides visible evidence that they have superior mental-processing powers; their teachers approve and their self-esteem is enhanced. Yet, if self-esteem is dependent on high exam marks, low marks will diminish it, which can put even the most brilliant pupils in the perilous position of having to score highly all the time – a risky goal.

Devising tests. A few essential points:
(a) *Validity.* The test should measure what it is intended to measure. Do the questions really search for answers in the subject under test, or is

THE BENEFITS OF ATTAINMENT TESTS

1. They provide short-term, reachable goals.
2. They oblige the pupil to do some preparation involving some learning (as well as memorising), and so act as incentives to increasing knowledge.
3. They provide developmental learning experiences in themselves as situations of trial.
4. Good results, if communicated promptly to the child, provide positive reinforcement of achievement and encouragement to continue learning.

HARMFUL EFFECTS OF ATTAINMENT TESTS

1. For teacher and pupils, they become goals in their own right and dominate education in schools. They then become currency with which to buy other forms of learning and, in effect, detract from meaningful education.
2. They are used to divide children, even of the same family, and sometimes for all their school lives, into different schools.
3. They are taken to represent a child's total development. Low marks can be discouraging and distressing to children, even to the extent of keeping them away from school, affecting their future progress, and evoking hostility and feelings of resentment, unfairness and so on. Low marks can also be allowed to interfere with good teacher/pupil relationships.
4. They interfere with other aspects of development, for example when a child is advanced a class or two in school with harmful emotional consequences.
5. They are sometimes the only indications of a child's progress which a school communicates to parents, and parents may not interpret the information in the way the teacher intended.
6. They are accepted as valid and worthwhile, when in fact they may be giving a completely false picture. This may be due to poor testing techniques, favouritism or antagonism between pupil and teacher. Some pupils may cheat (even with the tacit knowledge of the teachers) and the more honest pupils are thus penalized.

general knowledge, for instance, a large factor in the expected replies? Is the marking affected by other 'subjects', such as the lowering of marks due to bad spelling?

(b) *Reliability.* The test should produce much the same result if given again to the same pupil within a short space of time – it should be consistent. Every individual will vary at different times, leaving some room for error, but the acceptability of this error is limited. A test can be totally reliable, producing the same scores over and over again, and yet not measure what it was intended to, that is, not be valid. On the other hand, a test which is valid is always reliable.

Objective tests, which require short, ready answers, are the easiest to mark and are more reliable. It is in the essay-type answer that reasoning and selection are best measured. When essay-type answers are marked on specific points, the final marks can vary considerably between teachers, but a mark from a subjective impression of the work is, surprisingly, not very different and much quicker.

IMPROVING FEEDBACK FROM ATTAINMENT TESTS
1. Use appropriate and varying methods of measurement.
2. Be aware of the means by which a test can be constructed so that most pupils will score around the 50% range, or wherever the teacher wants them to score.
3. Make questions clear and specific, particularly for essay-type answers.
4. As far as possible, make the optional questions of equal value.
5. Be aware of simple statistical procedures, such as the standardization of scores and the difficulties involved in comparing the results of different tests.
6. On the basis of the results, provide a detailed summary of the strengths and weaknesses both of the individual and the class as a whole.
7. Provide oral or written observations to give substance and background to the bare marks.
8. Make use of peer-assessment, the pupils' assessment of each other's work, where possible.
9. Offer praise and encouragement for effort and work well done.

Variations of attainment testing. Continuous assessment is becoming more popular, but it has its limitations. Essentially, it means that the teacher keeps a record in marks or words of how each pupil progresses in many ways, such as calculating a total of all essay marks, or a note on the quality of cakes baked. It is not as decisive a grading as an examination and has all the bias of being marked by the examiner – who is also the teacher – but it can provide a fairer overall estimate of the pupil's abilities.

Open-book exams are another technique devised to avoid the examination of merely rote-memory in a formal setting. The examinee is allowed to bring any information thought appropriate into the exam room. This avoids sheer memorization of mathematical or chemical formulae, for instance, or of information which a professional would look up rather than remember. Pre-knowledge of examination questions is an alternative method in the same category.

Dissertations, projects or presentations of original work are now taking some or all of the role of examinations. They have the benefit of avoiding exam 'nerves', and also test the ability of the examinee to ask questions himself.

Self-evaluation is perhaps the least used and yet most important aspect of educational evaluation. Pupils who are partners in their own learning – helping to set up objectives, devising routes by which to reach them, and so on – will obtain the greatest benefit from self-evaluation and testing, which they have been involved in preparing. It is their very own feedback. If the pupil accepts self- and school-evaluation as an integral part of his education, and is not restricted to judgment by the system alone, then he will be more aware of what he is doing and for what goals he is aiming. Self-evaluation also provides the pupil with an important lesson in self-understanding – a vital aspect of education. The validity of self-evaluation is uncertain, however, since some personalities tend to over- or under-estimate themselves. Pupils will need help in this too, both in regard to insight and self-acceptance.

Psychological effects on assessment. The same form of assessment, given at the same time to a number of individuals, may be distorted for a number of reasons:

1. The pupil may misinterpret the test instructions. Such mistakes are not necessarily due to understandable reasons, but may have an unconscious motivation, such as failure as a deliberate form of rebellion against authority.
2. Some pupils are better at writing down what they know than others, possibly because of their positive attitudes towards tests, feelings of security and general intelligence.
3. Some pupils are better at recognition than recall, so that test results will also vary with the form of the test. For example, some questions ask the pupil to tick one possible answer in a multiple-choice selection, while others ask testees to structure an answer themselves.
4. Health, both physical and psychological, is very important in intellectual functioning. For instance, girls' marks are found to drop significantly when they are pre-menstrual; hay-fever sufferers do less well when the season is against them.
5. Motivation is crucial to the production of the best efforts the pupil can offer, but poor motivation has a variety of psychological causes.
6. External conditions, such as noise or heat, will affect some pupils' intellectual performance more than others.
7. Interaction between tester and pupil is known to affect results. In the United States, for instance, black children have been found to score more highly on intelligence tests with black testers than with white testers.
8. Pupils are liable, like anyone else, to have fluctuations in memory, attention or blockage of knowledge – often affected by differing lev-

els of anxiety brought about by the examination situation and all the above conditions.

School reports. The use of preset forms which teachers fill in two or three times a year to report on pupils' progress is under some criticism for the following reasons:

1. Children's marks are not usually shown in comparisons with a general standard for children of that age. Even when they are ranked in order of the class, parents cannot know what the general standard the class is. This means that, on the whole, marks or grades given in different subjects are not directly comparable – teacher A may be a 'stricter' marker than teacher B – and if several children have the same mark, then a position of tenth may be virtually equivalent to first.

2. Grades can mislead. The teacher has perhaps over a hundred forms to fill in within a couple of days and may err, but parents assume that the information is accurate.

3. They act against teacher/pupil co-operation because the teacher is directing information 'over the heads' of the pupils to their parents, instead of discussing their work with them.

4. Parents tend to become emotional about reports. Seeing something in writing about one's child from 'authority' can affect the calmest parent: children are, on the whole, their parents' representatives.

5. Teachers may not have meant to say what parents have understood them to say. What does 'fairly good' mean, for instance?

6. Form-filling is an extremely time-consuming and irritating ritual for the teacher, and teachers tend to copy their comments from each other. Hence, good reports become better, and poor ones worse.

Adequate, freely flowing home and school communication can dispense with reports, especially at primary level. A brief phrase on each topic can never be enough to provide understanding, yet misunderstanding can cause misery. When pupils, bright ones particularly, are given the respect and knowledge of having a place in the active educational team, they can report on their own progress. Such pupil reporting implies trust all round, between pupil, school and home – not a bad thing to aim for.

Under-achievement. Under-achievement is as prevalent as the common cold, and just as difficult to cure: current research indicates that the pupil may be the last person responsible for this condition, rather it is the tangled web of circumstances which impede progress in learning (Butler-Por, 1987). To break through it, the threads have to be separated, smoothed and redirected by both teacher and child. The overriding reason for children's under-achievement is the lack of provision for learning, whether in material, teaching or emotional support. The earlier the 'treatment' for under-achievement starts, the better; this should be preferably in the first few weeks of school, as even very young children can get firmly stuck in the rut.

Under-achievement can be diagnosed by teachers, who can identify the symptoms in children's performance, ability and behaviour, via records, professional help and the parents. There are two things they should do:

1. Genuinely listen to the child – to see if he has any advanced language and comprehension of abstract ideas, as well as any involvement in complex out-of-school activities. These can indicate intellectual processes which might not be exploited in school-type learning.

2. Involve the child in problem-solving – to judge how information is used in synthesis and analysis, and in different types of reasoning. It also provides the opportunity to see originality, creativity, organizational abilities, and the capacity for independent, self-directed learning.

It is particularly difficult to judge a child who has a high potential but is under-achieving, and teachers may need information from outside the classroom to help, particularly when the teaching is formal. High ability in under-performing children can be discovered by a feeling for how they are handling language, general knowledge, problem-solving and their personal interests, though some, who keep a low profile in class, can be discovered through standardized tests. To many teachers, the idea of under-achievement and high ability is a contradiction in terms, because children are usually judged by their products rather than their potential.

The first goal in treating under-achievement is to build up the child's feelings of competence, which may mean a transfer of some control from the teacher to the child to enhance intrinsic motivation. It should be taken one step at a time, not setting the targets so high (for teacher or pupil) that failure is likely, or so low that success will be dismissed as worthless. Suggested guidelines for reversing under-achievement are to involve the pupil actively in the choice of goals, setting appropriate activities to reach these, and giving rewards. It might be a good idea to draw up a contract for each area, specifying the goals of the learning. Teachers can be astonished at the enthusiasm of younger pupils whom they had all but abandoned, although progress is normally slow with adolescents, who may need longer-term reinforcement.

Teachers are the key to this process of improving achievement, both in their expectations and in the essential aspects of good teaching – involvement and commitment. In inner-city areas with a high teacher turnover, this is difficult, and teachers can suffer because they feel powerless to do anything about it.

SOME CHARACTERISTICS OF SUCCESSFUL TEACHING
* Respect for children.
* Concern for the whole child.
* Encouragement of collaborative and active learning.
* Setting open-ended tasks.
* Willingness to give children autonomy within defined boundaries.
* Clear criteria for what the pupils are expected to achieve.
* Use of modules to break up the subject for easier learning.
* A wide use of teaching methods beyond the traditional ones.
* Discussion and negotiation with pupils about their learning.
* Team planning, both within and across subject boundaries.
* Constructive, well-planned marking.
* An emphasis on what is positive in pupils' work.
* Well-planned homework.
* Elaborate assessment records.
* Clear feedback to pupils on how they are doing.

CHAPTER VIII

The flexible curriculum

CHILD OR SOCIETY CENTRED?

For most schoolchildren, the curriculum – the knowledge and skills that they are set to learn – is a mystery. It is not for them to question what or why they will learn it, or why it should be so. Yet the development of competence at school is very dependent on the curriculum, not only in its explicit learning goals, but also in the implicit outcomes of the way it is taught, in conceptualizing and reasoning, and the underlying messages. The curriculum plays a vital role in socializing pupils, taking them further along the path on which they set out at home towards a deeper understanding of their society and its values. Accordingly, curricular change, in both content and methodology, is seen as a powerful component of social engineering, a basic way in which to change the working of society (Eggleston, 1990).

In many developing countries, the curriculum is society-centred, and therefore greatly concerned with rules and with recognized ways of behaving. Its aims are often to pass on the basics of literacy and numeracy, and to accommodate children to the ways of the culture. On the contrary, in many industrialized countries a child-centred approach is more usual in which teachers are involved with pupils' individual needs. The key to this is more flexible organization, both in the structuring of the timetable and the patience and enthusiasm expected from the staff.

Integration. Especially in the secondary school, the curriculum is usually parcelled into separate subjects, unlike the integrated world of adults. So much so that sometimes the lesson that pupils learn best is that maths is what happens in maths lessons, and science in science lessons, and, what is more, that there are only the most tenuous connections between the two subjects, neither of which is relevant to modern languages or to art. It is often different in primary schools, where many teachers try to organize broad subject areas on integrated lines in such a way that content and ideas can flow from one to another. For example, they may take a central point for consideration, such as aspects of transport, bringing in history, geography, engineering and style, etc. This integrated subject approach also provides opportunities for knowledge and understanding to be co-ordinated with the child's needs and out-of-school life.

The question of which children are to be given an integrated style of curriculum is often decided on the basis of ability – lower-ability pupils take integrated studies, while brighter ones take a selection of specific academic subjects. This is because highly focused subject-centred educa-tion is strongly supported by employers and universities, for whom qual-ifications in the pure sciences, the arts or languages provide the only val-id credentials. Yet the ability to think in complex ways is not restricted to those of above-average intelligence. The basic skills involved in common forms of learning used by almost everyone, such as reading and writing, are now seen to be very complex indeed. Reading is a prime enabling skill, and so is writing, particularly if the teaching is concerned with the processes of argument, construction and evaluation, rather than only issues of literary expression. Mathematics, in particular the construction of formal representations and argument, is another potential enabling discipline.

A good basic school curriculum should contain a variety of areas to be studied up to school-leaving age, though closer focus on particular areas of interest of a more academic nature would not be excluded, and indeed would reflect and incorporate the broader areas.

EDUCATIONAL CHOICE

Young children soon become aware that they are better at some things than others, and constantly discover new abilities and attractions to com-pare them with. Before long, though, school authority, in the form of teachers and administrators, will make educational decisions for them, for example, in selecting them for particular learning groups. A more objective and personal form of educational guidance – sadly lacking in the world – has been found to improve achievement, increase their chances in higher education and work, and reduce delinquency.

Most school curricula were designed to promote vocational training for specific areas of work and, as a result, rather than emphasizing initiative, adaptability and creativity, they can often limit pupils' life-chances and the flexibility of their response to change. Gender-linked subjects are clear instances of this. In most cultures, when boys and girls are given checklists to say whether they think school subjects and jobs are mascu-line or feminine, their preferences show that there is a wide range of

---

THE CONTENTS OF A GOOD BASIC CURRICULUM

* *Scientific studies*: the history of science, scientific method, the major principles, and the moral issues raised by scientific progress and discovery.
* *Literature*: introduction to the world of literature, analysis and appreciation of its different forms, imitation of these and development of one's individual style in writing, oral skills (reading aloud, giving a talk, conventions of debate), the literature of other nations.
* *Aesthetics*: historical aspects of art, drama and music, opportunities for appreciation and performance, exploration of other media, e.g. photography and television, artists and musicians – the men and women behind the creation.
* *Thinking skills*: specific assistance in logical and creative thinking.
* *Technology*: the principles, uses, history and social implications of technological advances, alongside practical skills in handling, maintaining and (at a simple level) creating technological equipment.
* *Computer studies*: practical use of computers, the potential of computers and computing, issues in the use of computers in society.
* *Cultural studies*: national and international historical and current affairs, the critical use of the media, people and places in the news, human and economic geography, political boundaries, creeds and philosophies.
* *Life skills*: relationships, beliefs, religions, philosophies, morals and ethics, politics, aspects of law and economics, and the management of personal affairs.
* *Languages*: oral and written communication in one or more languages which are significant in the contemporary world.

---

subjects which are seen as distinctly one or the other. Feminine subjects include foreign languages, religion, biology, sewing, cooking, typing, commerce and office practice, and so girls are usually less interested and under-achieve in the physical sciences and mathematics. Masculine subjects, seen by both sexes as more difficult, include science and mathematics, technical drawing, drama, metalwork, engineering, car maintenance, physics and physical education. Art, music and geography are often seen as equally suitable for both sexes. Boys' and girls' different spheres of interest, and the boundaries between them, can be understood in terms of power relations; the tendency is for these boundaries to diminish in most modern industrialized countries (Archer, 1992).

The task of helping individual children with their educational choice may be taken up by a school counsellor, an untrained teacher, or it may be simply ignored by the school. The person who is providing this help should be aware of the variety of options and moves open to pupils, and at the same time be sensitive to each pupil and their way of life. Accidents of birth order, personality effects on achievement, personal problems, and so on, must be given due weight. For example, it may be helpful to support a youngster's strong determination, allied with modest ability, by finding alternative ways of reaching his goals and surmounting the shortcomings. Group pressure from peers can also be powerful in changing an individual's life-course, and can be used in group discussions about careers. All guidance counsellors should try to accept their clients as they are and not simply accept opinions from other members of staff.

Although the pressure to make a choice is inevitable, decisions made early in school life may be regretted later on. Because children develop at different rates and in different styles, they need guidance over time about their education. Unfortunately, important educational choices are normally made at the time of adolescent changes and emotional strife. Even with experience, it can be difficult to predict slow development, so that a child may be taking courses which are not an adequate preparation for later growth of ability. On the other hand, an early-maturing 14-year-old boy may develop an intense dislike for the restrictions of school, and either waste time until he leaves, or simply absent himself. Yet, educational guidance, which could help such young people in preparation for future training and work, is not available in most of the world's schools, or at best is only offered in the late teens. Most children have to turn to their parents or to subject teachers.

The highly able may have the less-usual problem of being able to do too many things extremely well – a mixed blessing – which leads to delay and wasting of time when different courses are tried out in turn. Choices within the school curriculum are a preliminary to those that the school-leaver must make. Although early selection of a subject area by a talented child may stimulate vocational thinking and eventual high levels of achievement, it also restricts future choice.

Some schools, are introducing 'work' itself as a subject on the curriculum, composed of a parcel of work experience, shadowing someone at work, simulated production and work ethics. In practice, children can study different occupations to build up a picture of what a job involves. They can look through newspapers to see what opportunities exist, noting stereotyping in job descriptions, and teachers can invite people from the local community into the classroom to talk about what they do. Later, pupils can make a positive search for possible careers, assessing them in real-life, individual terms, and discussing how these might affect the rest of their lives. For preference, the concepts and content of careers should be integrated into existing teaching, whether of languages, arts or science. These can be enriched by group discussions, debates, library research, work experience and other exploratory experiences.

Using guidance tests and lists. A qualified educational counsellor can use ability or aptitude tests as tools, either for selection by aptitude within a

---

THE EFFECTS OF EDUCATIONAL GUIDANCE

1. *Who am I?* Awareness and exploration of self and others. This includes acquiring information about one's own personal characteristics, and understanding that career development is a lifelong process. A sense of identity in a pupil implies the ability to ask, if not answer –
2. *Where do I want to go?* Awareness and exploration of career and lifestyle alternatives. This includes exploring and analyzing possible choices of leisure activities and family roles and settings.
3. *How can I get there?* Acquisition and use of decision-making and goal-planning skills.

---

school, or for guidance in helping an individual reach an educational decision. There are three main types of tests, all of which can be used to indicate possible future success or failure in comparison with other children.

1. *General mental ability tests*, which often result in an IQ score and are often only available to educational psychologists.
2. *Attainment tests*, which measure current attainment rather than potential.
3. *Aptitude tests*, which again measure performance with a qualified guess at future directions, such as those for manual dexterity, reaction time, musicality, space orientation, etc.

However sophisticated they are, tests can never entirely replace personal counselling, and may in fact prejudice advice given to the pupils because they are not always accurate. Yet test results can be used beneficially as a stimulus to continue to work in the area of choice, or to highlight unknown areas of ability by placing all the pupil's educational options on view, which can improve a child's self-concept and facilitate self-awareness. Testing can also be used as a learning process in decision-making, and pupils can choose what they would like to be tested in, followed by explanation and discussion.

Each person who attempts educational guidance will probably devise a scheme or checklist of their own. A comprehensive interest list, to be filled in by the pupil before an interview, is helpful; commercial ones are available which attempt to provide a sound, widely-spread system for coping with the multitude of educational choices.

School counselling. The term 'counselling' implies some form of trained intervention, but it is not teaching in its fullest sense, rather it is a concern with overall development and psychological adjustment of individual pupils. Unlike teaching, counselling is mostly, but not always, nondirective, offering little praise, blame or direct advice, but accepting what the child says. The appointment of a school counsellor implies that someone will be available to help pupils grow emotionally, and to arrange the best possible educational provision for them within the school's limits. Even so, school counselling is never restricted to the person appointed to the job; warm-hearted teachers will continue to be involved with their pupils in this way.

Learning about relationships and how to learn should be as much a planned part of the curriculum as numbers and letters. Plenty of potential opportunities already exist for teachers to help, for example, in group projects or physical education, nor is group discussion and evaluation after an exercise beyond the grasp of 5 year olds. Talking about an event often helps to put it into perspective and reinforces the experience. Older youngsters may need personal help of a kind which teachers and parents cannot always provide. Teenagers seem particularly glad to have someone to turn to who is not a member of the family. How much better it would be if all teachers were given some training in counselling as part of their initial teacher education.

A MULTICULTURAL CURRICULUM

A working multicultural approach often implies a thorough overhaul of the curriculum so that it genuinely provides education taking account of the resources of the children from a variety of cultures. Changes should encourage a mix of cultural ideas, recognizing the importance of cultural diversity, rather than total domination by the majority culture. Current multicultural education has come about from a response to poor race relations, and aims to raise awareness among both the prejudiced and the victims of prejudice that racism springs from fear and ignorance in which an individual's worth is seen as unalterable by education. But it should always be recognized that, in spite of the many varieties of multicultural education now on offer, there are very many once-disadvantaged and now successful people, who are extremely grateful for the formal education that, without any special provision or consideration, gave them a route out of culturally stifling conformity.

Cultural or ethnic factors cannot be entirely accountable for children's achievements in school, because there are marked differences between members of any such group. They will vary, for example, with regard to country of origin, values, economic status, number of generations in the host country and language of origin. Some groups may also convey more subtle cultural barriers to their children which, instead of preparing to change the future, can conflict with school achievement, such as living in the present and accepting fate, gender divisions and the centrality of the family. In some community-based cultures where the greatest value is placed on co-operation rather than competition, such as among the Inuit, concentrating on the needs of an individual child may create tension within the community. Religious authority can raise special problems, and the aims of any form of religious fundamentalism antagonistic to the education that is freely available to all are certainly not compatible with multi-culturation. Such influences mean that trying to find specific teaching strategies appropriate to each group presents a real challenge.

Since the 1970s, education for those who do not belong to the majority culture has been divided into the two camps of either 'assimilationist' or 'pluralist', which offer the distinct approaches of either intervention or empowerment to help schools teach their minority pupils.

Intervention. Intervention means changing the child, so that he or she can develop in the mainstream culture and compete at their true ability level for a place in further education, jobs and so on. Interventionist approaches assume that teaching can alleviate children's weaknesses and help them to fit in to the mainstream, which implies an existing deficit in them. The school attempts to assimilate the disadvantaged children into its majority culture by encouraging them to change their behaviour. In this way, working-class children must become 'more motivated', girls must become 'more scientific', while children from minority cultures must become 'more acculturated' and also 'solve' their language problems.

Assimilationists argue that, irrespective of background, children require mastery of higher-level and creative thinking skills in mainstream society if they are to become competent in it. To do that, the curriculum might be enriched with content which reflects cultural diversity (for example, history, literature, art), but would not deal overtly with issues of inequity, racism and discrimination. Thus, a successful curriculum would lead to the same outcome both for those who are differently cultured and for mainstream pupils.

Sometimes, this assimilation process involves the children's removal from the mainstream curriculum into special remedial sessions or classes. The decision is often based on a child's difficulties with the majority language, and a full return to the mainstream curriculum is only permitted when language skills have improved sufficiently. One effect of this remediation is to interrupt children's full participation in the curriculum, with the result that, although their language may be improved, their school achievement can remain poor. Another way to tackle this problem is to offer the pupils specially designed full-time curricula, considered suitable for their 'deficit'. This could be practical subjects for slow-learning children, 'girl's' subjects for the girls, or 'ethnic subjects' (community languages, music, crafts) for the ethnic minority pupils. This method may have had some success, but the relative advantage of the advantaged and the relative disadvantage of the disadvantaged tends to remain untouched.

Empowerment. Empowerment of children means changing the schools. This pluralist approach tends to support the original culture, while the school itself tries to accommodate to diverse individual experiences, valuing different outlooks, and watching out for social interaction, such as possible racism. With this approach, schools try to adapt teaching to the children's familiar styles of thinking, and look for their diverse strengths. Initial weakness in the majority language is not seen as a necessary impediment to successful study, and most learn it successfully as they go along. It also leaves children's beliefs and traditions relatively intact, thus providing them with a sense of personal worth.

For example, obliging a child who has only limited English to master English composition skills before trying to write creatively is ignoring native language and creative-thinking skills, and will possibly frustrate their expression. An alternative approach would be to encourage it through the child's strengths, which may be writing in the native language, oral story telling in either language, or developing a pictorial essay. Later, when the child achieves sufficient English proficiency, the teacher would require the creative writing to be in English, then build up composition skills through feedback and revision. Carefully planned in this way, the child's creative competence is respected, and stimulating outlets are offered for its expression, without the implication that there is a deficiency.

However, there can be a great variety of cultures – maybe more than a dozen languages in any one school – so that any attempt to offer each child special education in their own language can be impossible for reasons of time, money and, not least, co-ordination of the school's activities. More often, the largest minority group in the school is given this special treatment, and the minorities among minorities get nothing (Bennett, 1990).

In recent years there has been emphasis on collaborative learning among age-peers for culturally diverse youngsters. Co-operative strategies can result in greater pupil engagement: in addition to academic achievement, they can promote such outcomes as self-esteem, friendships with those of other ethnic groups, and the ability to co-operate, because pupils are brought together in working towards common goals.

This is particularly important for the highly able child. Even though children in some Asian groups are over-represented among the recognized highly able, they still constitute an ethnic minority and can face racial discrimination in non-school aspects of life, such as work, social relationships and housing. Pluralists who are concerned with social change would like to see a curriculum which would not only include academic achievement as a necessary component of empowerment, but would work towards social justice. For example, the history and experiences of oppressed groups, analysis of social institutions, conceptualization of the ideal society, and processes for effecting change could be added to the curriculum.

This could help the culturally diverse youngsters who face both personal identity issues and conflicts with peers, even though they are excelling academically. A curriculum for empowerment should benefit all the school's pupils, not only those from culturally diverse backgrounds, because it seeks to create awareness of issues related to social class, religion, gender, sexual preference, exceptional need and ethnicity, as well as promoting skills to effect change. The goal is to produce citizens who, through thoughtful reflection and critical analysis, recognize social injustice and will work towards the creation of a more equitable society. Democratic ideals, human compassion and informed personal choice will be served more consistently through such broad curricula and processes promoting critical thought.

CREATIVITY IN THE CURRICULUM

Creative thinking is part of every situation in which there is a problem to be solved – everyone does it every day – and emotion and personality are always involved. But there is always some conflict within creative endeavour, because the individual cannot then hide behind the security of a closed familiar environment where answers are already known, but have enough confidence and even sometimes courage to try new ways.

To be creative means acting in a purposeful way to that end, but not with special mental processes, the everyday ones will do, as they interact and are co-ordinated using the learned skills needed for the task. Many researchers have concluded that creativity works by what Simonton (1988) called 'chance-configuration', involving a large number of more or less random associations. But that is only the beginning; chains of these associations emerge in a series of logical small steps, for which knowledge of the field is vital (Weisberg, 1986). The essential creative procedure is the recognition of the emerging pattern as a solution to a problem and the clue to distinguishing real creative ability lies in disentangling the effort and the talent.

Being creative means being able to offer the world ideas or products which are novel. Creative ideas should contain the seeds of change, adding to the available ways of looking at things, and offering fresh approaches to knowledge. There has to be an element of quality in this, however; reproducing a great many examples of the same idea is not enough; there should also be breadth and depth to the creative product. Though it may not be obvious at first glance, the qualities of originality and value should become clearer over time with each reworking of an idea. The invitation to be creative is not the same as the invitation to be silly: context is important as well as applicability. It is useful to question whether the ideas are relevant to the problem under consideration.

The well-known stages of creativity described by Wallas (1926) are as follows:

–   *Preparation*: the information is collected and the problem
    determined.
–   *Incubation*: ideas ferment, often unconsciously.
–   *Illumination*: a solution is found.
–   *Verification*: testing the illumination.

Incubation and illumination are the 'soft' parts of creative activity – the pleasurable brain alpha rhythm, the easy-going style of right-brain activity which includes personality. Preparation and verification call for the firmer activity of the left brain – memory, classification and the ability to compare and contrast different elements using careful methodology.

Creativity was once seen as an aspect of high academic achievement, but Milgram's (1990) major review of research on IQ and creativity concluded that IQ cannot of itself predict real-life creativity. Talented achievement appears to demand something more. Many studies have settled on a figure of about 120 IQ as a minimum which is needed to shape ideas using higher order mental abilities, and to identify effective and worthwhile routes and products, either by the creative person or others. As a qualitative aspect of mental functioning, creativity can be considered to be a 'style' for applying intelligence, rather than as a separate ability (Cropley, 1993), or alternatively as intelligence in action. An attempt to clarify the relationship between creativity and high conventional intelligence has been made by Renzulli (1977). He designed a 'three-ring' model, composed of three overlapping circles labelled 'intelligence', 'creativity', and 'task commitment'. Although each constituent element is seen as necessary, it is not an adequate condition for high-level creativity; that is defined by the area in which all three circles overlap. A fourth dimension, the social environment, was added by Mönks et al. (1986).

CREATIVITY NEEDS COURAGE TO:
* Tolerate ambiguity;
* Defer judgement;
* Resist destructive criticism and rejection.

   It is based on:
* Security;
* Mental freedom;
   but includes:
* Anxiety.

Emotion and personality in creativity. The essential elements of both knowledge and feeling merge in the creative experience. It is through feelings that particular knowledge is selected, but feelings also constitute a form of knowledge which is at the heart of the process of creativity. Emotion is a way of knowing – what one feels is right – and this may change during the process of production. The feelings which lead in to the project, such as curiosity, may vanish as the work progresses, to be replaced by other emotions, such as the urge to display. Emotions can also mislead, or be inappropriate – so that what one feels is 'right' may not in fact be so.

Any ability that is identified as 'creative' has considerable overlap with many others, and measuring any creative activity while disregarding emotion and personality is the sort of sterile psychological exercise which creative people complain of. Studies of creative people in many fields describe them as having particular personality characteristics, notably flexibility, sensitivity, tolerance, a sense of responsibility, empathy, independence and a positive self-image. Indeed, the relationship between personality and creativity is one of the most consistently emphasized findings in the scientific literature. Creative people are usually not much concerned with making a good impression on others, which means they are less likely to be conforming, and so must risk personal problems – but without that independence, originality would be lost.

A glance at the childhoods of artists, writers and architects often seems to show that they had a lifelong tendency for unusual and creative responses, which diverged from the conventional ones, and were able to develop unique formulations of experience (Albert, 1983). Creativity thus appears to depend as much on personality as on ability – though no research has ever predicted a creative future from a child's measured personality.

Personality does not operate in a vacuum. Creative people have to be sufficiently independent in their judgement to formulate and stick to their own opinions. Because it is in the nature of a creative act to express rather than repress impulses, creative individuals must be relatively free of emotional repression and open to inner experience. This style of thinking can bring on social disapproval and (at least in creative scientists) is frequently associated with what psychologists measure as introversion at limited social adjustment, often accompanied by high anxiety.

In order to be creative, people may have to cut across the social stereotypes and be less affected than others by social disapproval. Aesthetically creative men, for example, are more receptive to their feelings than is normally acceptable for males in many societies. They may then be described as having a higher degree of 'femininity', allied to a super-ego or conscience. But the super-ego is not absent: the production of a creative work is a controlled process. The key state to aim for is flexibility – the relaxing of mental structures, allowing emotions, impulses and irrational and primitive thought processes to come to consciousness. It is possible that creativity is a form of immature thinking (Bruner, 1972).

In being open to experience, creative people need to have greater tolerance for the anxiety brought about by ambiguous and conflicting experiences. In addition, they often prefer complexity, such as complex asymmetrical designs over simple geometrical ones. This may be for two reasons:

1. In absorbing complex, disorganized experiences, the artist can then impose personal order on them, which comes from an intrinsic need for a unique ordering of experience. This need is part of artistic creativity.
2. The artist has an attitude which welcomes the new, instead of being overwhelmed by anxiety at the very idea of it.

Talent in the arts

The major problem of measurement of, for example, fine art and music, is that of aesthetic interpretation – often a matter of contention between 'experts' compared with the easier assessment of a performance ability, such as gymnastics. Tests of talent in fine art are very few, and those for musical ability are not always reliable, yet tests of musical fluency in children have been seen to predict an ability to engage in a musical career, rather than becoming a composer (Sloboda, 1985).

Technical assessment has its problems too. For example, Norman Freeman (1993) has shown how the drawing of young children is hampered by what he calls 'production problems'. The development of their ideas is not equalled by their graphic skills – neither their fine-motor skills nor their language are ready to carry out what is in their minds – making it hard to judge their attempts from the point of view of either appreciation or creativity. Added to that is a 'bio-mechanical' bias in graphic development, which is not apparent in music. For example, young children's scribbling tends toward the vertical, which is why legs are generally the dominant limbs in their 'tadpole men' – the familiar picture of a big belly with stick arms and legs, and a little head. Possibly this physical problem is the reason why infant prodigies are so rarely found in fine art, compared with the numbers playing musical instruments. Painters usually start their artistic work and reach their peaks much later in life than musicians.

Perception of the arts. In both fine art and music, perception begins with pattern recognition – the extraction of figure from ground – such as the theme in an orchestrated piece of music. Because the early patterns tend to become more rigid as perceptual habits, it is important to expose children as early as possible to variety. But in life, nothing is seen or heard in isolation, and the context in which children have their experiences has subtle and important effects on the perception of even the most meagre line drawings or notes from an instrument.

To understand the perception of the arts it is important to distinguish the effects on the child's senses of both physical light and sound, and the psychological effects of the environment. Light rays hitting the retina reach the brain in a psychologically 'processed' state, having come through a filtering process of expectations, approval, associations and so on. Each person's private impressions of sensations are shaped by both the physical reception of images in the brain and by experience, which includes language. As ideas change so does the living language, altering perceptions, imagery and the relationships of people with the world. Environmental pollution, for example, was little considered until recently, but the concept and the language now in use to describe it have altered the ways in which people feel and behave towards nature.

There seems to be a plasticity in human imagination, which the rest of the animal world does not share. A child may pretend to be a horse, for instance, but it does not happen the other way round. Playing, imitating ability, which can be described as 'perceptual participation', brings the world within a child's mental grasp, and sometimes calls for courage to explore unknown territory (Landau, 1985). This constant questioning and experimenting with the real world is based on early sensory experiences and is conducive to the production of improved and more complex schemas.

The creative use of language. Language is neither neutral nor is it simply a medium of transmission (see Chapter IV). Its artistic use has a similar tradition to that of listening to music or looking at paintings, where the aesthetic response is between the perceiver and the text. The way words

> **CREATIVE COMPARISONS**
> New information goes to:
>   old schemas – which lead to:
>   comparisons of sameness and differences –
>   which lead to: new perceptions – which result in:
>   restructured flexible schemas – which produce:
>   creative thinking.

are used is the culmination of centuries of ideas, taking in the changing meanings of the times, as well as from a personal perspective, picked up from experience – a joining together of vision and culture.

The appreciation of any art is always within the context of what we have already learned, and in both poetry and prose, there is a natural association of certain words. In a poem, these connections are used to set the reader's mind in the right mood with the title. People of the same culture depend on this process to ease communication, making familiar associations like the English 'bread-butter-jam'. If someone is asked to simply list words for a minute, many of them will be found to be connected in meaning.

Emotional words are used differently from neutral words, so that people give different answers when they are happy or sad. Meaning is usually more important than rhyme, for example, 'lion' is closer to 'cat' than 'hat'. Some words are unpleasant, like 'death' or 'blood', and these are more difficult to hear when one is listening. The words you choose to use about yourself tell others something of the way you think about yourself – the self-image. But people are realistic; even those with poor self-images do not choose all the nasty words to describe themselves, they select the most appropriate ones. The use of words is closely allied to intelligence: psychologists use them to test it: 'Cat is to mouse as lion is to . . .'. Personality also affects the way words are used; obsessional people are more narrow-minded.

Insight

Creativity can be thought of as the electricity of the intellect, and insightful thinking as the spark which appears to short-circuit reason in a flash of illumination. It is an ephemeral, satisfying joy with a magical quality (Bastick, 1982). It is part of all aspects of life, an experience common to everyone, no matter what their level of intelligence.

In its various guises, insight may take the form of an everyday hunch, offering a clue for making a decision, or it may be a deep moving experience. That vital spark often comes at times of relaxation, during easy familiar action: Isaac Newton observed the falling apple while musing; Archimedes discovered displacement, and cried out 'Eureka', when taking a bath; and Poincaré, the great mathematician, was getting on a bus when he made one of his discoveries. Millions of other insights have been responsible for practically every innovative human creation to date. Even Poincaré said that logic alone could create nothing new, nor lead to anything but tautology.

To be insightful is to be human. The computer, though it is a powerful tool used to analyze the most complex data, cannot ask even the simplest meaningful question by itself. Insight is basic to all levels of learning, and the most effective teaching constantly seeks to develop it. Yet the thinking styles required for most school learning do not help it. School problems normally demand responses from the analytical, sequential end of the thinking spectrum in order to cope with problems with specific structures and answers. Everyday matters require far more of the intuitive, flexible end, with sensitive and free use of feelings, because they are rarely so clear-cut, and sometimes several solutions are equally possible. In fact, just identifying the cause of the trouble, let alone the solution, is usually difficult, because it is part-and-parcel of living. Everyday problems are also very persistent: one decision sometimes only seems to pave the way for the next set of problems; one cannot just close the textbook and go away. Furthermore, solving a life-problem is one thing, but convincing other concerned people of the rightness of the solution is another, and the decision about whom you marry, or where you choose to live, can change your whole life.

At times, the highly able youngsters in the Freeman study (1991a) caused some consternation in class with their flashes of insight, especially the mathematicians, who leapt over the recognized stages of computation. Although it is often a valuable exercise for such pupils to have to retrace their calculations in a more careful way, too much back-tracking can also act as an impediment for the creative aspects of their thinking. Understandably, teachers are somewhat anxious to know how to help their high-fliers balance the desire to fly with the need to check their work. It was not only in mathematics, but in the arts too that a bright youngster would have a flash of insight, though unable to describe the reasoning behind it.

Insight springs from the ferment of both past and present experience, and because intuitive thinking involves the whole self, both emotion and intellect make up reactions to the mix of familiar and unfamiliar. Mild anxiety may build up before the 'flash', but after it happens and one knows the rightness of the insight, the feeling of confidence releases the tension. People have described it subjectively, but it can also be measured by changes in skin response, heart-rate and respiration. It produces a feeling of satisfaction, if not euphoria.

Encouraging creativity in schools

Potential does not simply mature into talent – it has to be taught and learned in a long process which may or may not reach a successful conclusion. One result of increased interest in this subject has been the search for methods of teaching creativity, though with modest success. What is clear is that improved knowledge and understanding of the subject area is the essential basis for creativity in that area. A competent musician, for example, who understands how music is produced is more likely to compose than someone who is without that understanding. But in addition, unless the whole context of the child's development nourishes that kind of activity, creative endeavour is unlikely to take place (Freeman, 1977).

Because creative thinking is part of all problem-solving, understanding the types of problems teachers set children – 'the problem of the problem' (Getzels, 1982) – helps to prepare the ground-work for encouraging creative problem solving. The more open-ended the possible solution, the more free the pupil is to think creatively, given the self-confidence and teacher's permission to do so.

TYPES OF PROBLEMS
* *The presented problem*: with a clear format and prepared answer, such as in mathematics.
* *The discovered problem*: where there is no known formulation or solution, such as asking of an event, 'Why did it happen?'
* *The created problem*: where no problem or relationship existed before, such as in abstract painting.

What of those children who react in unusually creative ways to the learning situation? High scores on paper and pencil creativity tests are viewed with suspicion (and with good reason) by teachers, who usually prefer to choose their exceptionally creative children themselves within their subject area. The main problem with tests of creativity is that they are designed to be completed in an hour or so, whereas real-life originality may need years, or even a life-time. Teachers usually look for such indicators as an unusual vocabulary, imaginative writing and original behaviour as signs of creative talent, although they might then miss the child with mechanical gifts. Intuitive feelings have their honoured place in identifying and assessing creativity, but are most efficiently used along with other methods to counter the teachers' biases from their own backgrounds and attitudes.

ASSESSING CREATIVITY
1. **Decide what you are looking for.**
2. **Use several measures which will include performance, such as auditions and displays. Look for potential, which may be found through the judgement of experts.**
3. **Assessment of creativity should be continuous.**
4. **Creativity is complex, so keep an open mind.**

Environmental influences which promote creativity differ somewhat from those for high academic achievement, and the creative needs of intellectually able children can sometimes be neglected because of the heavy load of accumulated knowledge they are obliged to digest. In Freeman's long-term study, many children who were highly successful academically, particularly in the sciences, were found to be creatively crippled because of the narrow focus of their schooling (Freeman, 1991a). It is too easy to let children who are keen to absorb more and more information to carry on doing so. Although it is the way to high scores in examinations, it is not the route to becoming a well-rounded adult. All children need their fair share of imaginative participation in art and writing, a touch of humour in everyday life, and a sense of proportion.

INFLUENCES ON CREATIVITY
Inhibitors:
* *Insecurity*: which makes one feel unable to risk stepping out of convention, since it may lead to fear.
* *Fear*: of offending other people's feelings, and of one's own ability to cope with the results of the creative act.
* *Pre-digested categories*: when other people have decided what should go with what, such as the school's distinction between history and geography, or physics and chemistry, which inhibits creative connections.

Reinforcers:
* *Emotional support*: can help a child over the fear and insecurity to reach out and be different.
* *Self-confidence*: to reach beyond what is assumed.

Although creative talent and academic success do not always coincide, almost all students are selected for high-level academic courses on the basis of their academic results, and yet are somehow supposed to be creative later on. There may even be conflict between the characteristics necessary for high academic achievement and those for creative work, so that some students may be wrongly chosen because of high academic marks, for example for university courses in architecture, where a creative outlook should also be looked for in the selection process. These apparently contradictory traits can, of course, co-exist in one individual.

PART THREE:
THE COMPETENCE-PROMOTING SYSTEM

CHAPTER IX

The education of teachers

During the 1960s, there was a widespread belief that social and economic progress could be ensured by wide-ranging change inside the education system. That optimism has not been sustained, however, and in the 1970s the thrust of this reform began to falter. Now, in the 1990s, growing youth unemployment in much of the world, together with the persistence of social inequalities deeply rooted in the social system – which educational reform on its own was apparently powerless to eradicate – have ushered in a sterner political climate, with new social theories to underpin it.

In many countries efforts are being made to improve the quality of teacher training in order to improve the quality of education, mostly by offering more difficult courses and extending the time taken to qualify. In the industrialized countries, however, this has coincided with three trends: the economic recession from 1974 onward; a fall in the rate of growth of the population; and a consequent fall in the demand for teachers. In response, most industrialized countries have cut back on their public expenditure on education, and there has been a fall-off in teacher recruitment, together with a general lowering of the status of their profession. In place of the goal of equality, which had been a feature of the 1960s, the emphasis is now on improving quality. This marks the difference in the ethical or moral commitment away from the euphoria of the 1960s, which underlies many of today's education policies, to a concern with quality.

The urge for improved quality includes teaching for basic competence – at least enough for all children to be able to get about in society. Consequently, the goal becomes not so much a sense of equal opportunity for all (an ephemeral idea with no specified standards), but rather that of higher quality for all. This also applies to the training of teachers because, with the drop in the number of posts available, there can be more careful selection of those who are appointed. It is also a reflection of the world trend in which knowledge and intellectual dealing has acquired a higher status than manufacturing as a generator of national income. All these changes of outlook result in changes in the content of teacher education.

In much of the world, teachers are suffering from an excess of changes in ideas and policy. As a result, their enthusiasm for new ideas may be somewhat exhausted, and some may feel that their profession is losing its integrity, and a more conservative 'back to basics' view is re-emerging – implying that such matters were not attended to in previous efforts to improve education. The very competence of teachers is under attack in much of the world; yet, to educate children for competence, the professional competence of the classroom teacher is paramount.

Inevitably, there is retraining to do, not least because many teachers practising today, and who will still be teaching in twenty years' time, were trained and appointed by tutors who were themselves trained in the 1960s and 1970s, if not well before then. They need some in-service help to adapt to the changes of teaching performance required for quality basic education; the inflow of new teachers will not be enough on its own. For that reason, many governments in the 1980s have been strengthening the provision for in-service training programmes to bring teachers up to date in their knowledge of specific areas or disciplines. In addition, there is a strong secondary aim of helping teachers to find out what they are good at, which might mean that their transfer to posts in subjects which are short of staff.

Higher salaries for teachers are not necessarily the best way to improve enthusiasm for teaching, even though, by any standard, teachers in many countries are badly underpaid. What clearly affects their contentment, however, are their working conditions. Roofs which leak, dirty staff washrooms, graffiti on the walls and tattered textbooks are all depressing – and destroy morale.

In order to educate rather than train children, teachers have to create an atmosphere in which rational and reflective thinking can take place. This means that they themselves must be able to use those abilities in their everyday teaching. Teachers are certainly most effective with pupils if they share a value system about what they are aiming for, and have respect for each other. Without it, or some sort of compromise, pupils are less likely to be interested in school-work and will drift away, either mentally in day-dreams, or physically by truancy.

Teachers are not always familiar with industry, and they would benefit by being more familiar with it, such as via work exchanges. This would also help them guide their pupils in vocational choice. It is important for educational bodies to invite workers, whether managing directors or trade-unionist leaders, into schools, and to take pupils into the work place for visits or work experience. Companies usually have materials and know-how which can be used by schools. They do also help finance special school projects and competitions.

TEACHERS

Men and women, of all kinds – young or old, stable or neurotic – can train to be teachers. They are a voluntary, self-selected population of people for whom neither the ability, nor even a real wish, to teach are required qualifications. In general, teachers have themselves enjoyed being taught and are often the children of teachers. But as they are often without much experience of the outside world, the teaching profession is sometimes said to be overly academic and inward-looking, which can produce a dulling effect in the classroom.

WHY PEOPLE BECOME TEACHERS
* *Security*: a regular salary for life in many countries.
* *Long holidays*: often quoted with envy by non-teachers – though these tend to get eaten away by extra-curricular activities such as in-service courses or second jobs. Short working days come into the same category.
* *Satisfaction*: the joy of teaching young minds can, at an extreme, become the love of power over a captive audience, although frustrated performers or autocrats can also be very good teachers. Satisfaction in teaching also includes meeting its constant challenge.
* *Respectability*: however hard the work, it is a clean job, and in developing countries can have a high-status, implying superior knowledge.
* *Fits in with school holidays*: this is a big pull for prospective or actual mothers, and so a 'natural' choice for educated women.
* *The system promotes its own*: to a person who has progressed through school and university, for example, with a degree in history or literature, teaching may appear to be the most obvious next step.

The objectives of training teachers. The role of the teacher includes that of a role model for imitation – 'text-book' teachers never get bad-tempered, disgruntled, bored and sarcastic, though real teachers do. However, as model adults, teachers should be better equipped with maturity, experience, knowledge and self-control than their pupils.

Qualifications. Details of the qualifications which teachers must gain to practise their profession vary from country to country. There are two basic routes, as well as other systems of apprenticeship in some developing countries.

PERSONAL REQUIREMENTS FOR TEACHING
* Teaching skills.
* Maturity and stability.
* Knowledge of the subject matter being taught.
* Understanding the processes of child development.
* Genuine concern and respect for pupils as people.
* Ability to fit in with the staff.
* Awareness of the school in its social setting.
* An open and lively mind.

University graduates usually take one further academic year to prepare for teaching. They study methods of teaching the specialist subject they had studied for the university degree, as well as educational psychology, and they also practice teaching under supervision. In addition, there will be outside lectures, seminars and visits to schools.

Colleges of education and higher education usually provide a three- or four-year training course for a qualification in education, whether for a certificate or a degree. A much wider variety of educational provision and teaching practice is possible in this time, though it must, of course, include the subject matter to be taught.

The training also forms an important part of the student's personal education. Many need it before they can enjoy teaching children, appreciate rediscovering the pleasures of learning and re-awaken dormant abilities in themselves. This applies especially to 'mature', late-starting students, who can be admitted on prospective merit but with lower exam successes than are required in younger candidates.

The essential content of courses

Though educational psychology is an integral part of all teacher-training programmes, it is rarely presented in the form in which it may be put to immediate practical use in the classroom. It is often rather over-burdened with theory and with psychological topics which are not entirely appropriate to teachers' needs. This means that its contributions to teaching skills are lost and teachers often hold it in low regard as being merely the academic contemplations of their tutors. It is not unknown for an inexperienced teacher, tutored mainly in the theories of teaching, to be given considerable responsibility in a very real classroom during teaching practice. But because teaching is almost entirely concerned with communication, the application of educational psychology based on research evidence as well as theory should be the core of all teacher training.

Field-work. Out-of-college studies can add valuable insight and effectiveness in the training of teachers, for example, in a child study. For this, students choose a child to study closely over a period of, say, two years and write up a detailed report. This includes a description of the child's home, relationships, school life and so on, and is entirely confidential. Shorter field-studies may involve evaluating groups of children or helping with 'difficult' children or visiting and evaluating institutions.

Field-work has the advantage of taking students out of the academic learning situation, at least for a while, into a variety of homes or educational places, and into other people's lives. The theoretical, examination-orientated aspects of educational psychology are complementary, but not a substitute for spending time with, adapting to and learning about even one real child. Students personally involved with both normal and abnormal children will be far more aware of children as individuals, and they normally report this spontaneously.

Micro-teaching. This is essentially a form of short lessons in small classes, which is being used more frequently in both the initial and post-experience training of teachers. A student-teacher prepares a ten-minute lesson for a small group of pupils while other students watch and take notes, or (if possible) record it on video. The student-teacher is given the feedback, takes note of any mistakes, and may remake the lesson to be tried again with another group of pupils. This method is considerably speedier and more effective than practice with a whole class; it is also applicable to many other types of training involving relationships, such as counselling or interviewing.

The benefits of learning through micro-teaching are impressive. The teacher's talking time drops by at least a third, including the number of times that questions are repeated, as well as the number of times teachers answer their own questions. They also interrupt discussions less frequently. As a result, the children's questions are more carefully thought out, and more complex, and they talk and learn more.

Assessment. Even with a basic understanding of psychological development, student teachers may emerge at the end of their course with little scientific basis for judgement of the children in their care. Unfortunately, it is possible for teachers to become qualified without the simplest understanding of statistics, such as the possible meanings of a comparison of children's scores on an achievement test or a class test (see Chapter VII). Furthermore, understanding an educational psychologist's report is not always straightforward for a teacher (although this may well be the fault of the psychologist).

Educational research. In general, appreciation of the fruits of educational research and the motivation to practise it are not given an important place in teacher-training courses. As a consequence, teachers place little value on research results, and are often antipathetic to research work in their schools. Researchers in turn tend to avoid the type of enquiry which disrupts the school routine, with the combined result that potentially valuable information, such as comparisons between the benefits of different reading schemes, tend to remain neglected.

Counselling and guidance. A teacher's self-understanding is the first step towards understanding others. Student-teachers who are able to make use of group counselling sessions, or to practise interviewing with feedback from others or on video, will be more aware of their performance, and better prepared for the role of developmental guide with children. Career guidance, for example, does not hinge on test results, but on the understanding of individuals. Since primary school-teachers have a particular responsibility for the emotional development of their pupils, it would clearly be beneficial if they were well prepared for this important aspect of their work.

The characteristics of practising teachers

Although teachers are as variable as any other people, the composition of the profession is partly defined by the routes taken to reach it. They bring their own amalgam of beliefs and experiences to school, but, unlike any pupil, they are in a position of considerable influence.

In many countries, the most obvious feature of teachers is their predominantly upward social mobility. It is a time-honoured route through which intelligent, hard-working, but poor, young people can enter a profession. It is also one of the few 'respectable' ways of earning a living for girls in some cultures. Even where women are emancipated, women student-teachers tend to come from a higher social class than the men, are likely to outnumber the men, and are likely to be better-achieving students. However, men are entering the profession in steadily increasing numbers, which has meant that they are tending more and more to assume the headships of mixed-sex primary and secondary schools, although the classroom teachers are more frequently women. The sex of a teacher affects classroom relationships, such as role identification, in both primary and secondary schools. Because the headteacher's influence is so pervasive, the effect of the changing balance of power between the sexes in schools deserves more research.

Teachers, not surprisingly, tend to value the education system which has benefited them. This attitude affects both their own aspirations and their perceptions of the way in which individual pupils fit in with the system. In fulfilling their role, most teachers speak to their pupils in a form of the language which is grammatically correct and considered suitable for imitation; this means that pupils whose morals, manners and out-of-school activities are clearly not in the approved style are likely to be at odds with the teacher's ideas of suitable styles of living. Research results indicate that teachers are more easily able to identify with and encourage pupils from social classes higher than themselves.

On the whole, teachers tend to be friendly, outgoing people who value human relationships more than objects or the way things work. They are often of well-above average intelligence, though they vary considerably in this respect. Greater differences have been found between the personalities of groups of teachers themselves than between those of teachers and the general population. Primary school-teachers, for instance, are happier when involved with children than are the teachers of adolescents, who sometimes have a tendency to involve themselves with their subject and see pupils simply as beneficiaries of it.

Teacher stress

Current educational concern is for teachers to be aware of their pupils as individuals, listening to them, and caring about their needs. No matter how adequate the other services available to the school, the teacher who is in daily contact with pupils must bear a large responsibility for their mental well-being, and it is probably true that most teachers are under some stress, whether physical or mental, as a result of their work. Daily contact with growing, active groups of children, together with the variety of human relationships implicit in an organization of any size, demand constant energy and ingenuity. Within a school, other members of staff can be supportive or destructive depending on the prevailing atmosphere.

No teacher can expect a perfect meeting with the minds of thirty or more children, but some meetings are less perfect than others. Many teachers are very distant from their pupils and have devised impenetrable psychological defences, teaching in a rigid formal way year after year, sometimes spending even less than the allotted period in the classroom. They are out of touch both with their pupils and the times. Although no new teacher would want to be like them, they appear to have coped with stress in their own ways. Perhaps it is the caring teacher who is more vulnerable to the various stresses of the work.

Insecure teachers, who retreat from seeing their pupils as people, may hide behind institutional pupil/teacher roles, and teaching in a role-bound way can be counter-effective. An extreme example of this might be an ambitious, middle-class teacher practising in a poor district. She might neither talk to her pupils in their own 'language', nor recognize their life-styles as being essential to them – either during the school situation or when they go home again. Alienation and mutual unhappiness are then all too likely. Communication is not only verbal: enthusiasm, eye-contact, loving physical contact with little ones, and so on, are all parts of getting the meaning across.

Not all teachers welcome their position of authority. Refusal to accept it and crude attempts to identify with pupils as equals can be very confusing for pupils, who are capable of rejecting unhealthy teacher friendship quite bluntly – a blow to the teacher's self-image. At the other extreme, true authority which is based on respect may be unjustifiably assumed. A teacher must be in charge of the classroom, and failures of teacher self-discipline, such as constant lateness, an observable dislike of the work, bad technique, shortage of knowledge, and so on, will detract from authority and order, inviting chaos into the classroom and lowering pupil learning.

Teachers appear to suffer greatly from monotony in their teaching and the inertia that goes with it, the lack of will to change things, killing the joy that should be part of teaching and learning. Bored teachers create bored pupils and lead to the attendant classroom problems. The reasons for this include giving the same lessons to a different set of similar names and faces every year, the constant repetition of teaching points in the same classroom situation, the persistent need to play the teacher's role, and the energy needed for daily enthusiasm. It is brought about by having to wait for equipment that never comes, or by accepting boring ways of teaching as normal.

To do their best in the daily grind, teachers need encouragement, which can be brought about by putting more (not less) power in their hands. This would necessarily involve greater control over spending: most schools do, in fact, have some free money to spend above what is needed for basic running costs, which comes either from careful housekeeping or from local fund-raising. This requires greater co-operation between the staff, which can draw them together at the same time and improve their team spirit.

Classroom teachers need enough freedom to use their own initiative. Access to a 'resource fund' for independent research or innovative ideas and enterprise would be valuable, with prizes awarded for such successes as improvements in the curriculum, reduced running costs or better school organization. Easier transfer between the different roles in education – for example, administration, inspecting and research – should be built into contracts of employment.

In each school, there should be a group devoted to teaching entrepreneurial skills – if not the whole staff. They would meet regularly to come up with new ideas for the management of learning, as well as those who are currently looking at the curriculum. They should look for ways of using locally available facilities such as those available from parents and employers. Teachers should know the school's specific aims, how it works, and how they can play a part in it.

Difficult as it may appear, teachers can be helped to deal with stress by applying the lessons they may have learned in educational psychology to themselves.

STRESS REDUCTION

* *Self-awareness*: Teachers, like pupils, should have access to a trained counsellor to help them put their actions, successes and failures into perspective. Group discussion between teachers is often helpful, especially out of the school setting, say at a teachers' centre. Techniques such as role-playing of problems in groups can help to promote insight. Headteachers are often in lonely positions and could reap special benefit from group meetings.

* *Respect is a two-way process*: When teachers have genuine respect for others in the school, as well as expecting it themselves, they are less likely to have stress problems.

* *Rest*: Teachers need real breaks during a working day. Free time should not be filled by marking exercises and preparing lessons. A teacher who finds that most evenings are spent on school work should examine his or her methods of work and the school's expectations. Over-conscientious teachers are not always the best at making human relationships.

* *Variety*: Overcoming monotony calls for constant extra effort, such as changes in teaching routine, altering the emphasis within the syllabus, refresher courses and an experimental, creative approach to teaching, etc.

* *Leaving*: If teaching is constantly distressful, the head seems a petty dictator, the regulations like a maze of tripwires, and the school atmosphere stifling, it would seem wise to change schools. Otherwise, a long, if not permanent, break from teaching might be the answer.

TEACHING FOR HIGH ABILITY

There are always special needs in teaching which require special attention, and although student-teachers are often in a position to learn about the teaching of slow-learners, it is rare to find courses for them on how to teach children of high potential (see Chapter V). This lack of focus in training may either come through unawareness or as a deliberate policy – attitudes may be deliberately vague or positively hostile because of perceived elitism. As a result, most classroom teachers who are faced with teaching the potentially highly able are unlikely to have the expertise to plan and adapt lessons specially for them and to adjust to their learning processes, even if they have given the matter much thought themselves.

Providing the educational facilities and care that are needed by the highly able is one aspect of creating better education for all children. It calls for something different from the regular provision and depends on the school staff having a flexible outlook, as well as patience and enthusiasm, to help children make the most of their educational experiences. Increased awareness of the need to identify potentially bright children can enhance the teacher's sensitivity towards individual differences in general. Indeed, changes in the curriculum on behalf of the highly able are usually conceptual, and can improve the cognitive level in the classroom. With teachers' enthusiasm, special help can be offered to highly able children in ordinary schools, sometimes in unusual subjects. The teacher is in a position to enhance creative thought with an open, questioning, and challenging style of teaching, providing a safe atmosphere in which the highly able might try out their intellectual wings.

At a basic level, a further reason for the relative neglect of the highly able is that the responsible authorities are rarely in agreement about what to do about them, especially with regard to the content of courses, so that the role of teachers in dealing with these pupils is ill-defined. Many educators actually believe that it is enough to give able pupils extra work on top of what they are already doing and, even where special provision does exists for them, it usually takes the form of yet more information, rather than improved thinking skills. It should be recognized that teaching initiatives for highly able children benefit all pupils, since they involve the overall improvement of the teachers' classroom skills.

Indeed, the educator who is confronted with the task of providing for the highly able finds it too easy to retreat behind the very real problems of definition and identification. In many countries, school principals are apt to deny the needs of their exceptionally able pupils, believing that all the children are already catered for as individuals. If all else fails, an ailing economic climate can be used as a reason for lack of action. Teacher training in this area is also hampered by a lack of research to show exactly what is effective. Additional features which militate against effective training include the pressure of time in one-year, post-graduate courses, and the fact that many training college staff are not themselves acquainted with this 'minority' area of educational studies.

Sometimes, educational authorities do have good intentions for their brightest pupils – courses are planned, policies formulated and intentions expressed to appoint specialist advisers, 'when the economy improves'. The aims which may be formulated include opportunities for schools to get together and experiment with new courses or teaching methods, opportunities for acceleration, enriched curricula, weekend activities, guideline booklets for teachers, specialist schools for specific abilities in the arts, co-operative ventures between schools and higher education institutions, and a real interest from the schools' psychological services. But often there is little real progress towards realizing those ideas: genuine mixed-ability teaching and learning which is tailored to individual needs are still not common.

Training for teaching the highly able

It is important that the teachers of the highly able should be of sufficient calibre in knowledge and skills. There are many ways of improving teachers' ability to deal effectively with their brightest pupils – either during first-level training or as in-service courses – and none need involve heavy expenditure. For example, existing teachers' centres could be used to improve awareness and stimulate ideas through information about such pupils, including such resources as enrichment materials. Contact and co-ordination on these matters between different local education authorities would assist in defining criteria by which the provision for such children might be assessed on a national level.

Any course of training for future or practising teachers of the highly able should aim to cover the following elements:

Identification skills. Experienced teachers often claim to be able to identify able pupils by 'instinct'. Some common pointers which they can use for this purpose include:
–   the speed with which able pupils grasp concepts;
–   their ability to think out problems;
–   their obvious above-average ability to cope with the learning material;
–   their speed of thinking;
–   their ability to ask intelligent questions;
–   their initiative;
–   their relating of new work to things which have gone before;
–   their ability to draw out implications and conclusions and to assimilate facts quickly;
–   their possession of lively and enquiring minds.

Other similar checklists can be valuable, if used with the proviso that they are not decisive indicators. Because a child's social behaviour is as heavily influenced by his environmental circumstances as is his ability, teachers also need to be aware of social aspects of testing procedures, such as the relative merits and interpretation of tests of attainment, intelligence and reading. Though some tests require a qualified person to administer them, a teacher should be able to make a fair judgement about the meaning of the scores on pupils' records.

Under-achieving bright pupils are especially difficult to identify. They may be bored, restless, orally fluent but poor in written work, friendly only with older pupils or adults, excessively self-critical yet apparently also quick-thinking. There are those who are creative, able to solve problems, ask provocative questions and think in abstract terms. Sometimes highly able under-achievers may have been bullied by their school-mates into mediocrity, and it is important – both academically and in terms of the emotional climate of the classroom – for teachers to be aware of the current emotional and potential educational problems of such children.

Managing the curriculum. It is part of the repertoire of all teachers to be able to guide what children learn. For highly able pupils, the curriculum is too often based on an inadequate model of knowledge, and needs to be enriched with more stimulating and complex cognitive demands. To do this, teachers not only require a sound knowledge of cognitive development, but also a grasp of the aims, intentions and objectives of the curriculum they are offering, along with those of individual schemes of study and individual lessons. The abilities essential for teachers of the highly able are to formulate clear intentions, provide interesting and provocative learning experiences, and assess the nature and extent of the learning which results from them.

Too often, initial college training stops short of curriculum building in favour of syllabus construction, and newly qualified teachers are assumed to possess the very skills they have not yet acquired. Faced with pupils who read voraciously, reason quickly, absorb information rapidly, question, invent problems, provide creative solutions, and cope with concepts and abstract ideas at a young age, many teachers are left floundering. It is then, while concentrating on the slower learners, that they tend to fall back on simply providing extra work of the same kind for those children, as a defence against the challenge of what seems to be an insuperable problem.

Using language appropriately. For teachers of highly able pupils, certain skills are particularly useful on a lesson-by-lesson basis, especially verbal interactions between teachers and pupils. The spoken language of classrooms revolves around three main transactions: teachers' talk; teachers' questions; and pupils' responses or initiations. The cognitive demand of a lesson – a significant factor in the satisfaction of the able pupil – can be recognized by the level, the speed and quality of verbal transactions.

The relative proportions of low- and high-level talk, and questions and responses which go to make up a stimulating, effective lesson for able pupils are open to argument, yet the teacher can use these means to stimulate the able pupils while not losing or alienating the others. Because high-level thinking, shown by verbal interactions, represents only a small percentage of normal classroom life, the following teacher-skills may be particularly important for improving this picture:

- clarity of explanation;
- conscious use of language at an appropriate level;
- the ability to raise pupils' thinking levels by more demanding questions;
- a problem-solving approach to learning (as opposed to a data-based approach);
- the skill of handling individualized learning.

Improving task demand. Any impartial observer, looking over the tasks which children are set in the classroom, might be forgiven for concluding that some of them are trivial and that the cognitive demand they make on youngsters is often relatively slight. Highly able pupils are capable of and want increased cognitive stimulation.

An example is offered by a study theme which can be taken at any level – colour in nature: such as colour for camouflage, colour for display, and colour for communication in herds or by individuals. Additionally, each of these aspects of the study can be pursued in depth. Colour for camouflage may examine the use of a single tone, of pattern, of mimicry and of change, as well as pursuing questions about the effectiveness of each strategy; why it is likely to have evolved, and how the adaptation works in practice. Relationships between the various aspects of the study would be pursued, for example, to point out conflicting evolutionary needs for camouflage and display which may account for sexual variations in the plumage of some common birds.

This type of study could be made to highlight the conceptual framework which is necessary for proper understanding – an appropriate use of technical language, and a problem-posing as well as a problem-solving approach to thinking. Tasks emerging from a study that was planned in this way would be likely to have both immediacy and a relevance to observed phenomena; and they would also be unlikely to result in simplistic classroom activities, such as copying, drawing and passive listening or regurgitation.

Enrichment materials. The highly able need to have access to special enriched curricular materials to occupy them when they finish assignments early, even if it is not directly related to the lesson. This extra material could be shared by a group of schools, or it could be housed in the school library and the child given permission to go out of the classroom to use it. In fact, that sort of reward, implying work well done and responsibility for oneself, also offers valuable motivation to do well.

Highly able children like a challenge, and they usually enjoy thinking creatively round a subject. For example, they could be set an essay on 'What would happen if the temperature in the world changed?' or 'What if there was always daylight?'. They often love playing with words, especially using proverbs and idioms. One exercise could be to draw everything you can think of beginning with the letter 'A'. Commercial toys and games are also available to teachers as teaching resources, many of which are designed to increase children's skills of observation and planning. Teaching thinking skills, by whatever means, should not be an added extra for children of high ability, but an integrated part of the learning context for all children.

Organizing the education of the highly able

Acceleration. Acceleration is a form of individual selection in which a highly able child is promoted above his age group by a year or two. It is undoubtedly the easiest move administratively, but is not always successful because children's psycho-social maturity can lag behind their cognitive development. Indeed, Freeman's (1991a) research in the United Kingdom found that acceleration is often harmful, both emotionally and academically, although American experience is more favourable to this move, and there are probably other cultural differences which would make the integration of younger children into older age groups easier.

It is often assumed that acceleration is a form of enrichment because it exposes the child to a more advanced level of knowledge and thinking. In practice, the older children in the new class may simply be working on the same intellectual lines as before, but with an additional year's acquisition of information – arguably, some of the intellectual excitement the move brings to the highly able child is making this up with little tuition. Thus, although the accelerated, highly able child may be able to make progress in picking up what has been missed, advanced intellectual stimulation cannot be assumed. Moreover, because of the obligation to speed up the learning, there is no certainty that its foundations are firm and accurate. Certainly, as far as the child's non-scholastic emotional development is concerned, the idea has to be approached with extreme caution, and probably as a last resort.

Educational selection of the highly able. One or two talents of a particular kind seem to call for special full-time education. Most specialist schools for the highly able around the world are for music and the performing arts, notably dance, but there are also others for technology, mathematics and languages. There are also schools which select children by their general intellectual capacity and, although they are not 'officially' schools for the gifted, the intake of children is of an extremely high level. In fact, few such schools offer specialist education for these potential intellectual high-flyers, and the education provided is usually designed simply to see them through their examinations at an earlier and higher level than their age-peers.

It is undoubtedly true that grouping bright children together for teaching helps them make better progress in their school work. It must also be true that such children have to mark time in most mixed-ability classes without careful differentiated teaching. The vast majority of bright children, however, are neither separated into special schools, nor do they receive true mixed-ability teaching. They are more likely to be sorted into differently sized groups of roughly the same ability, usually by school tests and teacher opinion (as described in Chapter VII).

Provision for specialist groups of highly able children can be made by restructuring the school timetable to include periods of independent learning for them. But this can also be carried out less formally by individual teachers. For example, if the geography teacher has noticed that her top few pupils seem to be keen to get on with the subject, she should be able to approach other members of staff who teach them to suggest that they be allowed to work on specific projects, either in the geography room or outside. She would have to be sure that they knew the current work well, and that what she set them to do was not simply more of the same, but was rather of a compatible and enriching nature.

Part-time withdrawal. The idea of taking children out of normal classes for remedial teaching is normally accepted and acceptable because the children are recognized as having a need for special education which overrides that of keeping them with their classmates all of the time. Withdrawal, unlike after-school activities, is not voluntary; pupils are given it at the school's discretion, and so it is an integrated part of the school curriculum.

In the United States it is not unusual to find gifted children withdrawn from normal classes for special education, though this is rarely done in other countries. Teachers fear that, by selecting some children as bright, it will detract from their class-relationships by promoting jealousy and snobbery. But perhaps deeper than this is the implicit threat to the teacher's own competence. Such feelings may be quite unconscious, but many teachers cannot help but feel offended that somehow taking the children out of their class for something better implies that they are not good enough. They complain that routine is disrupted by such moves and the child misses ordinary lessons.

Despite such objections, the benefits of withdrawal are beginning to be documented (at least in the United States). These benefits are not only in higher academic achievement, but also in terms of the children's' self-confidence and interest, more positive attitudes towards school and school-work, and even greater modesty. Withdrawal seems to be both beneficial and much appreciated by the children concerned, and it does not seem to have the side-effect of upsetting the others in the class unless it is tactlessly done: it would be insensitive, for example, to take the gifted children out for an exciting field trip while the others have to stay indoors and do arithmetic.

Giving intellectually highly able children the opportunity to work at their own pace, even for a while, may mean that they need more concentrated supervision during that time. This does not have to be a problem if it is acknowledged that such help is not entirely dependent on teachers. Parents can step in on specialist subjects in which they are experts; older pupils too can be very helpful, if the school has the kind of atmosphere in which co-operation, rather than competition, is encouraged.

The highly able in the mixed-ability classroom. Like any other pupils, the highly able need the pleasure and stimulation of variety, and the excitement that can be generated from different combinations of ideas. That is why when lessons are too easy, as in most mixed-ability classrooms, the highly able are excluded from the rewards that other pupils get – the satisfaction of tackling and resolving problems. To compensate, they may deliberately make trouble, either in their own minds or among others in the classroom, just to taste the spice of stimulation. Without that, school-work becomes a rather boring matter of taking in and reproducing what the teacher says, and the flame of discovery burns low. The answer, of course, is to provide the highly able with education that is appropriate to their needs.

A major problem for the highly able in a mixed-ability class is in adapting socially with classmates, yet remaining intellectually alive and different from them. Expecting a child to think at a level of brilliance, while others around are behaving normally, demands enough exceptional maturity to show gifted behaviour at times and conformity to social norms at others. If, in addition, the deep-thinking child regards lessons as somewhat pointless and deems the system less than relevant, probably more than other children, he may well feel some sense of alienation and purposelessness.

The normal classroom is a fairly structured place of activities focused on content, so that the pupil's performance is correctable. Pupils who are interested in ideas for their own sake require time to think and can benefit from a looser structure in their learning. The very essence of their high potential is at risk, and expecting them to conform to social norms in the classroom can be detrimental to their uniqueness. Pupils who feel obliged to subdue their own personalities in that way may also suffer damage to their self-concept.

The highly able are particularly vulnerable to the 'three-times problem' (Freeman, 1991a, and Chapter V). In a normal classroom the teacher frequently gives out information three times. She says it once to introduce it, again to remind the children, and a third time to summarize and reinforce. The highly able hear it and remember it the first time round. They do not want the tedium of hearing it again and again, so they sometimes devise a technique of listening to the new material the first time and switching off for the next two. This a very high level of skill, which involves listening without registering.

The danger is that when they have discovered this way out of the 'three-times problem', they practise this skill to such a standard that it can function almost automatically. While they are reaching this point, they are likely to miss some of the teaching the first time round. Hence, they may leave out some of the building blocks in the learning process and miss vital information. Fortunately, this is not always a problem in a class of reasonably mixed-ability, as the lesson will doubtless be repeated the next day, and they can catch up if they are listening. Nevertheless, this switching off can become a dangerous habit: it becomes easier to remove themselves into dreamland, into solving a problem of their own devising, than simply to accommodate new information. The learning of the highly able can thus seem erratic, and with bits of material missing, they can come to wrong but firmly held conclusions.

Even in a selective school, the 'three-times' teaching rule still holds, although at a higher level of teaching. Since it is likely that the information will vary more on each telling it will retain some intrinsic interest. But, even in such a school, there is always a difference in ability between various members of the class, so the switch-off problem will still function for some pupils in every case.

CHAPTER X

The school
in the community

SCHOOL FUNCTIONS

All over the world, education is associated with improved cognitive development, and when schools have been closed due to war, political disruption or natural disaster, children's measured intelligence has been found to drop. The relative importance of the school, however, varies with children's circumstances: those from poor backgrounds can sometimes suffer a drop in IQ even during the long summer vacation, when their active participation in school life stops (Husén & Tuijnman, 1991). When a variety of secondary schools in London were assessed for their effect on children's attitudes to learning, optimum results were seen to have been achieved by a combination of two factors: the pupils' active learning experiences; and a social atmosphere in the school which promoted self-confidence and an interest in learning outside the formal environment (Rutter, 1985). Children, however, do vary in sensitivity to their environments, and the extent to which a school can foster effective learning also depends on the attitudes pupils bring with them from home.

In education, politics are unavoidable, not least because most of the world's children are educated at public expense with the not unexpected result that there is contention about what should be taught. Some favour a core curriculum of the 'three Rs' – reading, 'riting and 'rithmetic – while others want to broaden it to include subjects like peace or anti-racism. Then there is the battle over the pupil intake of schools: should it be selective or comprehensive? Within the schools, too, there are the many ways of subdividing children, such as streaming or setting, which can strongly affect their daily lives and self-concepts. Both local and national education authorities demand particular kinds of education, as do influential bodies such as religious groups – with their different subdivisions – while universities and colleges require specified kinds of preparation for their courses. Employers want literacy and mathematical skills, while intellectuals insist that children should learn to think.

Education is about power; in particular, the relative control of central or local government over the curriculum and the way it is taught. Many central governments control school curricula, public examinations, the core curriculum, subject teaching, regular testing, and the in-service training of teachers. Such centralization is, however, often resisted by the local education authorities, the schools and their teachers, who see it as an erosion of individual initiative and responsibility, and thus a threat to the very nature of education. Strong local control means that the quality, style and provision for education throughout a country will vary with the outlook of each local authority and what it wants as the end-product, as well as due to the inevitable competition for money between education and other services.

SCHOOL ORGANIZATION

In the child-centred approach to teaching, current in many advanced countries, the concern is that schools should offer pupils opportunities for educational satisfaction and personal growth. To be child-centred, a school attempts to provide a variety of differentiated activities centred on each child's learning needs, although it is the teachers who carry a large share of the burden of pursuing these aims. Introducing meaning into children's learning with individual projects and interests means replacing a rigid timetable with careful preparation for teaching guided by the child's individuality. In the society-centred school, which is more usual in developing countries, more attention is paid to rules and to recognized ways of behaving – past and present – and it is particularly orientated to passing on basics skills, such as numeracy and literacy, taught in traditional ways.

There is as much need in poor countries as in rich ones for well-educated and able leaders, who need the appropriate educational provision as children for that role when they grow up. In the developing world, where resources are stretched to the limit, concern for the highly able is rare, because educational provision is constrained not only by lack of money but also by culturally shaped points of view. And yet, even in rich countries, governments are reluctant to provide special education for the more able.

In the long run, the principal goal of any school should be to enable children to continue learning when they are outside its direct influence. No school is merely a machine for passing on information, since it always acts to some extent as a developmental guide. Part of its function is an attempt to uphold and instil the values of the society from which the pupils come, and which it represents. Some schools leave room for pupils to grow in their own way, while others act as coercing funnels from which the emerging young person can be recognized as acting in the approved manner. While they may reflect society at large, individual schools inevitably develop a 'personality' of their own. Moral standards in schools tend to be higher than family morals; for example, taking food from the school kitchen is normally regarded as stealing (an attitude which is unlikely to have the same value at home), or dirty clothes on children may indicate moral deficiency to teachers, and politeness – 'please' and 'thank you', and opening doors for teachers – may be more important at school than they are considered to be outside.

The pupil's sense of obligation with regard to school learning – in fact with regard to all school behaviour – depends on the extent to which he feels that the school and the teachers are doing their best and fulfilling their part in the implicit learning contract between them. For example, children will be more obliged to put greater effort into learning when they feel that the school provides an appropriate and efficient framework for their development, and that the teacher is conscientious about her work and proficient at it.

The teacher's influence on a child's motivation obviously interacts with other factors, but it particularly affects the pupil's learning orientation – the goals for which the pupil aims. The combination of motivation to high achievement and good learning strategies will lead to success in most subjects and at most levels of ability, as can be seen in Japan, for instance. This is particularly relevant in countries where strict admission quotas control entry to university, so that students who aim to enter university must be at their peak of efficiency to be accepted. Schools can help best by guiding pupils to discover good learning procedures and by encouraging their motivation to aim as high as they can.

The school is an artificial situation, dominated and authorized by adults for children. Researchers have found that children initiate activity in school very much less frequently than they would consider doing at home. Children with a drive to be creative, expressive and to think for themselves, are likely to be particularly distressed by the rigid structure of many schools which seem to be organized for the benefit of the teachers rather than the pupils. Like any other institution, a school which is unable – or unwilling – to cope with individuals, but attempts to mould them to the system, will probably provoke antagonism in those who are lively and searching.

As in many organizations, a school is structured as a hierarchy. The people at the top have more status than others lower down; power filters down from the head via the staff to the pupils, and maybe then to the domestic staff. Unless the process of spreading information and the recognized power of every person in the hierarchy are clearly understood, considerable distress can be caused, which may be reflected in the teaching. Much of the atmosphere of a school reflects the personality and vigour of the headteacher, no matter what the official style. The head always has the job of key decision-making, even in the leadership of a democratic school in which pupils and other members of the school may have some say in what happens. More unusually, a school is run by a committee, the intention being to operate as a co-operative rather than a competitive institution. Chairing the committee is difficult, and takes a great deal of time in discussion. Research on school organization finds that a school's smooth running depends largely on how the head is perceived to behave by the rest of the school staff. Paradoxically, an autocratic head may be regarded as 'fair', while a democratic one may appear to be 'uncaring', and the latter is often seen as the greater fault.

There is immense variety among the world's schools. Most secondary or high schools are comprehensive, bringing all the neighbourhood children together under one roof, but they may also co-exist alongside schools which select by intellect, technical skill, or other special abilities such as music. Complaints about comprehensive schools centre on the lack of attention from teachers for individuals, poor intellectual discipline and stimulus, and poor curricular provision. Schools in culturally poor areas tend to be less ambitious for their pupils, whereas complaints about highly selective academic schools often relate to the over use of children's learning abilities. When examination pressure is great and the pupils' own values and interests have a low priority, the result can be sterile thinking and, ultimately, direction and instruction rather than a broad education. Because most selective schools assume that their pupils will go on to higher education, practical subjects usually have low status.

No one kind of school can be wholly better for all children than another, because no school is adequate to meet all the pupils' needs all the time, or to be totally responsible for all their learning. For example, it is mostly verbal skills which are advanced in school, whereas the visuospatial skills are more often acquired in the incidental learning of daily life. There are many different ways in which children could learn new skills, such as sampling adult work, through specialist out-of-school activities, or even by spending time in other kinds of schools.

Schools in deprived areas and developing countries have a particularly heavy responsibility when parents cannot provide a sufficient contribution. In such situations it helps to think of the school as being 'without walls' – not to think of education as confined to the school building. Within the school, however, the pupils' sense of efficacy and competence can be enhanced by giving them responsibility in working for the school community. With some help, they can be involved in administration, the accounts and especially in designing the syllabus, as long as it is done in such a way that the children do not lose money by it. Both governments and industry could support such schemes by paying the children as much for their work in the school as they would have earned working outside – otherwise they cannot afford to stay in school.

An example of such a scheme is Project Mala, which was set up in 1988 in Uttar Pradesh in India to free children from the exploitation of the carpet-weaving industry. Six schools were due to be opened, offering education together with vocational training and health care, and paying a small wage to replace the money earned from weaving. Despite the help of the state government, only one of these schools now exists, and the national government shows no sign of expanding the project.

THE MOST IMPORTANT GOALS OF A GOOD SCHOOL

1. **Making a distinct effort towards reaching academic and vocational goals for all the pupils, demonstrated by a large proportion of the teachers' time being devoted to active teaching, group planning of the curriculum, regular setting and marking of homework, and checks to be sure that the intended practices are being followed.**
2. **Promoting efficient learning by good classroom management, such as lessons beginning and ending on time, clear feedback to pupils on their performance, minimum disciplinary interruptions and effective teaching techniques.**
3. **Aiding high morale, for example by generous but discriminating use of praise and encouragement, adequate materials and conditions for learning, good examples of behaviour in teachers and good care of the school buildings.**
4. **Maintaining a balance of abilities in the children coming into the school, where this is possible, and setting suitably high expectations of all pupils by teachers.**
5. **Providing opportunities for most pupils to take some responsibility and participate in the running of their school, including out-of-school activities shared between staff and pupils, so that they can work in harmony towards achieving educational goals.**
6. **Encouraging the pupils to feel that the school and the teachers are doing their best to fulfil their part in the learning contract. This affects pupils' sense of obligation and orientation to learning, which is reinforced when they feel that the school provides an appropriate and efficient framework for their self-development, including their general attitudes to education.**

Schools in operation

Pupil roles. Just as a child must learn that there is one way to behave at home and another at the grandparents' house, so must the pupil learn about school too. Children who go to nursery school before the age of 5 have already made considerable adaptation to being in a group, and so 'settle down' much more quickly when they get to 'proper' school than those who have not had that experience. A certain amount of socialization is essential if children are to participate in activities with others, but an over-rigid school, where the low level of noise gives the impression of permanent examinations, may evoke a feeling of unease in them. The effects of repressive schooling can be seen in the children's creative work – dull, neatly written, and correctly spelled essays, with cross-repetition of set phrases from the teacher. Art-work, too, tends to be stereotyped in these circumstances, as children learn which style gains the highest approval.

In a school where overriding importance is attached to the transfer of information, along with the imposition of discipline, children who play their role well are attentive and retentive of learning. But lack of internally controlled discipline and the stifling of intelligent curiosity in pupils is a sad educational price to pay for a smoothly running institution. Nor is the high moral behaviour expected of good school role-playing necessarily that of a real conscience which will function well in adult life. Genuine awareness of social behaviour is a product of maturation and experience; it is an aspect of rational thinking and works independently of external social demands. Such mature, rational behaviour in adolescents can appear to teachers as rebellion against the petty dictatorship of school rules, and a refusal to play the obedient-pupil role.

Schools often accentuate sex roles. In most mixed primary schools, for example, girls are separated out for girls' subjects, such as needlework, and boys learn technical skills, such as woodwork. In schools which are divided by sex, any subject matter considered appropriate for one or the other will be emphasized or omitted on that basis.

School discipline. When children begin school for the first time, they bring along a ready-made set of attitudes from home, and because schools have their own values and standards, difficulties can arise when those from home are not the same. What may seem minor matters to the world outside, such as girls' jewellery or length of boys' hair, can erupt into bitter home/school disputes.

When behaviour at school is very different to that at home, children may be expected to take some time to adjust to being pupils. The amount and form of control that parents have used in early upbringing, whether strict or easy-going, will notably affect the ease with which the child adjusts to the requirements of the school. Children from homes where strong physical punishment is used are likely to be more aggressive in behaviour but, on the other hand, lack of control at home also leads to a type of aggression associated with frustration, when a child is unaccustomed to the school restrictions. External control always comes before internal control; the two seem to combine most effectively in a loving and supportive environment. Some internal control, the earliest form of conscience, is usually in operation by the time a child starts school.

Many schools rank obedience and discipline as a first priority for their pupils. The child from a more authoritarian home will not find this too difficult, but one from a democratic home may well be confused; spontaneous questioning must be curbed, for example, and a certain autonomy forfeited. The spread of more democratic behaviour from the infant school upwards is overcoming more rigid types of secondary schooling in many countries, so that children are becoming less bound by rules and fear of punishment, and even very young ones are closer to actively participating in planning their own education.

School/home relationships. A child who spends half his waking hours in a school which all but refuses to recognize parental influence is being cheated of some educational opportunity and is obliged to split his developing psychological life in two. Many children are caught in the psychologically harmful dichotomy of 'Teacher says this' and 'Mother says that', where Teacher and Mother never talk about their different approaches.

Quite apart from the financial benefits of parents' involvement, schools which work closely with parents are often able to use the educational assistance which they are mostly glad to give. A parent who can listen to children read, take a class round a factory, or describe how a car engine works, is bringing the real world through the school gate. Schools which deny the role of parents as educators or who fear that by opening the door to them the status of their teachers will drop, appear to have little faith in their own expertise, which may be apparent in a greater degree of rigidity and control.

The opposite problem, parents who are without interest in their children's schooling, is less common. Yet there are times when, in spite of every effort by the school staff, there is virtually no communication between home and school. Some schools organize home visits by teachers and social workers, but these are extremely time consuming and expensive, if not actually impossible in widespread school catchment areas.

A type of school recently developed to bridge the gap between home and school is the community school, which exists in several countries. In the most open examples, parents and children are able to sit in lessons together, including evening tuition and participation in other activities, which are also open to everyone. Although still partly experimental, this effort at educating a whole community could have a beneficial effect, both practical and psychological, on all concerned.

The school does not operate in a social vacuum, any more than the home does; both are engaged in continuous interaction with the surrounding society. At the same time, they are the two most important influences on the (far from passive) child. When either of these educational influences is inadequate, the child is the loser. Should both home and school fail to provide some aspect of educational enrichment, such as music or art, then apart from chance opportunities, the child may remain impoverished in those areas. To avoid such omissions both home and school should be equally free to supplement each other, where there seems to be some lack of provision.

School buildings. The age and layout of school buildings inevitably affect the type of teaching which can take place within them. Team teaching, for instance, works best in an open space, and the older type of school, built with classrooms faced with glass around a central hall, can discourage new forms of teaching. When buildings are old and facilities poor, the imagination of the teachers is the prime resource for educational opportunity.

ENRICHMENT IN EDUCATION

Educational enrichment is the deliberate rounding out of the basic curriculum subjects with ideas and knowledge that enable a pupil to be aware of the wider context. It is not a supplementary diet which depends on whether there is enough money for 'extra' material and tuition, but should be an everyday part of school provision. This is a particularly important aspect of education for highly able youngsters who have the potential to go far beyond the elements of any particular area of study, relate it to other areas, and play with ideas so as to come up with new ones. The teacher's task in enriching the curriculum is to provide the groundwork, and to guide and encourage pupils to explore this further. Because enrichment does not always take place either in the school buildings or during school time, teachers may have to make an effort to be involved, or at least familiar, with what pupils are doing elsewhere.

Enrichment activities, unless they are taken in groups, should be tuned to the learner's interests and learning styles. Youngsters must be sincere in wanting to follow a particular topic or activity which they themselves have chosen to take further; when the interest is one's own, it guarantees motivation and makes success more likely. This can take place in the school classroom using extension learning materials, in the school or public library, in the community, or even through a correspondence course in which the student and the instructor never meet. Youngsters will need some introduction to areas that they have not considered before, and enough unpressured time to choose before they commit themselves to time spent working on it. Others, although they believe they know what they want to do, should also be made aware of related subjects with which they may not have had any contact, to broaden the scope of the project. It should be made clear to the pupils from the outset that they are expected to pursue their explorations purposefully and that, after a suitable period of time, each one will be responsible for analysing the experiences gained, and coming up with some new ideas for further study.

In schools which have a policy of providing enriched education, the professional staff are encouraged to develop their skills through in-service courses and workshop activities. Additionally, during the school day, teachers will be able to co-ordinate different subjects, for example, relating the basic material in one subject area to that of others; this is more likely to be beneficial to the learner than further detailed study of the same subject. An example would be when history and geography specialists, whether in their own classrooms or together, co-ordinate their teaching about the Second World War, which would give a more rounded picture of events than either one working alone.

There are many ways to loosen up the rigidity of formal teaching, where each child is locked by age or school-class into the same lessons, timing and homework, regardless of ability and maturity. Many human aptitudes are better developed outside the classroom than in it. Bright children especially can benefit greatly through contact with professionals who are not primarily educators: artists, performers, agricultural and industrial scientists, scholars, craftspeople and others. It is not always lack of money which prevents them doing this. It needs a fresh outlook, a real concern, a willingness to alter routine – to think differently. Even though the kind of learning which takes place outside the scholastic setting is not always obvious and not easy to measure in conventional academic assessment, it usually results in improvement in school achievement. The wider gains for the child lie in the advantages of improved understanding, and relating and forming new ideas, along with the positive personal rewards of enhanced self-concept and improved ability to cope with life.

There seems to be a fear among teachers that if you give children an enriched education they will do less well in their formal exams. The likelihood is, in fact, that when they spend more time on enrichment, they do better in their exams, particularly at scholarship levels, which calls for a rounded approach to the subject, and not merely a repetition of learned facts.

IDEAS FOR EDUCATIONAL ENRICHMENT

* *Integrated teaching.* Integration of what is taught in a school implies harmony in acquiring knowledge, in both breadth and depth. It means that teachers form a 'learning web' for the pupils, starting with one subject and pulling in other fields and ideas. Another image is a wheel with spokes: the hub is the nucleus of the area, such as the local football team, with the spokes being what is associated with it, the design of the players' clothing, the rules of the game, the stresses and strains to be considered in building safe spectator stands, and so on.

* *Time.* Children need different periods of time to learn different things. Time can be employed in many ways, and dividing it up into equal lengths for teaching is not always the best way. For example, in a small or primary school children could spend the whole day painting, rather than the normally specified number of minutes or school periods.

* *People.* Parents and others can come in to school to share their expertise and ideas, and also take the children out to where things are happening, such as local events and work places.

* *Communication.* An integrated enriching school is where people talk to each other, and parents and children are encouraged to continue doing so at home. Children should share in the preparation of topics for teaching, the planning of events, such as a school trip, and maybe they should take parents along too as it helps them to see their own child from a different perspective.

* *Group activities.* Children's co-operative group activities can be expanded for enrichment, such as in the production of a class newspaper or a study of the local community, during which each child must take responsibility for his or her own part of the project. The pupils should be allowed to talk, argue and reach their own conclusions. Alternatively, a separate group could be taken out of the regular class for a specialist assignment. Small groups of, say, six children with a teacher, could choose from a limited range of topics which would not appeal to the whole class, such as the nature of poetry, stamp collecting or ideas in mathematics. In the tutor group, the pace would be faster and the search deeper. This type of specialist group work can be enhanced when children from several schools with the same interests get together from time to time to work on themes and projects – such as a Mathematics Day, to consider crossword puzzles or the dimensions of space. This is exactly what is done in sport when athletes or teams come together for practice, and it works well around the world.

* *Learning centres.* Open learning centres for exploring new areas of interest could be provided in school or community buildings as far as finances and organization allow. The centres can be used either in or out of school hours, and with teachers and equipment available for all who want to use them, that is, without selection. They should be well co-ordinated with school life. These resource centres would also provide teachers with specialist practice, both before graduation and on an in-service basis. They would not only have material on the basic school subjects, but could include numerous variations like puppetry, landscape architecture, anthropology and civil rights. The difference between such centres and a library is that teachers and other adults who work in the centres are present to guide and help youngsters to choose and explore areas of interest.

THE BENEFITS OF ENRICHMENT
1. Enrichment benefits all children, since each individual takes what is available at their own level.
2. Each child can follow personal interests in the subject areas.
3. With appropriate extension material pupils can work independently of the rest of the class, either when their investigations have taken them further or because they are more able and work more quickly.
4. Children working in their areas of interest can meet others in the same field and discuss ideas at their own level.

Enrichment support systems in the community

What is available will obviously vary, but teachers and parents can share skills and organize a system of contacts with both local and national bodies. There may be local associations or clubs and societies which run activities and would welcome the participation of schools, such as those for highly able children or young mathematicians. There may be museum and library courses providing art classes for children at weekends. Competitions run by private groups, such as newspaper poetry competitions or, for instance, the international Mathematics Olympiad, are open to all children. Colleges or other higher education establishments often welcome bright children to use their laboratories, while businesses and places of production may be willing to help.

Vacation courses. Everyone likes to be with people who are like themselves, where they can relax and feel comfortable. Children with special

---

THE BENEFITS OF VACATION COURSES
* The enjoyment and stimulation of being with others of comparable ability, vocabulary and interests.
* The relief from the boredom of being held back.
* The freedom to be themselves, to make mistakes, to have different interests and to form a more realistic image of themselves and their capabilities.
* For the highly able, the discovery that being top of the class does not come automatically, that they need to work.
* Personal and social development, and a strong sense of cohesion with other group members.
* Raised career aspirations, particularly in those from families where education has not been highly valued; those who would have left school at the earliest opportunity may stay longer.

---

interests, notably the highly able who take part in weekend and holiday courses, describe with pleasure the relief it is for them to meet others of their own kind. For the duration of the course the children can become openly enthusiastic and discipline problems are rare; the overriding atmosphere is one of working together.

Youngsters could be invited to a summer school for a week, with a theme such as plant productivity or theatre productions, including visits to the local places of interest; they could consider, for example, different kinds of world diet and conduct research a novel sources of food, or they could study some psychology, such as the different ways in which people perceive the same events.

FUTURES STUDY

One of the problems with all education is that it tends to look backwards; that is, teachers teach what they themselves have learned, often during their own childhood education, which depends, in turn, on what their teachers had learned, etc. There is a joke in teachers' circles that it takes three generations for new ideas to reach the classroom – hardly the way to keep pace with the demand for rapidly developing skills and information in a changing society. Even though understanding the past is always essential for providing for the future, an education which does not take trends for the future into account, but only dwells on the past and the present, is not equipping youngsters adequately.

Futures study, or forecasting, is a form of educational enrichment which comes from practices in business and industry. It can be woven into the pattern of all teaching; indeed, in the sciences, futures teaching is already part of many courses, or it can be an independent part of the timetable in all areas. The basic premise is to look for creative possibilities to encourage more sophisticated perspectives on present-day knowledge. Because change in outlook must involve the whole person, futures study must be an all-encompassing process, concerned with self-development and human interaction – with very many beneficial developmental side-effects.

Education, by its very nature, should be future-orientated, since educators supposedly prepare children and youth for the future. Futures study, with its emphasis on the mastery of processes such as creative problem-solving and higher-level thinking, will be useful throughout an individual's life. The first step is to involve teachers during their training by focusing on the goals and strategies of futures study, so that the course content can be expanded to include futures topics and processes, and to identify real world problems for the pupils' own research topics.

In order to focus on educating pupils to be citizens of the future, teachers need to modify the classroom and to select materials and learning experiences that will help their charges analyse, synthesize and evaluate information. In addition, to create the classroom of the future, teachers should stress flexibility in thinking and attitudes, not least by presenting themselves as models. A major aspect of this operation is to offer pupils the challenge of reaching decisions from incomplete information and from a variety of sources to simulate real-life creative problem-solving. This can be done, for example, by setting up problem 'scenarios' of events, such as a siege or negotiating a business deal. In addition, youngsters can gain considerably from meeting people who are real problem-solvers and hearing how they tackle their daily challenges.

In futures study, as in other aspects of enrichment, the student can gain strongly from investigating real problems or topics, using appropriate methods of enquiry. This is not the same as, for example, following a story in several newspapers to compare the different ways each reports it, or using summarized references such as encyclopedias in libraries to co-ordinate other people's work in a written essay. Those are school-type activities resulting in a relatively formal report about conclusions reached by other people. Investigating real problems could mean working with raw data, perhaps discovered through field work or found in a national or local statistical office. With such knowledge of the chosen field, the school-student can think and work like a professional researcher, rather than merely completing a pre-organized, school-type exercise. The students have to design their own procedures, reject irrelevant data, and draw conclusions and pointers for the future from their own work. This makes them producers rather than consumers of knowledge.

Techniques for futures study are well recognized as effective in many other areas, although they need to be focused and co-ordinated for the purpose in hand (Sisk, 1993). It can often be difficult for youngsters in rigid school systems, who have been trained to reproduce information rather than to think for themselves, to use these techniques; they may need much help to break free of old habits of thought. The teaching of thinking with a futures perspective calls for critical and creative processes. These might be relational skills, which compare and contrast, say, the styles of different areas of society or the policies of nations. It demands decision-making skills for defining and structuring the problem, as well as identifying and quantifying alternatives. In the same way as a clothing business would make investigations about the coming fashion before putting money into a new sales line, futures study involves analysing trends and considering what they mean in practical terms. One typical technique is scenario writing in which a fictionalized forecast is examined from a future date and envisaged backwards over the period between then and now, as if it had already occurred. Using informed imagination to simulate or to pretend situations, whether in acting out roles or written work, can focus on general problems such as war and peace or energy, or specific matters of policy. Through such integration exercises, pupils will experience the excitement of learning with a futures perspective (Sisk, 1981).

MENTORING

Mentoring is a focused form of enriched learning. It provides a highly specialized education for youngsters whose needs cannot be met within the education system, and can include, for example: observing and assisting the daily work of a lawyer, a factory manager, a sculptor or an engineer; discussing it afterwards and devising a related project for the young person to carry out under the mentor's guidance. Although mentoring bears some resemblance to the old idea of apprenticeship, it neither implies the social hierarchy nor the long-term commitment which that involves. The relationship is rather more diffuse than an apprenticeship, because there must be respect on both sides for it to work; the student or 'protégé' is not obeying instructions, but is encouraged to challenge himself or herself in the process of realizing individual potential. This kind of teaching relationship is particularly beneficial to the highly able, because it allows for the mutual exchange of knowledge in a learning partnership. The mentor should be aware that a talented student can comprehend the subject area in a greater depth, and breadth and at a faster pace than most other students. The closeness of the personal relationship, in which the pair might be on their own in a number of situations, means that mentors have to be very carefully chosen to be trusted with youngsters.

Mentoring has been known in business, the arts and in education for many years (think of Socrates and Plato, for instance), although rarely in the school context outside the United States. A mentor is anyone with the qualities and commitment to take on the responsibility of helping to educate a protégé. Both must share an interest in the subject matter, in which the mentor has greater expertise. They must also be in agreement on the degree of difficulty of the material, the level at which the protégé will begin work, and the degree of authority accorded to the mentor. Parents are usually the child's first mentors, so hardly any child is too young for mentoring to start (Daloz, 1986).

The challenge of mentoring is to find the right match between the two people involved; personality is an important factor. In some subject areas, more than one mentor may be needed to attend to different aspects: such as administration, co-ordination, design, evaluation and communication. Since the mentor/pupil relationship involves a delicate psychological balance, both should be clear about their role expectations before they begin. Not only must the mentor be secure and competent in the appropriate skills and abilities, but also aware of any embryonic jealousy, competitiveness and frustration. Both mentor and protégé should agree on a work contract outlining their commitment to the project. This should describe what the project will be, how the student envisages doing it, the estimated time to complete it, what the end-product would be, how it could be shared with the rest of the school and, lastly, who is going to evaluate the project. Ideally, the teaching style on one side and learning style on the other should be compatible: some mentors might use a gentle, encouraging style, while others hold highly idiosyncratic views about the teaching process.

Boys usually look for other males as mentors, and girls for a female model. This makes it more difficult for girls to find a mentor as women experts are less easily found. Boys generally prefer a mentor who is a skilled expert, hard working, and able to motivate and provoke them to excel, whereas girls generally prefer one who encourages and praises, acts as a friend, instils confidence and inspires them. Both boys and girls want someone who is honest, gives realistic appraisal and criticizes constructively.

Organizing mentoring. Since the protégé must have easy access to the mentor, time is the biggest single problem; beginning with finding sufficient time to put a compatible pair together and co-ordinate their activities. Mentoring itself may mean a large time commitment and, since mentors, by the very nature of their success in their work, are usually very busy people, it is sensible to give a time-scale for the activity, such as one school year. After that period, it is up to the protégé and the mentor to decide if they want to continue.

A great deal of time is devoted to communicating, timetabling and after-school supervising, but there also has to be enough for learning and completing the work involved, as well as co-ordinating the provision of any teaching supplies. Continuous discussion between mentor and student is essential, even if a report is not regularly kept up-to-date. Because mentorships are on a part-time basis, everyone needs to be regularly and clearly informed about how things are going. This means that parents must come into school at least once a term to discuss the mentoring project, and must respond quickly to letters or telephone calls about it at other times.

Mentoring in school calls for suitable arrangements and flexibility in time, so that teachers know they can allow pupils to leave their classes occasionally to work with their mentors: however, it can also be done before school, during the lunch-break or after school. Outside school, it could take place at the mentor's place of work or home or at the pupil's home, when it might involve the whole family in a research project, which can be enriching for everyone. A teacher might continue with whatever she has been teaching in the classroom by acting as mentor to keen pupils after school, or a specialist teacher could extent the mentoring role to a small-group project, such as the production of a play.

Highly able children can act as peer-mentors, for example, in a creative writing project or the learning of computer languages. The same rules would hold for them as for adults – the mentor must be able to present a valid, honest critique at the end of what has been done together, both as a teacher specialist and as a friend. However, there is a danger in peer-mentoring that advanced pupils may be exploited. Instead of spending time on their own learning, they are obliged to help others who are less advanced, and it must be clear that the pupil-mentor really wants to be involved and does not feel coerced into it.

EDUCATIONAL ASPECTS OF MENTORING

* *Modelling.* This offers the protégé the mentor's personality and level of skill or knowledge with which to identify.
* *Keeping tradition.* Mentors not only provide a knowledge-base, but also pass on the processes of acquiring it, including curiosity and cultural thinking about the area.
* *Offering direction.* A good mentor helps students to develop their own plans for the future and ways of achieving them.
* *Suggesting a new language.* The students are offered new ways to think about reality: their frame of reference may expand to take on extra meanings, as they learn to look at familiar problems in new ways.
* *Providing a mirror.* The mentoring relationship should expand students' awareness of the self through honest feedback, allowing them to analyse their thinking and their own development.

Emotional aspects of mentoring. The mentor must be willing to share, listen, care, encourage and accept the protégé's mistakes, and above all to act as a role model. It does not matter about the age difference: the most important aspects are the blend of personalities and mutual interest in the topic being studied. Students must show respect for their mentor by attending promptly for sessions and acting responsibly. Since young people may not realize the value of the mentor's gift of time and experience, the teacher who arranges the agreement must clearly define these boundaries. Students must also understand that the attention of a mentor does not guarantee success, but it does imply extra work.

When the protégé realises he has reached a point of diminishing returns with that mentor, the relationship must end or it will stagnate; although this does not necessarily mean that the connection ends, only the mentoring state. The mentor must be able to let the relationship drop, to recognize its limitations and perhaps to allow the protégé to move on to another mentor. Some people may find it difficult to relinquish their domain over a protégé who has been intellectually nurtured and assisted, especially with one who is keen and highly able; or the mentor may have to acknowledge that he or she is not of the highest level, but merely a middle-level expert, and the student must now pass on to a higher level.

With so many problems of time and responsibility, why should anyone be willing to be a mentor? At best, the answer lies in altruism, the benevolence of one human being towards another, and also in the satisfaction of teaching and watching a protégé develop. But clearly, care must be taken in watching out for adults who want to be in a position of control, or who are offering to be in close contact with a young person for other, unacceptable, personal reasons.

The ways in which mentors can build trust are mainly concerned with the manner of giving advice, and with their integrity.

Advice: The ability of the protégé to develop is dependent on his positive self-esteem, which is not at risk when asking for advice, but which can be threatened if it is constant and unsolicited, possibly to meet the mentor's needs. An idea can only be offered once or twice before its repetition becomes uncomfortable, and it can be more effective to wait until the need for it is felt and asked for, because this indicates the protégé's readiness and openness for learning. If advice is offered before the right time, it may not be understood by the protégé.

Any rejection of the mentor's ideas should not be taken personally. More often than not, rejection relates to the degree of readiness to learn, and so is a valuable clue about this aspect of the protégé. Protégés should be encouraged to think for themselves, especially with questions which promote higher-level thinking and problem-solving. Time is needed to discuss these decisions. The mentor is bound to make some mistakes of timing or approach, even though the ideas involved may be very good. When that happens, it is important to be open about asking for feedback and to learn from it.

Integrity: The mentor should always be positive and supportive, and should continually reinforce the confidential nature of the relationship. The protégé should be thanked for confidences, which are signs of a deepening relationship and trust. The need for the protégé to have some free time outside school hours must also be acknowledged, so the contract should permit time for some social diversions and involvement with other areas of life. The mentor can offer to support other matters concerned with the administration of the mentoring, such as making arrangements for visits, but responsibilities that belong to the evaluator or others should not be taken over. Discussion of the protégé with other staff or administrators should be approached with caution; the perception that discussion has take place can affect the relationship. It is best for discussions to take place in the presence of the protégé.

WAYS OF STARTING UP MENTORSHIP IN SCHOOL

* Start small, with a few pilot projects.
* Build a community resource file of possible mentors. This probably means going into the community, asking parents, asking at the public library and letting the search be known about in appropriate places. In finding good mentors, it is important to describe what is expected of everyone involved, and to acknowledge the existence of other support, such as extra classes that the student may be attending.
* The integrity of the mentor in this position of trust is vital: it may well be necessary for schools to obtain references before a mentor is recruited, while the activities must certainly be monitored by some other responsible adult, preferably in the school.
* Allow enough time for administration, finding, thanking, travelling, discussing, evaluating and so on; this is likely to be much more than expected.
* Arrange a programme so that the organizer can communicate to all interested persons. Keep copies of all written and verbal communications. Important notices should be posted to all concerned.
* Try to interest the rest of the staff in the school. A regular time should be kept in staff meetings for telling them about it.
* A volunteer, probably the teacher whose idea it was to start the scheme, should explain to staff, parents and students what mentoring is.
* It is important to be flexible in developing the programme, so that others will become convinced of its value.

PARENT/SCHOOL CO-OPERATION

Parents and teachers always have to work actively together with a child to get the best results. Teachers are in a position of expertise and can therefore help parents to improve their impact by sharing their educational knowledge so as to promote the development of the child's learning and thinking in everyday life.

School-talk with and about children

When children are getting ready for school in the morning, conversation is usually confined to what they need for the day. It is usually better to talk after school, focusing on the day's events. Careful conversation between parents and children can reach deeper and more effective levels than is possible with teachers during the school day, and this can ease children's progress through school (see Chapter IV).

SOME TALKING POINTS
For parents talking with children:
* Help children to find out more about what they are interested in by asking questions which show a real concern.
* Be ready to listen to any problems, and find out how they are being attended to at school.
* Encourage talk about the really satisfying experiences at school.
* Ask what kind of teaching the child would prefer if he had his way, and discuss how he feels about the approach his school takes to pupils' learning.
* What does the child feel about the marks he receives at school? Are they about right, or could progress reports be improved somehow?
* Talk about the ways that teachers and parents communicate, and how they might be improved.

For parents talking with teachers
* Generally, ask how children are getting on at school.
* Suggest ways of providing something extra in the basic day's teaching to enrich the children's learning.
* Suggest ways in which the child's interests can be developed at school, perhaps by specializing to some extent.
* Discuss how the children's horizons might be broadened to alert them to new interests.
* See where possibilities of learning can be shared with others in the class.
* Discuss some priorities, such as whether one or all the children in the class could benefit from special attention; for example, are there enough highly able children to form a group?
* Understand that children may not be as enthusiastic as their educators over all aspects of their education.

THE IMPORTANCE OF PLAY

There is no such thing as a free natural play, because there are always environmental constraints, whether physical or psychological. This is because all human behaviour is embedded in its social context, which sets limits on an individual's physical and psychological freedom. Wheth-

WHAT PARENTS CAN DO TO HELP THEIR CHILDREN SUCCEED IN SCHOOL

1. If parents place a high value on education, their children probably will too.
2. Aim to supply children with the basic material to work with and learn from, like plenty of paper and pencils and a corner of their own at home.
3. A peaceful home is a place where a child learns more easily and so will do better at school.
4. Pre-school education, whether at a playgroup or nursery school, is known to improve children's success when they go on to formal schooling.
5. Working with the child's teacher produces the best results for the child. Talk to the teachers about educational matters which concern you.
6. Teaching a child at home in a way which contradicts that in use at school is confusing to the learner; check that both styles are in accord.
7. Emotional support at home is invaluable to a child who aims high, especially if the rest of the class disapproves of hard work.
8. Try to keep your expectations for the child in line with his ability. The art is in getting a child to try hard, without placing the goal so high that failure is inevitable. For example, although a child may be reading fluently, it may still be important to take each progressive step in a reading scheme: jumping one of the course books can create a learning gap which is hard to fill in later.
9. Parents should try to maintain their children's interest in what they are supposed to be learning, and nothing kills off the will to learn more quickly than boredom. Learning must be seen to be relevant to the learner, if it is to be of interest and taken in well.
10. Allow the child to stumble on the road to learning. Don't correct every little error of grammar while talking and reading.
11. Reward good learning with affection and occasionally perhaps a present, but only when the child's efforts merit it. Reward for no real effort loses its effect.
12. Encourage children to follow their ideas through, to persevere as far as they can.
13. Show initiative and give attention to what children are trying to do. Take them to places of interest, such as historical sites, to fill in the background of their topics, but do not overdo it; it is the child's interest which should be the guide, not the parents' keenness to be good parents.

er they are aware of it or not, adults limit some of their children's actions and promote others while directing their development (Smith, 1984).

Play is an activity which might appear to be purposeless, during which children often act out behaviour out of context in a different way from work, but it could be a form of practice to improve later performance or to perfect existing skills. On the other hand, it can be seen as helping flexibility in performance, such as spatial skills which are improved through playing at fighting. It can be a testing of the environment, or a try-out of behaviour in a safe way – for example, you cannot be scalded by 'pretend' cooking, and a 'pretend' teacher can be controlled. Play allows children to try out new relationships between objects, such as putting dolls together in different combinations, and thereby enhances creativity. One could even say that, like creativity, play is a form of cognitive style.

In the animal world, the higher the intelligence, the more the young play – and the longer is infancy. Social play evolved with social living, but only human play is symbolic, and consciously so – a child knows what it is to pretend, and can use 'nothing', such as a space, as though it were something. Human play is also culturally transmitted – it improves co-operation and social behaviour and the ability to control it. It serves to make good some deficiency in an inherited potential by filling in with individual experiences. Whatever practice a child has in fantasizing relationships, these do eventually have to be tried out on real people for real control, which creates the problem of how to bridge the gap between fantasy and reality. Children who have spent time in playing with relationships, such as in a nursery school play-house, have been shown to be happier, more mature and less aggressive with other children because they are more skilled at negotiating. Even tiny children make sound signals to tell parents that it's not for real: when fighting is just playful the screaming is high-pitched, and when a toddler is starting to play chasing with mother, there's a great deal of laughter with it. Fantasy is a positive means of preparation for social skills.

Intellectual and emotional maturity comes from the experience of both success and failure, and in learning how to cope with either. Such experience begins with play. A small child building a tower of bricks, for example, is learning about mathematical and physical concepts – a tower supported by several bricks can be built higher than one based on a single brick – and that patience and perseverance is more likely to be rewarded with success than carelessness. Even play which may appear to have no purpose is a form of practice that aids flexibility in intellectual and physical performance. Feelings about other people are worked out through play-acting, a procedure which is also a recognized source of creative endeavour for both young and old.

There are many ways of using play to develop active minds; each one has advantages and drawbacks. Although fantasy play was once thought of as irrelevant, it can provide a more flexible part of education for the future than conventional education. For example, it offers innovative learning experiences, which help children to form strategies of behaviour that can be used in other, as yet unknown, circumstances. Conventional learning is inevitably bound to the present, and so must often become obsolete even as it is being taught, because of the rapid changes going on in many societies.

Just as there is a difference between dreaming and imagination, so there is one between play and creative imagination; for example, a repeated action, no matter how playful or enjoyable, is not imaginatively creative, although it might set the scene for true inventiveness. Play is always a 'framed' event; it involves special signals (displayed by animals too) without which the play might break down into violence and anxiety, as indeed it sometimes does. There are standard forms of play in all children, such as making a 'zuzzing' noise when playing with toy cars. Play contains repetition, exaggeration, miniaturization, changed atmosphere, stock characters, special location and guaranteed illusion: it is a transition from one mental state (of being entirely in the present), to another (in the realm of make-believe).

There is an alternative, idealized view of play, which is seen as time to do as you wish, so that anything which is not work is deemed play – television, sex or a night out. Children's play is particularly idealized as the essential form of freedom, but this is not true since it is limited by the equipment they have to hand, by adults, and by environmental influences such as advertisements for toys (Singer, 1973). Team sports are also idealized as a form of play which provide social skills and competence in other areas, although this is also a way of bringing some form of group cohesion, and it has never been proved that games build easier social relationships more than any other form of group activity. Play also has a less attractive side, seen in unpleasant teasing, bullying and the struggle for power in class.

The differences between work and play are diminishing. Mihaly Csikszentmihalyi (1982) describes a quality of 'flow' – a play-like state of pleasure – which can be found in the context of any activity whether work or play, such as chess, rock climbing, gardening or surgery. It is a state of extreme motivation which happens to people functioning at high levels where other matters, apart from the goal one is aiming at, become merely background. 'Micro flow', he says, is found in the pleasure people get from shopping, walking round art galleries or whatever. Play is thus no longer seen as trivial or irrelevant, but rather as a positive and pleasant aspect of human character, intelligence, pleasure and freedom, and the root of creative endeavour. The connection between imaginative play and creativity holds good throughout life. Questioning and searching for ideas involves a quality of playfulness, in enjoying contradictions and rearranging them into speculative combinations. But play cannot be taken for granted, even in small children, because it can be inhibited by environmental influences, with consequent poor outcomes for creativity.

The dilemma for educationalists is that when children are selected for more intense, highly structured academic programmes by virtue of their ability to pass examinations, development of a playful, creative approach to their work and in their general outlook can often be stunted. An environment in which the exceptionally able child can prosper all round must be a balanced one; it requires enough time with other people to make good social relationships, develop interests outside study areas, and take part in school and other community activities. This needs recognition and the will of parents and teachers to make sure that the non-examinable side of their pupils' lives is adequately promoted.

Children who have to work from an early age and others living in very poor circumstances suffer from lack of play. Although such children may appear very 'grown-up', if not world-weary, this superficial display of adulthood is no substitute for real maturity. Maturity needs slow, steady, trial-and-error development of the kind which allows decisions to be made on the basis of knowledge gained from experience. Role-play is enormously important in giving children a balanced view of themselves so that, in their imaginative worlds, they can take turns at being Mother, Father or Teacher, and develop a feeling of control over their own lives. Young working children often grow up learning only that they must do as they are told by figures of authority, such as their boss, so that they lose that sense of self-control. This is a situation, needless to say, which is entirely detrimental to their competence in other situations.

CHAPTER XI

Competence in different cultures

THE SOCIALNESS OF HUMANS

Human beings are social by nature. They come together in groups which have their own particular cultural identity, made up of what their members have learned and how they behave. Cultural influences, such as historical origins, mythology and religions, legitimatize this behaviour, as in the division of labour or the status of each sex. Culture filters downward through generations, but also spreads horizontally, as when it affects other cultures (notably the world-wide American influence); it can even move upward, as when new expressions in language, coined by the young, are absorbed into general speech. Changes also come from creative endeavour, for example the psychological ideas of Sigmund Freud or Pablo Picasso's new concepts of art, which are absorbed by the cultural network. With all these currents and cross-currents, the culture inherited by a particular generation is not the same as the one it passes on.

With any cultural change, the language changes accordingly: new words are introduced, and others become obsolete or disappear altogether. In 'oral' cultures, story-telling is not only entertainment, but can have a rich educational role, informing people about their mythological past, the nation's history, or how to conduct themselves. The stories that are told over and over again are memorized by the listeners; the teller can then improvise on the old patterns to comment on current situations, such as in the Wayang puppet performances of well-loved stories in Indonesia. Because people know them so well already, they can recognize any new messages, but unless the message fits into the cultural framework of ideas and experience of the audience, it will be lost.

In almost all countries, people are marked as belonging to different sub-cultures by using different words and dialects within the common language, and their ideas about social values are accordingly diverse. One person may belong to a number of sub-cultures, grouped around such activities as a profession, a religion, an age-group or a political tendency, which will affect their daily behaviour.

Non-verbal, physical expressions, such as the way people greet or insult each other, are as culture-based as language is. Some forms of dress or haircut can be more informative than any words in identifying people within sub-cultural groups, although sounds and speech are generally more powerful. The number of words used to describe anything indicates how important it is in a society: when a particular food crop is dominant, it will carry many words for its variations, while others may use only one. Some tropical cultures may have dozens of words for sweet potatoes, or for rice – 'in the field', 'uncooked' or 'boiled' and so on – as well as different words for forms of behaviour by particular relatives. Similarly, the Inuit have very many words for water lying on land.

To understand each other, people have to learn the specific codes, signs and language of their culture. Communication has developed through writing, with the gradual improvement of writing materials such as paper and pencils, typewriters, computers and printing techniques. Instruments like radio, television and the telephone have widened the possibilities and range of communication immensely. As a result illiterate people can be reached in ways other than the written word, and writing is becoming less important. Recorded messages can reach later generations of people, but the availability of the various media in developing countries differs widely. In some, the daily circulation of newspapers is less than one per thousand inhabitants, while others do not have a national TV broadcasting network or a reliable telephone system. Egypt, for example, is a country fighting to keep its literacy rate above 50 per cent. Although 766 new children's books were published there in 1989, this will still not satisfy the needs of the country's 22 million children.

THE PROMOTION OF LITERACY

Literacy is the ability to read and write to some extent; numeracy is sometimes included in it. The cultural context is important in defining literacy: in some areas, it may mean simply being able to read the letters of the alphabet or sign one's name. In others, however, which are more technically advanced and which demand a higher level of literary competence in daily life, even someone who has had a primary school education may be seen as functionally illiterate. In general, the more complex a society's economic and social structures, the more an individual is obliged to read and write to a higher and even technical level (Street, 1990).

Being literate means being able to present ideas using the written word, and understanding, storing and analyzing words to react appropriately. UNESCO (1988) defined literacy as 'the application of a set of skills to a set of general knowledge areas, which result from the cultural requirements that are imposed on the members of a culture'. Their breakdown of this definition is presented as follows:

(a) *Literate*: a person is literate who can with understanding both read and write a short simple statement about his everyday life.

(b) *Illiterate*: a person is illiterate who cannot with understanding both read and write a short simple statement on his everyday life.

(c) *Functionally literate*: a person is functionally literate who can engage in all those activities in which literacy is required for effective functioning of his group and community, and also for enabling him to continue to use reading, writing and calculation for his own and the community's development.

(d) *Functionally illiterate*: a person is functionally illiterate who cannot engage in all those activities in which literacy is required for effective functioning of his group and community, and also for enabling him to continue to use reading, writing and calculation for his own and the community's development.

These definitions place literacy firmly in the context of the society, but they can be broken down further to more specific sub-cultures (Dubbeldam, 1991):

The family. A literate family both improves a child's chances of going to school, and encourages familiarity with the written word. Education, especially basic literacy, is identified with status, self-esteem and empowerment, which can be unfortunate, because not all members of the family are seen as having the same need. For example, where women's' lives are restricted to the home, they may be denied literacy; spoken communication is thought to be enough for them, as all other communications with the wider (male) society are filtered through to them by their male relatives. But literacy for women has proven value: important research in areas of high illiteracy, where one group of mothers were taught to read and a control group was not, found that women with even a little education produced healthier and cognitively brighter children (Hundeide, 1991). Despite these findings, in societies which are repressive to women they are the least likely to be educated. Such information suggests that the education of poor females should take precedence over that of poor males.

Village level. Without literacy, a village is decidedly limited in the information it can receive from outside, such as directives about farming, health or population planning. Literacy can stimulate economic development in the form of small businesses and co-operatives, and can support political development if sufficient information from brochures, newspapers and magazines is available.

Cities. The more dense the population, the more literate people have to be. They must be able to read street names, traffic boards, and prices in shops, while forms have to be filled in for licenses, membership cards and so on. The poorest people, however, have less need of literacy, because they are more likely to go to street markets than supermarkets, to earn a living in some way that does not call upon literacy skills, and are less likely to have social encounters in which it is an essential part.

National context. Literacy is increasingly a requirement for many types of employment; a labour force which can read, write and calculate can find better jobs and produce more. Furthermore, as more and more people gain those skills, it becomes increasingly difficult for those without them to find employment. Literacy is essential in order to improve life economically in terms of health, welfare and the use of public facilities. Without literacy, there is always some degree of dependence on others, although clearly other skills are needed. It is possible that by the year 2000, the literacy rate in the world will be 46 per cent of all adults. The poorest developing countries have the highest illiteracy rates, mostly in the densely populated areas of Asia, where the combination of low income with high population growth is a strong negative influence. When people are fully occupied with surviving, there is hardly enough energy left for learning to read and write.

Motivation for literacy

Motivation always comes from the individual, although its results may be for the benefit of the community. The tried and tested message to those who want to promote literacy in a community is that if people are to participate, they must want it for themselves; they will neither learn nor maintain the skill if it does not fulfil what they feel they need. There are three major reasons why people might want to aim for literacy:

1. Literacy strengthens people's social position, increasing the ability to receive information, while enabling them to contribute their own ideas. Being unable to read and write is generally equated with ignorance, devaluing people's traditional knowledge, social skills and individual ideas. This is why most new literates say it has dramatically increased their self-esteem.

2. Literacy provides hope of economic improvement, whether in finding employment or in running one's own business more effectively.

3. Literacy provides access to information about gaining individual satisfaction: reading, moving about the country, writing one's own name instead of a thumb print, mastering numeracy so as not to be cheated, knowing one's own rights, and teaching others.

Literacy through schools. To have the strongest effect, the message implicit in lessons must fit the conceptual framework and life experiences of the learners. In primary schools, potential conflict between national and local interests can hamper literacy because what is taught is different from children's basic learning needs; learning how to prepare food may, for example, seem to be more important than reading. A growing number of educationalists propose that governments should provide only a skeleton curriculum, delegating much of the substance of the teaching to the local school, teachers, and community. The primary school is the most powerful of educational instruments, reaching the largest groups in the population when they are still at a receptive age – including girls. Yet universal primary education is not within reach in all countries, implying that each year the number of people world-wide who have missed formal school education and reach adolescence in an illiterate state is increasing.

Adolescents or adults who have been late in starting to read are much more difficult to reach. Since they may not be highly motivated to learn, the programme should be specifically designed to attract people to it. Lessons must be delivered at a time that suits people's rhythm of labour. They must be offered in a flexible way, to preserve the framework of methodology but leave much of the content to be filled in by local teachers, who will find ways to link up with the specific interests of the learners, such as the way they live. When the teaching is over, there is little to read for many of the learners; newspapers or magazines are hard to obtain, and may be read by very many people in turn, long after the day they appear. Except for the more well-to-do families, many people have no reading material in the house, except perhaps government pamphlets or religious tracts; such material rarely reflects the cultural heritage of the readers, such as their own stories, songs and writings.

The content of literacy lessons. Good literacy teaching encourages the newly qualified to continue reading, but if the ideas presented to them differ too widely from what they already know, there may be misunderstanding, loss of interest and poor learning. Worse, it may actually widen the gap between the indigenous culture, associated with illiteracy and ignorance on the one hand, and modern society, associated with literacy, knowledge and progress on the other. In mass campaigns, therefore, governments should provide the facilities and organizational structure, but not the details of the curriculum. The contents of the lessons can be designed most efficiently by involving the people concerned in deciding on local priorities and how to put them across.

The usefulness of literacy depends on the continuous access people have to reading materials, without which there is relatively little point in the exercise. In order to make literacy so sustainable and stimulating that it becomes a habit, educational authorities and funding agencies may have to promote the production and distribution of reading materials that either provide information of practical value to the individual reader or raise his or her interest with culturally and socially relevant information; this may be specifically directed at, for example, women, or ethnic or occupational groups. There is a real need for research to be directed towards identifying the needs, methods and sustainability of literacy, with or without post-literacy programmes. This must include the means for disseminating research results, and to start with, the building up of an adequate research capacity.

Education in different societies

For the foreseeable future, the education systems of both developed and developing countries will be dominated by the need to produce a higher proportion of better educated and trained young people than in the past, stimulated by increasing international competition and relatively declining resources. The fact is that in many previously colonial countries the character of the education system has not changed as much with independence as might have been expected. This is not only because it may still be too soon for a real challenge to emerge to those firmly founded systems (whether missionary or colonial), but also because in some areas, such as in South-East Asia and Africa, they have become part of the culture, especially in the sphere of examinations, language policy and local financing. Greater state control may only serve to reinforce old ways, and even if the state would like to change them, there may not be the means to do so. As a result, there is a tendency to rely on private, community and local initiative to deliver what are meant to be national systems.

The character of schooling in different societies is determined by popular attitudes towards human potential and the role of the teacher. In some, the 'hidden-curriculum', which is concerned with the promotion of attitudes in pupils, is quite open. Malaysia, for instance, has recently introduced a moral education curriculum to promote a group of character traits. In China, Japan and several other countries of eastern Asia, it is widely believed that high-level attainment is open to all children if they work hard enough, an attitude which affects the role and expectations of the teacher, and promotes both a uniform curriculum, and high expectations by parents and teachers of children's examination results.

While education systems are being remade, wide variations are emerging between central and local administration policies, although they all have to use money which comes from taxation, whether local or national. Local education authorities are concerned for pupils and students in their area, and the level of spending is guided by their numbers, the provision of teaching staff being by far the most costly item. To save costs, the head of a small primary school might teach regularly, but in a large secondary school the head may take a largely managerial role, with very little, if any, teaching. One school may be located in different buildings and need extra staffing, whereas another might have a high incidence of pupils with a different mother-tongue from the majority, needing additional help with language teaching and other functions.

Spending on teaching materials – books, equipment, stationery and so on – is also related to the number of users. Money is also needed for the maintenance of the school buildings, possibly for school meals and transport, as well as the professional support groups – advisers, inspectors, welfare officers, careers advisory officers and paramedical staff. Not all authorities will pay for essential office supplies, and fewer still cover entry fees for public examinations.

According to Benjamin Franklin, two things are certain – death and taxation. As far as education is concerned, there is the added fact that there will never be enough money or resources to do what we would like to do. At the same time, international comparisons suggest that Germany and Japan are able to reach higher standards of achievement than most other countries, using a smaller proportion of their gross domestic product. If this is so, management must become increasingly important in education as a means of narrowing the gap between resources and expectations. Evaluation, in turn, will become increasingly important, since without it the better management that is needed simply cannot take place.

The education of teachers

There is an international view that educational standards are slipping, and that the fault lies with new methods in teacher education, promoted by 'experts', which have failed the pupils. The assumption is that standards were higher in a golden past when order and obedience reigned, and that if we return to the old ways, children will learn better. This attitude is accompanied by calls for legislation to reverse the present tide. But it all depends on how the evidence is interpreted. For example, if more pupils pass an examination, then the correct conclusion might not be that the children's education has improved, but that the examination standard has fallen. There is a difference between real teaching and lecturing, between guiding and inspiring pupils on the one hand, and telling them what to remember on the other. One of the outcomes of the current distrust of teachers is a tendency to turn teaching back to lecturing, so that children absorb information without thinking.

There are three main international trends which teachers are currently expected to be aware of, and incorporate in the presentation of their lessons and management of their classes, however varied their circumstances:

1. *Modernization* – industry and urbanization, their organization and the development of technology.
2. *Individualization* – concern for the development of individual differences, learning processes and assessment.
3. *Internationalization* – awareness of different cultures, styles of education, and expectations of life, as well as caring for the environment of the world.

Teacher training. Whatever the constraints of local circumstances, the best way to improve teaching is to relate it to the pupil's perception of their own needs: while improvement cannot be confined to those perceptions, neither can it be divorced from them. The European ministers of education recently gave priority to the promotion of excellence in teaching as a means of raising standards in education; the support for this was to come mainly from improved initial and in-service teacher education (Council of Europe, 1987). The ministers were concerned with the particular contemporary challenges which teachers face:

1. It is becoming more difficult to apply differentiated teaching strategies because of the extension of compulsory schooling, increasing cultural diversity, changes in family structure, and the integration of children with special needs into mainstream education.
2. There is a growing complexity in society, the economy and technology, which means that teachers are expected to ensure that the mass of the population is able to perform at levels of competence previously required of only a minority. The content of education has expanded, with the explosion of new knowledge and skills in all fields, and has become more diversified with the appearance of new subjects such as education in human rights, health, environment, computer studies and so on. Because so much is available, teachers must make choices as to what and how they teach, but they often receive little guidance in extracting the most appropriate parts of the curriculum for their needs.

3. Teachers face competition from alternative sources of learning, which can convey contradictory information and values, particularly the mass media. They must somehow take this mass of information into consideration and turn it to educational account. They are also expected to teach pupils how to discriminate among the mass of alternative information, so that they may draw on parts of it for their own learning.

4. The introduction of new technologies in teaching (computers and interactive video) has affected the teaching and learning process in ways which no teacher can afford to ignore; it challenges them to acquire higher classroom management skills.

5. Schools are opening up to the outside world, so that there is a greater development of all-round education for all, challenging teachers' pedagogical and co-operative skills. The community generally (for example, parents, industry and commerce, trade unions, the mass media) has sought to extend its influence on education. Teachers are faced with such a variety of expectations that the results of their work are subject to conflicting judgments.

The report recommends that initial training should prepare teachers for a very broad and sound general education, and aim to make their own intellectual basis adequate to meet these new challenges. It recognizes that student-teachers need personal and social skills for communication, adaptability, creativity, self-confidence, as well as empathy for classroom management, team-work and relations with parents. All this assumes that teachers will also know their subject and have the basic skills to be expected of a teacher.

In-service education should be an on-going, integrated part of qualified teachers' lives, responding to their needs as well as those of the pupils, and it should be co-ordinated with other forms of information at national, regional and local levels. It should also be co-ordinated between schools so that teachers can experience many different forms of teaching and out-of-school experiences, particularly in industry and commerce. However, since there is no accepted standard measure of good teaching, its appraisal should be wide and flexible; particular regard should be paid to how it fosters the personal development of pupils and equips them to take an active, responsible and constructive place in society. This is as true for teachers in particular positions, such as headteachers who may need special help in management, as for those who train the trainers of teachers.

Training of teachers has to be adapted to both market forces and central control. If central control is not too tight, there is usually some internal choice for the student in different systems of teacher education. This can be further broadened if the teacher training institution develops close links with local or central education authorities, as well as with the schools in their areas. To be most effective, initial training and probationary work in schools should be smoothly integrated as one process. The institutions could, in fact, be directly involved with schools on a regular basis, contributing help for their wider needs in improving their effectiveness.

Evidence of the development of children's competence

Developmental research findings are clear that cumulative social and economic influences strongly affect the individual's competence and consequent levels of performance in the way that it biases their expectations of life opportunities. Although it is seen that different school methods and settings produce different results, there is still a need for more information about the precise effects of instruction within and outside school hours, and of different kinds of educational organization: the effects of teacher's expectations on pupils' achievements, and the accuracy of their personal assessment of children's capabilities are now in doubt.

Certainly, research findings need to be given more practical and more easily understandable relevance: there is too much emphasis on theoretical views and discussions, and too little on field-work and practical experience. Sometimes this is because the investigating agencies are universities, which merely circulate the results among themselves, or because political issues can arouse hostility when national and international programmes are found to be less effective than was expected. Education in its cultural context is a sensitive issue, and many authorities do not allow the kind of evaluation that would lead to the publication of criticism.

Research projects are not always clear in their evaluation, especially in large-scale field-work, so that conclusions are buried in unread reports, or too ill-defined to be workable. This is often because, out of a whole project, the money available for evaluation may be restricted to only a small percentage of the total, and the larger the project the lower the relative share for evaluation is likely to be. There is rarely full publication of what research has been done and how the results were translated into action – if at all. It is often difficult to discover how often scientific research has been carried out, or how the design, content, methodology, implementation and evaluation of the project has influenced the outcome. Research on education, especially in the developing world, demands a multi-disciplinary approach: it concerns both technical and linguistic aspects, as well as cultural, social, and economic aspects.

**ACTION THAT SHOULD BE TAKEN TO IMPROVE
COMPETENCE FROM RESEARCH EVIDENCE**
* Information about ways of improving pupils' learning has to reach teachers and pupils.
* Concern for the disadvantaged should include specifying the kind of education which is most appropriate for their circumstances.
* More flexibility is called for in the organization of special help for pupils with special talents.
* Educational policies should be explicit, drawing from research results to promote competence.
* Counselling and vocational guidance should be part of general education.
* Enrichment in education should be recognized and implemented, to improve children's competence.
* Education in thinking skills should be focused within subject areas.

The most important questions to which educational research should address itself in the future should be taken in a developmental and cultural context, and are as follows:

1. What are the best ways of offering help to those who, because of their circumstances, do not fully use their abilities?
2. What proportion of a country's budget would be needed to aim for competence for all its children?
3. Is it better for children of high potential to be identified and treated differently, or should they be encouraged to find their own way, given adequate educational material and tuition?
4. Do teachers hold children back because their training has taught them that there are defined stages of development? Would anyone tell a child not to learn to speak because she has not reached the right stage yet?

A POLICY FOR PROMOTING COMPETENCE

A policy for the promotion and actualization of competence must be flexible enough to serve many cultures, and yet sufficiently well structured to be of use in a single one, including individual local education authorities. It should try to distinguish which procedures are beneficial to the education of the child and which aim to promote a particular point of view, although each will influence the other (Freeman, 1993).

Politically driven reforms of various kinds can be to the 'left' or the 'right' of the political spectrum, although always supposedly for the good of the child. There were, for example, the largely left-wing 'discovery methods' of the 1960s and 1970s, in which the learning environment was taken to include most of what a child needed to learn with. Critics maintained that if children were supplied with bricks and encouragement, they should have been able to work out the principles of architecture for themselves. But teachers were not adequately prepared for this kind of teaching, so that children's educational progress was restricted by lack of basic instruction, such as in reading, the development of learning skills, and the foundation knowledge they needed as a springboard to discovery. On the other hand, right-wing and/or religious governments in several parts of the world officially prohibit freedom of speech – if not of thought. Strong beliefs of teachers can bias the way they present information, and can also damage the development of children's own thought.

All children should have the right to aim for excellence, which is what a supportive society can offer through fostering their different aptitudes and enthusiasms. Often enough the resources already exist, but in circumstances where money is in particularly short supply, parents and teachers feel satisfied if most of the children receive a basic education. Youngsters who have left education early may find it difficult to make it up later.

Making changes. There are two distinct ways to initiate and co-ordinate the changes in educational practice, that are aimed at enabling children to become competent and reach their own level of excellence (Timar & Kirp, 1988). The first is from the more usual direction – 'top-down'. This happens when experts, such as educationalists and administrators at the top of a hierarchy, work out plans and instructions for others lower down to follow: such changes usually come from the government, whether central or local. Since instructions given in this way do not first seek a consensus from those who are to carry them out, some conflict is possible, which can disturb the smooth running of schools.

The alternative is the slower and more cumbersome 'bottom-up' approach, which is likely to be more effective. These more democratic policy decisions may be taken either at local authority or school level, where all staff could be involved, for example, administrators, teachers and counsellors. But it is also important to take heed of the opinions, hopes and wishes of the pupils; involved and motivated pupils will be keener learners than those who are simply told what to learn, particularly the brightest. Efforts to change attitudes are unlikely to be effective without the involvement and agreement of the people concerned (Lewin, 1947).

To have the greatest effect, action should be of both kinds. A 'top-down' approach involving administration and government could start with an official working party to co-ordinate and manage information and ideas that are already available, as well as seeking out new ideas for the testing and enrichment of educational methods. In a 'bottom-up' approach, the practitioners could organize co-ordinating meetings and workshops in schools and institutes of higher education, as the start of an awareness and information campaign about the use and improvement of local facilities for all the children of the neighbourhood.

All societies need the involvement of their brightest people in trade and industry, such as scientists and engineers working creatively and productively. A firm industrial base, run by a flexible workforce which can grasp new technological opportunities, can offer goods of variety and quality, and can compete in the world market. A nation's ability to produce its own goods and services enables it to pay its way, and to provide for the needs of its nationals; without that, their earnings and consumption will both be at a low level. The same is true for the management of any workforce; the most valuable manager is not the one with the most qualifications or the longest experience, but one who can achieve high levels of commitment, care and concern among workers. There is a special need for high levels of skill in work which is potentially boring and yet essential; the able manager will be able to engender a sense of involvement and purpose in the people who do this.

Guidelines for a policy for competence

All children are entitled to their fair share of the available resources of material provision and time from parents and teachers to enable them to develop fully; this includes those with exceptional needs who need specialist provision. The ability of young people to act positively comes from a sturdy self-confidence and the courage to use experience in new ways. This is greatly helped by mutual respect between teachers and pupils.

Formal education should not be seen as the only route for developing the highest levels of expertise. If the skills and talents needed by society are limited to an elite, then, whatever way the elite is selected, there will inevitably be talented individuals whose potential contributions are not recognized and so are lost. Because it is not possible to predict the kinds of talents that will be needed in the future, there has to be a wide variety of skills and outlooks available. Providing for individuals to develop their exceptional talents not only benefits each of them, but is more than repaid to the society which has helped them.

In some areas, mere mention of the idea that some children may be more highly able than others courts accusations of elitism, and in such circumstances schools are more likely to oblige all pupils to conform to the average. A local education authority can help schools to cater for all pupils by encouraging an atmosphere in which attention and provision for highly able pupils is normal and natural, to be carried out along with other policies and work in the schools. Although individuals may well be motivated to help the most highly able, unless there is clear concern from the government at all levels, that help is unlikely to be enough: it will exist and function well in certain places, but is likely to miss a high percentage of those in need of special assistance.

The aim of any educational policy which promotes competence should be to enable every child to attain knowledge in a manner which is meaningful, and which can be used in many situations in a creative manner. Individuals have to learn to work with others; they can practise this at school in group activities, leading to greater interpersonal understanding and possibly an influence on society for the better. Flexibility in education, concern for the individual child, the provision of free, high-quality education, as well as non-school educational provision for all who want it – all are facilities which enable excellence to develop in people from all walks of life.

Educational administration for competence

It is often difficult to extricate a nation's cultural outlook from its specific educational practices. If a change of style and of provision is to be achieved, so that children can gain an increasing ability to learn, be competent, and be creative, there must be effective planning. This involves making use of whatever facilities are available (no matter how little there seems to be), and seeking whatever improvement is possible in the circumstances. Because all education systems exist within a society, they must to some extent reflect it, and attempts at change must take into consideration such influences as religion, tradition, poverty, and discrimination.

In educational planning, it helps to involve other 'stake holders' – people who are involved in the system – into the policy decisions:

- *at government level* this might mean co-operation with other governments in recruiting foreign experts or in encouraging teacher exchanges;
- *at local authority level,* this might mean contact with the leaders of industry;
- *in a school,* this would mean consulting the teaching staff and the school governors, as well as parents. The pupils also need an accurate picture of what is provided and expected of them, if they are to be motivated to aim for the appropriate goals. This also implies that they should be given the freedom to negotiate for what they feel they need.

**WAYS IN WHICH THE LOCAL EDUCATION AUTHORITY
CAN GIVE SUPPORT**
Provision:
* Specialist advisers, possibly as a team, for educating those with special needs, as part of providing an encouraging atmosphere for differentiated learning.
* Courses and events for pupils to enrich their learning.
* In-service courses for all teachers.
* Specialist teachers for individual work with pupils.
* A bank of curriculum enrichment materials and teacher education materials in a resource centre which is open out of school-hours.

Co-ordination:
* Education co-ordinated in specific areas, such as between schools, or with colleges, universities, or industry.
* Co-ordinating between teachers who are forming their own curriculum enrichment materials and who have ideas and experiences to share.
* Out-of-school activities for pupils from different schools in the area, such as weekend activities or summer camps.

CONDITIONS OF DEPRIVATION

Very poor children often grow up in an unhealthy environment, with effects that are damaging to them both physically and psychologically. This is likely to result in the loss of many chances of developing their abilities, and so maturing into fully competent adults. They also risk losing their childhood, in any real sense. Inadequate food increases the odds stacked against a poor child's development. International study has concluded that improved nutrition leads to an improvement in children's IQ scores, correlated with increases in their head size and height (Lynn, 1989). Clearly, the better-nourished child will function better at a biological level, and this can be expected to support a higher level of mental functioning. This effect is recognized in many countries, such as Brazil and some areas of the United States, where feeding very poor children is an important part of school life; indeed, some children are motivated to come to school to eat.

Children may also be deprived of the less obvious nourishment of the social environment. In many parts of the world, the least attractive work is done by immigrants – and their children – who often suffer from the major handicap of not speaking the host language as their native tongue. Although some studies have shown that bilingual children can have greater cognitive flexibility, social sensitivity, and adeptness at creative thinking than the monolingual (Wiles, 1985), that research was conducted with children attending full-time school. Deprived children, especially those who work, have neither the time nor the attitude needed for learning.

As we approach the year 2000, a conservative estimate of the number of children worldwide under the age of 15 in full-time work is more than 50 million. Child soldiers are recruited in many countries, and children as young as 6 years old swell the ranks of prostitutes. By the end of the century, half the world's population will be under 25, and the chances that most of them will receive the education they need to achieve their full potential are minimal.

Babies are affected by their environments before they are born (see Chapter I), and the effects accumulate thereafter. A study of all British children born between 3 and 9 March 1958 (The National Child Development Study) showed that at 5 years old, those from socially disadvantaged backgrounds differed not only in being physically smaller and having more medical problems, but also in their more difficult behaviour and poor educational attainment (Butler & Golding, 1986). It is known that, within certain limits, there can be recovery from mental deprivation when the conditions for intellectual growth improve, but millions of economically and culturally impoverished children must be handicapped for the rest of their lives by their very early disadvantagement.

In a survey of educational programmes for children in deprived circumstances, notably in developing countries, Lansdown (1990) reported considerable progress. Although the gap between human needs and the resources to satisfy them is often very wide, there are relatively low-cost techniques for meeting those needs. Improvements always need time, but they can be speeded up if parents themselves have had some education, and slowed down by poor communication and collaboration between government agencies.

In poor circumstances, home-based programmes are the most effective, but parents and representatives from the community concerned have to be *actively* involved in their planning and implementation. It helps if homes are regarded as a sources of activity and enrichment, and not simply as a deficit factor: outside professional activity so often ignores local wisdom. Instructing parents, however, does not necessarily bring about a change in their behaviour; their confidence and self-esteem can be at least as important in effecting change, implying a need for their psychosocial support. Such positive attitudes to parents can increase the likelihood of their children going to school regularly, as well as on their better adjustment when they get there, so improving their attainment during the early years. Food supplements may also be necessary.

Working children. Children who have to work from an early age may by-pass some stages of vital psychological development, producing

HOME-BASED EDUCATIONAL HELP PROGRAMMES

The advantages:
* One-to-one interaction between children and parents.
* Direct teacher communication with parents.
* Teaching skills to children in terms of their own environments.
* Immediate feedback to parents.
* Adjusting intervention to the family's own timetable.
* Widening discussion to include other (non-educational) problems.
* Positive changes in the attitudes of fathers.

The disadvantages:
* In cultures where there is a strong family hierarchy, visits can be seen as a form of threatening interference, undermining the position of one or more parents, and the position of the oldest member. These problems can be overcome, for example, by working first with grandparents to overcome their antipathy to any new approach, although the costs can be relatively high, since such programmes are labour-intensive. They can, however, be less costly than some institutionally based programmes, and can be reduced when several services (health and nutrition as well as education) are incorporated. Not enough information is available to come to a conclusion on the most effective frequency of visits to families, although once a week is a possible ideal.

stunted maturation. This psychological deprivation results not only from the children's own experiences, but is also usually inter-generational: other family members have probably built up similar poor attitudes about themselves during their own lives, as a result of the same social and physical circumstances. Limited perception of their potential by both children and adult relatives has a strong effect on whether or not there is to be any improvement in the next generation's economic status.

A particular difficulty for children who start work very young is that although they may learn to cope with everyday obligations, they are likely to have difficulty in thinking and planning beyond the present – and the younger they are when work begins, the worse the problem is likely to be. Child workers are often given the most menial and boring tasks, during which they survive by 'switching off' mentally, so damaging their developing ability to think and to acquire a feeling of control over their lives. Just as babies leave the cradle to stand on their own feet, working children need help towards taking the psychological steps to autonomy. On the other hand, the time that working children spend in school, limited as it may be, can have lifelong value, if it is used to enhance their sense of self-efficacy and competence.

Work bondage (in which a worker is bound to his employer for many years without the freedom to change) is not uncommon in some parts of the world for both parents and children; pitiful earnings ensure that the cycle is perpetuated, because bonded labourers can only obtain their freedom by pledging their own children into bondage. Working conditions for these children invariably lead to disease of one sort or another, and often bring early death. Even though not all working children face such dangers at the workplace, they are highly vulnerable to the many problems of poverty.

Working children who fall behind emotionally, educationally and creatively are unlikely ever to catch up with the missed stages of their development. Even if information is acquired later, it is received into a changed mental framework from that of the younger child, and the end-result is bound to be different from that of normal children. For those who are aware of their loss of development time, it may be important to express it and grieve for it consciously, just as one should with any loss, before moving on to make the best of the circumstances. Recognizing this, it is of critical importance to help children who are either working or likely to work very early in their lives.

The loss of schooling

Almost all longitudinal research has shown that the two essential factors in the formation of children's competence are family and school. It follows that when children attend school rarely, the family becomes even more important. But the two vital influences which enable bright children to reach their potential – the provision of learning materials and parental involvement – are often the most difficult to provide in very poor homes (Freeman, 1991b). As a result, very poor children can unfortunately be deprived of both sources of help – home and school.

A very poor home is often a difficult place in which to provide effective outside help, because it may be relatively inaccessible and also because the parents may reject professional assistance. They may feel inadequate at providing what might be asked of them, particularly if they themselves cannot read or write. They tend to put up a subtle barrier, agreeing to a home-study programme, but failing to carry it out. Social workers in poor districts often encounter a real problem of ignorance and prejudice against schooling. Since girls particularly may suffer educationally from their parents' cultural attitudes, there is a very high illiteracy rate in some countries among very poor girls, relatively few of whom have access to printed reading matter.

For the children who work in damaging labour, not only is their sense of self-worth diminished, but time at school is minimized. Although this is bad for all children, it is particularly detrimental for those with the potential to develop their abilities to an exceptionally high level. Schooling can be almost an irrelevance in the daily battle for survival: there are no choices or career goals, and hence no incentive to persevere with formal learning. Absenteeism from school, whether voluntary or not, has a poor long-term prognosis even in a relatively rich country like the United Kingdom, where longitudinal research found that children who missed school were more likely than the average to have breakdowns in marriage, health and achievement (Hibbett & Fogelman, 1990). This individual human loss is enormously significant in world terms; in a country like Brazil, for example, where more than 40 per cent of the population live in poverty, 50 per cent fail to finish their fourth year of primary school (Alencar, 1988).

The majority language of a country embodies many of the ideas and attitudes on which its culture is based, and partly indicates loyalty to a common culture. When children are brought up without that language basis, they are to some degree excluded from those ways of thought, and so may effectively remain 'foreigners' in the country of their birth. The children of immigrants may also come up against the teacher's unconscious prejudices against them, reinforced by the children's lack of verbal fluency - which may appear as stupidity. Under-achievement has been identified amongst immigrant children, such as Gypsies in Hungary or Turks in Germany. This is not to say that all immigrant children succumb to such problems, as evidenced by the brilliant performances of many Vietnamese and Korean children in California, or of Jews in Western Europe and North America in the earlier part of the century. Among families where children have to work and miss school as a result, the essential difference between success and failure seems to depend on parental attitudes to education: if there is some alternative form of education at home, children can still be successful (see 'Multicultural education' in Chapter VIII).

In most societies, upward social mobility is facilitated by education, especially the kind which aims for autonomy and competence. School should be the most effective place for helping poor children, even though they are only there part of the time. But the picture of school education given by studies of poor societies is that the children are often given a limited, knowledge-based curriculum and are expected to learn passively. This is seen when children unthinkingly recite the lesson, or when the teacher asks questions which require a preordained answer. It produces an education which is convergent, factual and confined to accepted knowledge – certainly not the best way to develop lively minds.

The loss of schooling deprives children of basic enabling skills, such as reading, understanding how numbers work and basic scientific methods. It also isolates them from other educated children of similar ability, with whom they could have shared thoughts and experiences. It is possible to manage in life without tuition and practice in cognitive skills, with enough superficial information to earn a basic living, but not to reach the higher levels of thinking of which bright children are capable – analysis, synthesis, evaluation, and creative problem-solving. Relatively speaking, their educational loss is greater than the average child's.

Breaking the chain

In developing educational provision, administrators may have to consider methods used by managers and industrial psychologists for nearly fifty years. Experimental work by Kurt Lewin, begun in the 1930s in America, showed the way that individuals react to pressures in their environments (Lewin, 1947). His 'field theory' showed how people's outlook could be changed by using indirect rather than specific instructions; he used discussion and interaction as the means to move people to greater acceptance of the instructor's point of view. It is now well recognized that this feeling of being both involved and effective is of fundamental importance to changing opinions, an approach which applies equally to children and to adults.

Very many people may be required to change their attitudes if the poor children of the world are to be helped. Of course, employers might help their child employees from a sense of philanthropy, but they could also be encouraged to see the real benefit to themselves: for example, those children who can read and write are likely to make a more useful contribution to the workforce, and for this reason alone are worth bringing to full potential. Help could come from the provision of attractive open-learning centres, where equipment and teachers can be available outside school hours; these should attract children of high potential who left school early, helping them to develop methods of learning which would enhance their futures.

The cycle of deprivation which afflicts successive generations is, for many, impossible to break. Children who live in a situation of grinding poverty do not share the aims of teachers, who are themselves often struggling in poor circumstances. And yet, if there is any way out for the bright poor child, it must be through education – taken in its widest sense of enabling children to develop and use their abilities to the full. The failure of the Headstart programme in the United States, designed to motivate very poor children, was probably because it started when the child was already too old, and because it did not provide adequate help at home and in later life.

Reasons given by various governments for restricting spending on education are normally to do with the shortage of money, although that is a short-term view. Considerable evidence has now accumulated to show that early care and education are the best economic investment, but it is an expensive ingredient, and difficult to add to the food parcels. An educational basis is vital for the future prosperity of countries in which there is a highly subsidized yet narrowly educated elite, but where a high proportion of children do not finish primary school. A fear of allowing people to learn and be creative at a high level may in fact be more influential than lack of money. That fear is deep-seated, and usually serves to keep certain groups in a position superior to others. In many parts of the world, even minimal education is severely restricted for low-status people, especially girls. If people are able to learn, who knows what they might do with their learning?

Plans, based on field-work experience for alleviating children's deprivation in bad circumstances and using Feuerstein's mediation techniques, were extended by Professor Pnina Klein of Israel. She has adapted these plans (as the MISC Programme) to early infant development, and together with the Norwegian, Professor Hundeide, has also included care-givers (Hundeide, 1991). This approach is not so much content-oriented, but rather a process of sensitization and consciousness-raising. Thus the mediation is not imposed from outside, but offers a change of emphasis and some empowerment to the care-giver.

In spite of these schemes, there are cultural limits to the changes that can be made even in basic education. In a traditional community, for example, the most respected people, seen as the wisest and most intelligent, are also the most socially conforming, so that in those societies 'cleverness' has negative connotations, often implying immorality. This is so in rural Africa, for example, where problem-solving must be part of everyday reality, and intelligence as defined in the West is largely meaningless. Alternatively, street children, whose main aim is survival, often find intellectual planning impossible, and need help which is beyond what they might be offered in a school, even if they could get there.

Despite their varying needs and ways of life, all peoples have problems to solve, new situations to meet, and it is probable that they can cope with these more effectively through logical thinking of the same kind of complexity as that built up in the Western world. Yet Western tests of intelligence will fail to sample many skills which are more valued by the peoples themselves, for example, effectiveness in hunting or agriculture. These may be of a lower order of complexity, but generally play a larger part in daily life than does symbolic thinking.

It *is* possible to do something to help many very poor children to become competent productive adults, and at the same time make the world a better place for everyone. But real help for the brightest children in the worst situations has in the end to come from the top – from the governments for their own people.

References

Abroms, K. (1985) Social gifted-ness and its relationship with intellectual giftedness. *In:* **Freeman, J., ed.** *The psychology of gifted children.* Chichester, UK, John Wiley.

Albert, R.S. (1983) *Genius and eminence; the social psychology of creativity and exceptional achievement.* Oxford, UK, Pergamon Press.

Alencar, E. (1992) Developing the potential of disadvantaged pupils in Brazil. *In:* **Wallace, B., ed.** *Worldwide perspectives on the gifted disadvantaged.* Bicester, UK, AB Academic Publishers.

Archer, J. (1992) Childhood gender roles: social context and organisation. *In:* **McGurk, H., ed.** *Childhood social development: contemporary perspectives.* Hillsdale, NJ, Lawrence Earlbaum.

Bandura, A. (1977) *Social learning theory.* Englewood Cliffs, NJ, Prentice Hall.

Bastick, T. (1982) *Intuition: how we think and act.* Chichester, UK, John Wiley.

Bennett, C. (1990) *Comprehensive multicultural education: theory and practice.* Boston, MA, Allyn & Bacon.

Bennett, S.N. (1976) *Teaching styles and pupil progress.* London, Open Books.

Bernstein, B. (1972) *Class, codes and control.* London, Routledge & Kegan Paul.

Bettelheim, B. (1989) *A good enough parent.* London, Thames & Hudson.

Binet, A.; Simon, T. (1908) Le développement de l'intelligence chez les infants. *L'année psychologique, 14,* 1-90.

Blagg, N. (1991) *Can we teach intelligence?.* Hillsdale, NJ, Lawrence Erlbaum.

Blatchford, P. (1992) Academic self-assessment at 7 and 11 years: its accuracy and association with ethnic group and sex. *British journal of educational psychology, 62,* 35-44.

Bloom, B.S. (1985) *Developing talent in young people.* New York, NY, Ballantine Books.

Boekaerts, M. (1987) *Psychologie van de leerling en het leer-*

proces. Nijmegen, Netherlands, Dekker & van de Vegt.

Brooks, R. (1985) Delinquency among gifted children. *In:* **Freeman, J., ed.** *The psychology of gifted children.* Chichester, UK, John Wiley.

Bruner, J.S. (1972) Nature and uses of immaturity. *American psychologist, 27,* 678-708.

Butler, N.R.; Golding, J. (1986) *From birth to five: a study of the health and behaviour of Britain's five year olds.* Oxford, UK, Pergamon.

Butler-Por, N. (1987) *Underachievers in school.* Chichester, UK, John Wiley.

Butterworth, G. (1984) The relation between language and thought in young children. *In:* **Nicholson, J.; Beloff, H., eds.** Psychology survey 5. Leicester, UK, British Psychological Society.

Buzan, T. (1988) *Master your memory.* London, David & Charles.

Cattell, R.B. (1965) *The scientific analysis of personality.* Harmondsworth, UK, Penguin.

Ceci, S.J. (1990) *On intelligence . . . more or less.* New Jersey, NJ, Prentice Hall.

Chomsky, N. (1968) *Language and mind.* New York, NY, Harcourt, Brace & World.

Clarke, A.; Clarke, A.D.B. (1976) *Early experience; myth and evidence.* London, Open Books.

Council of Europe (1987) *News-letter/Faits nouveaux, 4.*

Cox, M.V. (1991) *The child's point of view.* Brighton, UK, Harvester Wheatsheaf.

Cropley, A. (1993) Creative intelligence: a concept of true talent. *In:* **Freeman, J.; Span, P.; Wagner, H., eds.** *Actualising talent: a lifelong challenge.* Göttingen, Germany, Hogrefe.

Csikszentmihalyi, M. (1982) Towards a psychology of optimal experience. *In:* **Wheeler, L., ed.** *Review of personality and social psychology, 3,* 13-36.

Daloz, L.A. (1986) *Effective teaching mentoring.* San Francisco, CA, Jossey-Bass.

Davidson, N., ed. (1990) *Co-operative learning in mathematics.* Menlo Park, CA, Addison-Wesley.

de Bono, E. (1991) The direct teaching of thinking in education and the CoRT Method. *In:* **Maclure, S.; Davies, P., eds.** *Learning to think: thinking to learn.* Oxford, UK, Pergamon.

Dochy, F.J.R.C. (1992) *Assessment of prior knowledge as a determinant for future learning.* Heerlen, Netherlands, Open Universiteit.

Donaldson, M. (1986) *Children's explanations: a psycholinguistic study.* Cambridge, UK, Cambridge University Press.

Douglas, J.B.W. (1968) *All our future.* London, Peter Davies.

Dubbeldam, L.F.B. (1991) Literacy and socio-cultural development. [Paper given at the international conference *Attaining functional literacy: a cross cul-*

tural perspective. Tilburg, Netherlands.]

Eggleston, J. (1990) The curriculum, contemporary issues, perspectives, and ideologies. *In:* **Entwistle, N., ed.** *Handbook of educational ideas and practices.* London, Routledge & Kegan Paul.

Elshout, J. (1993) Talent: the ability to become an expert. *In:* **Freeman, J.; Span, P.; Wagner, H., eds.** *Actualising talent: a lifelong challenge.* Göttingen, Germany, Hogrefe.

Entwistle, N.J. (1987) *Understanding classroom learning.* London, Hodder & Stoughton.

Erikson, E.H. (1963) *Childhood and society.* New York, NY, Norton.

Evans, B.J.W.; Drasdo, N. (1991) Tinted lenses and related therapies for learning disabilities - a review. *Ophthalmic and physiological optics,* 11, 206-217.

Eysenck, H.J. (1971) *Race, intelligence and education.* London, Temple Smith.

Eysenck, H.J. (1985) The nature and measurement of intelligence. *In:* **Freeman J., ed.** *The psychology of gifted children.* Chichester, UK, John Wiley.

Feuerstein, R. (1980) *Instrumental enrichment: an intervention programme for cognitive modifiability.* Baltimore, MD, University Park Press.

Feuerstein, R. (1990) The gifted underachiever and mediated learning experience. [Paper given at the second conference of the European Council for High Ability, Budapest]

Flavell, J., et al. (1968) *The development of role-taking and communication skills in young children.* New York, NY, John Wiley.

Flynn, J.R. (1987) Massive IQ gains in fourteen nations: what IQ tests really measure. *Psychological bulletin,* 17, 171-191.

Fowler, W. (1990) Early stimulation and the development of verbal talents. *In:* **Howe, Michael J., ed.** *Encouraging the development of exceptional skills and talents.* Leicester, UK, British Psychological Society.

Freeman, J. (1977) Social factors in aesthetic talent. *Research in Education,* 17, 64-76.

Freeman, J. (1991a) *Gifted children growing up.* London, Cassell.

Freeman, J. (1991b) *Bright as a button.* London, Optima.

Freeman, J. (1992) When earning interferes with learning *In:* **Wallace, B., ed.** *Perspectives on disadvantaged children.* London, AB Academic Publishers.

Freeman, J. (1993) A policy for actualising talent. *In:* **Freeman, J.; Span, P.; Wagner, H., eds.** *Actualising talent: a lifelong challenge.* Göttingen, Germany, Hogrefe.

Freeman, N. (1993) The emergence of pictorial talents. *In:* **Freeman, J.; Span, P.; Wagner, H., eds.** *Actualising talent: a* *lifelong challenge.* Göttingen, Germany, Hogrefe.

Gardner, H. (1985) *Frames of mind: the theory of multiple intelligences.* New York, NY, Basic Books.

Gardner, H. (1991) *The unschooled mind.* New York, NY, Basic Books.

Getzels, J.W. (1982) The problem of the problem. *In:* **Hogarth, J., ed.** *New directions for methodology of social and behavioural science: question framing and response consistency.* San Fransisco, CA, Jossey-Bass.

Guilford, J.P. (1967). Some new views of creativity. *In:* **Helson, J., ed.** *Theories and dates in psychology.* Princeton, NJ, Van Nostrand.

Harlow, H.F.; Harlow, M.K. (1966) Learning to love. *American scientist, 54,* 1-29.

Harlow, H.F. (1958) The nature of love. *American psychologist, 13,* 673-685.

Hartup, W.W. (1978) Children and their friends. *In:* **McGurk, H., ed.** *Issues in childhood social development.* London, Methuen.

Hibbett, A.; Fogelman, K. (1990) Future lives of truants; family formation and health related behaviour. *British journal of educational psychology, 60,* 171-179.

Hinde, R. (1991) Causes of social development from the perspective of an integrated developmental science. *In:* **Butterworth, G.; Bryant, P., eds.** *Causes of development: interdisciplinary perspectives.* Brighton, UK, Harvester Wheatsheaf.

Hoffman, M.L. (1986) Affect cognition and motivation. *In:* **Sorentino, R.M.; Higgins, E.T., eds.** *Handbook of motivation and cognition: foundations of social behaviour.* Chichester, UK, John Wiley.

Howe, M.J.A. (1990) *The origins of exceptional abilities.* Oxford, UK, Blackwell.

Hundeide, K. (1991) *Helping disadvantaged children.* London, Jessica Kingsley; Bergen, Norway, Sigma Forlag.

Husén, T.; Tuijnman, A. (1991) The contribution of formal schooling to the increase in intellectual capital. *Educational researcher, 20,* 17-25.

Jensen, A.R. (1972) *Genetics and education.* London, Methuen.

Karraher, T.N.; Karraher, D.W.; Schliemann, A.D. (1985) Mathematics in the streets and in schools. *British journal of developmental psychology, 3,* 21-29.

Kelly, A. (1988) Gender differences in teacher pupil interactions: a meta-analytical view. *Research in education, 39,* 149-163.

Kelly, G.A. (1955) *The psychology of personal constructs.* New York, NY, Norton.

Kohlberg, L. (1978) Revisions in the theory and practice of moral development. *In:* **Damon, W., ed.** *Moral development.* San Francisco, CA, Jossey-Bass.

Landau, E. (1985). Creative questioning for the future. *In:* **Freeman, J.,** ed. *The psychology of gifted children.* Chichester, UK, Wiley.

Lansdown, R. (1990) Intervention programmes in early childhood care and development. [Paper for the Division of Maternal and Child Health, World Health Organization, Geneva, Switzerland.]

Lehwald, G. (1990) Curiosity and exploratory behaviour in ability development. *European journal for high ability, 1,* 20-210.

Lewin, K. (1947) Group decision and social change. *In:* **Newcomb, T.; Hartley, E.C.,** eds. *Readings in social psychology.* New York, NY, Holt.

Lewis, M.; Louis, B. (1991) Young gifted children. *In:* **Colangelo, G.A.; Davis, G.A.,** eds. *Handbook of gifted education.* Boston, MA, Allyn & Bacon.

Lorenz, K.Z. (1965) *Evolution and the modification of behaviour.* Chicago, IL, University of Chicago Press.

Luria, A. (1959) The directive function of speech in development. *Word, 15,* 341-352.

Lynn, R.; Hampson, S.L. (1986) The rise of national intelligence: evidence from Britain, Japan, and the United States. *Personality and individual differences, 7,* 23-29.

Lynn, R.; Shigehisa, T. (1991) Reaction times and intelligence: a comparison of Japanese and British children. *Journal of biosocial science, 23,* 409-416.

Lynn, Richard. (1989) A nutrition theory of the secular increases in intelligence; positive correlations between height, head size and IQ. *British journal of educational psychology. 59,* 372-377.

Mackintosh, N.J. (1986) The Biology of Intelligence? *British journal of psychology, 77,* 1-18.

McClelland, D.C., et al. (1953) *The achievement motive.* New York, NY, Appleton Century Crofts.

Milgram, R. (1990) Creativity: an idea whose time has come and gone? *In:* **Runco, M.A.; Albert, R.S.,** eds. *Theories of creativity.* Newbury Park, CA, Sage.

Mischel, W.; Shoda, Y.; Rodriguez, M. (1989) Delay of gratification in children. *Science, 244,* 933-938.

Mönks, F.J., et al. (1986). The identification of gifted children in secondary education and a description of their situation in Holland. *In:* **Heller, K.A.; Feldhusen, J.F.,** eds. *Identifying and nurturing the gifted.* Bern, Huber.

Montessori, M. (1964) *The Montessori method.* New York, NY, Schocken.

Nisbet, J. (1991) Methods and approaches. *In:* **Maclure, S.; Davies, P.,** eds. *Learning to think: thinking to learn.* Oxford, UK, Pergamon.

Nisbet, J.; Shucksmith, J. (1986) *Learning strategies.* London, Routledge & Kegan Paul.

Oden, M.H. (1968) The fulfilment of promise: 40-year follow-up of the Terman gifted group. *Genetic psychology monographs, 77,* 3-93.

Okuda, S.M.; Runco, M.A.; Berger, D.E. (1991) Creativity and the finding and solving of real-world problems. *Journal of psychoeducational assessment, 9,* 45-53.

Ornstein, R.E. (1972) *The psychology of consciousness.* New York, NY, Harcourt, Brace, Jovanovich.

Palincsar, A.; Brown, A. (1984) Reciprocal teaching of comprehension - fostering and monitoring activities. *Cognition and Instruction, 1,* 117-75.

Papert, S. (1980) *Mindstorms.* Brighton, UK, Harvester.

Piaget, J. (1953) *The origins of intelligence in the child.* London, Routledge & Kegan Paul.

Piaget, J. (1971) *Structuralism.* London, Routledge & Kegan Paul.

Pickering, J.; Skinner, M. (1991). *From sentience to symbols; readings on consciousness.* Brighton, UK, Harvester Wheatsheaf.

Prawat, R.S. (1991) The value of ideas: The immersion approach to the development of thinking. *Educational researcher, 20,* 3-10.

Pringle, M.K. (1970) *Able misfits.* London, Longman.

Radford, J. (1990) *Child prodigies and exceptional early achievers.* Brighton, UK, Harvester Wheatsheaf.

Raven, J.C. (1965) *Advanced progressive matrices.* London, H.K. Lewis.

Renzulli, J.S. (1977) *The enrichment triad model: a guide for developing defensible programs for the gifted and talented.* Wethersfield, CT, Creative Learning Press.

Resnick, L. (1990) Instruction and the cultivation of thinking. *In:* Entwistle, N., ed. *Handbook of educational ideas and practices.* London, Routledge & Kegan Paul.

Rosenblith, J.F.; Sims-Knight J.B. (1989) *In the beginning; development in the first two years.* London, Sage Publications.

Rosenthal, R.; Jacobson, L. (1968) *Pygmalion in the classroom; teacher expectations and pupil's intellectual development.* New York, NY, Holt Rinehart & Winston.

Rotter, J.B. (1966). Generalised expectancies for internal versus external control of reinforcement. *Psychological monographs* (whole no. 609).

Rowe, K.J. (1991) The influence of reading activity at home on students' attitudes towards reading, classroom attentiveness and reading achievement: an application of structural equation modelling. *British journal of educational psychology, 61,* 19-35.

Rutter, M. (1985) Family and school influences on cognitive development. *In:* **Hinde, Robert A.; Perret-Clermont, Anne-Nelly; Stevenson-Hinde, Joan, eds.** *Social relationships and cognitive development.* Oxford, UK, Clarendon Press.

Rutter, M., et al. (1979). *Fifteen thousand hours.* London, Open Books.

Ryan, Richard M.; Connell, James P.; Deci, Edward L. (1985) A motivational analysis of self-determination and self-regulation in education. *In:* **Ames, C.; Ames, R., eds.** *Research on motivation in education. Vol. II: The classroom milieu.* New York, NY, Academic Press.

Shon, D.A. (1987) *Educating the reflexive practitioner.* San Fransisco, CA, Jossey-Bass.

Siegler, R.S. (1991). *Children's thinking.* Englewood Cliffs, NJ, Prentice Hall.

Simonton, D.K. (1988) *Scientific genius. A psychology of science.* Cambridge, UK, Cambridge University Press.

Singer, J.L. (1973) *The child's world of make-believe.* New York, NY, Academic Press.

Sisk, D. (1993) Thinking with a futures perspective. *In:* **Freeman, J.; Span, P.; Wagner, H., eds.** *Actualising talent: a lifelong challenge.* Göttingen, Germany, Hogrefe.

Skinner, B.F. (1972) *Beyond freedom and dignity.* London, Jonathan Cape.

Sloboda, J. (1985) *The musical mind: the cognitive psychology of music.* Oxford, UK, Oxford University Press.

Smith, Peter K. (1984) *Play in animals and humans.* Oxford, UK, Blackwell.

Span, P. (1993) Self-regulated learning. *In:* **Freeman, J.; Span, P.; Wagner, H., eds.** Actualising talent: a lifelong challenge. Göttingen, Germany, Hogrefe.

Sperry, R.W. (1961). Cerebral organisation and behaviour. *Science, 133,* 1749.

Stedtnitz, U.; Schar. A. (1992) Psychosocial dimensions of high ability: a review of major issues and neglected topics. *In:* **Freeman, J.; Span, P.; Wagner, H., eds.** *Actualising talent.* Göttingen, Germany, Hogrefe.

Sternberg, R.; Kolligian, J., eds (1990) *Competence considered.* Binghampton, NY, Vail-Ballou Press.

Sternberg, R.J. (1991) Death, taxes, and bad intelligence tests. *Intelligence, 15,* 257-269.

Sternberg, Robert J.; Davidson, J.E. (1986) *Conceptions of giftedness.* Cambridge, UK, Cambridge University Press.

Sternberg, Robert J. (1985) Cognitive approaches to intelligence. *In:* **Wolman, Benjamin B., ed.** *Handbook of intelligence.* Chichester, UK, John Wiley.

Street, Brian V. (1990) *Cultural meanings of literacy.* Paris, UNESCO:IBE.

Tanner, J.M. (1978) *Foetus into man.* London, Open Books.

Terman, L.M. (1925-29) *Genetic studies of genius.* Vols I-V. Stanford, CA, Stanford University Press.

Terman, L.M.; Merrill, M.A. (1961) *Stanford-Binet intelligence scale: manual for the third revision form I-M.* London, Harrap.

Timar, T.B.; Kirp, D.L. (1988) *Managing educational excellence.* Brighton, UK, Falmer. (The Stanford Series on 'Education and public policy')

Tizard, B.; Hughes, M. (1984) *Young children learning: talking and thinking at home and school.* London, Fontana.

Tulkin, S.R. (1977) Social class differences in maternal and infant behaviour. *In:* **Leiderman, P.H.; Tulkin, S.R.; Rosenfield, A.,** eds. *Culture and infancy.* New York, NY, Academic Press.

UNESCO. (1988) *Compendium of statistics on literacy.* Paris, UNESCO, Office of Statistics.

Ve, H. (1991) Children and teachers in exceptional learning situations. *In:* **Radford, J.,** ed. *Talent, teaching and achievement.* London, Jessica Kingsley.

Vernon, P.E. (1969) *Intelligence and cultural environment.* London, Methuen.

Vigotsky, L.S. (1962) *Thought and language.* Cambridge, MA, MIT Press.

Vigotsky, L.S. (1978) *Mind in society. The development of higher psychological processes.* Cambridge, MA, MIT Press.

Wallace, A. (1986) *The prodigy.* London, Macmillan.

Wallas, G. (1926) *The art of thought.* New York, NY, Harcourt Brace.

Wechsler, D. (1949) *Wechsler intelligence scale for children.* New York, NY, Psychological Corporation.

Weisberg, R.W. (1986) *Creativity.* New York, NY, Freeman.

Wellman, H.M. (1990) *The child's theory of mind.* Cambridge, MA, MIT.

Wertsch, J.D. (1990) *Voices of the mind: a sociocultural approach to mediated action.* Brighton, UK, Harvester Wheatsheaf.

White, B. (1985) Competence and giftedness. *In:* **Freeman, J.,** ed. *The psychology of gifted children.* Chichester, UK, John Wiley.

Wiles, S. (1985) Learning a second language. *In:* **Wells, G.,** ed. *Perspectives on language and learning.* Brighton, UK, Falmer Press.

INDEX

The following words have not been indexed since they occur on a very large number of pages: ability, child, children, development, education, learning, pupil, parent, school, skills, teacher, teaching, thinking.